WHEN A CHILD DIES

when a child dies

HOW PEDIATRIC PHYSICIANS
AND NURSES COPE

Robert S. McKelvey, M.D.

UNIVERSITY OF WASHINGTON PRESS

Seattle and London

University of Washington Press
P.O. Box 50096, Seattle, WA 98145
www.washington.edu/uwpress

Library of Congress Cataloging-in-Publication Data
McKelvey, Robert S.
When a child dies : how pediatric physicians and
    nurses cope / Robert S. McKelvey.
p. ; cm.
Includes bibliographical references and index.
ISBN-10: 0-295-98653-0 (pbk. : alk. paper)
ISBN-13: 978-0-295-98653-X
1. Terminal care. 2. Children—Death—Psychological aspects.
3. Physician and patient. 4. Children and death. 5. Terminally ill
children. I. Title.
[DNLM: 1. Death—Personal Narratives. 2. Grief—Personal
Narratives. 3. Adaptation, Psychological—Personal Narratives.
4. Medical Staff, Hospital—Psychology—Personal Narratives.
5. Pediatric Nursing—Personal Narratives.
WS 105.5.E5M478W 2006]
R726.8.M355 2006   618.92'0029—dc22   2006016880

CONTENTS

ACKNOWLEDGMENTS

I have been interviewing my colleagues for this book for the past three years. During the process I have gotten to know many wonderful people, each with a deep and heartfelt love for children and their families. I have not interviewed a single person that I did not come to like and respect, and a few have become friends. Some of the narratives touched me more deeply than others, perhaps because the people I spoke with were more open with their feelings and less guarded in their responses to my questions, but every one of them had a rich and moving story to tell. At times when I reviewed the materials on which the book is based I found myself struggling to hold back tears, illustrating for me that there is nothing as heart-wrenching as the loss of a child and the grief of its parents.

My wish for this book is that it convey a clear and convincing picture of the depth of my colleagues' spirits, for the feelings of pain and loss that are a part of their daily lives, and for their efforts to cope with tragedy while continuing to care for children and their families. If it does not it will be my failure and not theirs.

My greatest debt of gratitude is to those who volunteered to participate in the interviews for the book and who gave freely of their time both during our meetings together and in reviewing their sections of the draft. I also very much appreciate their encouragement of the project and their desire that the book accurately mirror their work and their emotional responses to their patients and their families. I apologize to those whose interviews could not be included in the book because of space considerations.

As always my chief source of support is my wife, Jill, the best-natured and warmest-hearted person I know, who is unfailingly encouraging and tolerant of my activities. I am very grateful, too, for the presence of my children and their spouses in our lives and for the gifts of our grandchildren, Alexandra, Taylor, and Isabel.

ROBERT S. McKELVEY
Portland, April 2006

WHEN A CHILD DIES

INTRODUCTION

I clearly remember my first experience of a patient's death. I was an intern on a medical service and the patient was an older man, probably about my age now, with severe respiratory difficulties. I did not know him and only became involved in his care because I was on call. He died as a result of my inexperience, exhaustion, and poor judgment. No one helped me to cope with his death. The only one who talked with me about it was my senior resident. In front of the rest of the medical team he pointed out clearly and angrily what I had done wrong. Surprisingly I do not remember feeling especially burdened by that death. My emotional reactions to it were repressed. What I did feel was numbness, inadequacy, guilt, and shame for the public exposition of my failure.

My first experience of a child's death was more disturbing and traumatic. I was rotating through pediatrics and one winter night I was working in the emergency room. A fire department ambulance pulled up to the entrance and the firemen told us there was a child inside that had been run over by a snowplow. Someone had to go out and pronounce him dead. We looked hesitantly at one another and finally someone said to me, "You've got to do it. You're on pediatrics." I had never pronounced a child dead before and had never had any instruction about how to do it. As I climbed into the interior of the ambulance I saw a little African American boy lying on his side. His skull was split open and much of his brain was lying outside of his head. I remember thinking, "He looks dead and you can't live with your brain outside of your skull, but is there something else I should do?" I was so stunned that I had trouble processing a logical course of action. By some strange twist of fate, I later cared for the child's mother when I was a resident on the inpatient psychiatry unit. She was suffering from a psychotic depression triggered by the death of her son.

The most painful deaths in my training were the ones that I experienced during my psychiatry residency. These were two patients I had worked with who committed suicide within a few months of each another. I had been part of the team treating one of them for over a year and knew him well. The other I had just met in a support group that I had taken over from another resident. The first patient, a chronically suicidal young man who had made many serious suicide attempts, killed himself by taking an overdose in a remote area. The newspaper reported that mushroom hunters had found his decomposed body in the woods. The second patient, a chronically psychotic man in his twenties, killed himself by jumping out of a window at his sheltered workshop. I received a frantic phone call from the staff member there who had just restrained him from jumping from an eighth-floor window. While calling to ask for help, he had left the man unattended, and the patient went back to the window and leapt to his death. All I heard at the other end of the phone was someone saying my name, the sounds of furniture moving, a shout, and then nothing.

The horror of those patients' suicides and the fact that I knew them as people made their deaths devastating for me. It was early in my career and my confidence and professional identity had not yet consolidated. Their deaths made me question whether I should be in the psychiatric field at all. I became depressed and, while still able to do my job, performed much less effectively than I had done, especially with suicidal patients. I wanted assurances from them that they would not commit suicide, assurances they were often unable to give me. Faculty in our program did their best to help me. They talked with me and gave me things to read about the uncertainty of our work, about our lack of control over what our patients do, and about our inability to predict the future. Time, psychotherapy, and experience finally helped me to deal with those deaths, to learn from them, and to move on with my career.

It is not surprising that given my own problems coping with those early patient deaths I should be interested in how others deal with the loss of their patients. However, I needed many years before I had the knowledge, maturity, and sophistication to examine the topic objectively.

The immediate stimulus for this book was my experience in leading a support group for hematology-oncology nurses in a tertiary-care pediatric teaching hospital. The group members were predominantly young women; many were only a few years out of nursing school. Their job was to care for children with cancer. While the cure rate for pediatric cancers is generally much higher than it is for adult cancers, many of their patients (approximately 30 percent of those with leukemia and other solid tumors and 50 percent of those with brain cancers) died. How, I wondered, did these women, often themselves the mothers of young children, cope emotionally with the deaths of children they had cared for and come to know intimately over weeks, months, and sometimes years?

A nurse in a pediatric cancer or intensive care unit is with the patient for eight, ten, or even twelve hours a day. She or he is a constant presence at the bedside and is continuously exposed to the anxiety, depression, fear, and anger of patients and their families. Unlike the physicians involved in the child's treatment, the nurse cannot leave the room to care for other children, to attend an educational seminar, or to conduct research. Given chronic nursing-staff shortages, she or he often does not even have time to go to lunch. Over the course of days and weeks the nurse frequently becomes a surrogate member of the child's family, developing strong emotional bonds with the parents that may not end with the discharge or death of the patient.

I also function as a consultation-liaison psychiatrist to the pediatric hospital. My duties are to evaluate and recommend treatment for children and families who present behavioral or emotional challenges to the doctors and nurses who care for them. As I came to know the hospital's physicians, pediatric residents, and pediatric nurses better, I sometimes also became an informal and occasionally formal consultant to them about their personal concerns or reactions to their extremely demanding jobs. Some, and especially the residents who were young and new to the field, spoke of the intense emotions they experienced after a child's especially difficult or painful death and of self-doubts about their role in and possible responsibility for it. Others discussed hurt feelings after the critical outbursts of distraught family members or insensitive remarks by professional colleagues or supervisors. Still others expressed concerns about continuing in professions that are so demanding of their time, energy, and emotions. Given my early career experiences with patient deaths these were concerns that I could fully understand and with which I could completely empathize.

Like the nurses and physicians I interviewed I continue to find myself unsettled by the tragedies I encounter among the hospital's patients and their families. I am old enough to be mindful of my own death, and the deaths of children remind me that sooner or later everyone's time, including my own, will come. I am a parent and grandparent and when I see young people suffering and dying I also worry about the health and safety of my loved ones. And when I witness the pain that is borne by so many children and their parents I am assaulted by the sorrow and unfairness of fate's seemingly random cruelty. I used to think that my pediatric medical and nursing colleagues, who appeared to deal with such deaths so stoically, were made of sterner stuff than I am. However, as I came to know them better, I realized that beneath their superficial calm and confidence were unanswered questions, personal and professional doubts, and a depth of incomplete mourning.

Shortly after the suicides of my patients, while I was still struggling to understand and deal with their loss, I spoke with a medical-school friend about how powerfully they had affected my work and me. His response was, "But isn't that why we went to medical school, to learn how to deal with patients' deaths?" If so, it was a lesson I had not learned, and in the course of interviewing the physicians and nurses for this book I have become convinced that medical professionals, despite their extensive and grueling training, are often still very susceptible to the traumatic effects of repeatedly experiencing the deaths of children. As one of my nursing colleagues put it, "there's nothing right about a dead baby." The frequent isolation of physicians and nurses within their professional roles and the lack of support provided to them by their supervisors, programs, and institutions make them even more vulnerable because they are often left to deal with their feelings alone. In many respects they are like soldiers exposed to combat, sharing with them a tradition of moral toughness in the face of death and an externally imposed need to move on to the next challenge rather than to stop and grieve. Expressions of emotion at a patient's death may be viewed by one's colleagues as signs of weakness or unprofessional behavior, leaving medical and nursing personnel with a reluctance to acknowledge that what they have seen and dealt with is, in its individual details, often horrible, tragic, and potentially overwhelming. What happens, I wondered, to all those bottled-up, unprocessed, and unresolved feelings?

The following excerpt from my interviews with Katie, a twenty-five-year-old nurse in the Neonatal Intensive Care Unit (NICU), illustrates the shock and revulsion experienced by young professionals during their first encounter with a child's death. It also shows the tender and loving concern of a nurse for her patient and the devastating impact on her of that patient's death.

"The baby was born at twenty-six weeks. She was a twin and very sick at birth. I like to care for sick babies and that often puts me in the situation of having to face the baby's death. This particular baby was initially not expected to live, but she did. She kept getting better each day and the staff and her family started to have some hope. I was the first person to hold and bathe her. She had facial anomalies, but I was attracted to her because of her sad face. There was something about the way she looked at you and absolutely melted when she was held. She loved being held, but for a long time she was so sick that she couldn't be. I tried to give her extra attention because she'd gone without physical contact for so long. Multiples [twins, triplets, etc.] are always paired so I also cared for her brother. After a few months she improved enough to go to the level two [less intensive] side of the nursery. She'd beaten the odds, and we planned to send her home along with her brother after they learned to eat.

"Unfortunately, hospital-acquired infections occur even in our unit. She got a virus and it consumed her. The little reserve she had was quickly expended and ultimately she died. A part of me is very angry about that. I feel that she didn't have to die. She had conditions that could have caused her death later in life, but to have her die of a hospital-acquired infection was very frustrating. Her brother got sick too, but he had much greater reserves and he lived. We tried her on different types of ventilators, but nothing worked and eventually her body systems started shutting down one by one. When the ventilators were no longer able to keep her blood oxygenated the doctor called her mother to come in during the night. It was so painful to see the mother holding her dying baby. I'll never forget the horrific wailing sounds she made as she held her and bargained with God, pleading for her daughter's life.

"Eventually the parents decided to take her off the ventilator. We withdrew support and gave her morphine as a comfort measure during the dying process. I was unprepared for what happens to babies' bodies when they die. Secretions come out of their noses and mouths and any other areas that have been punctured, like IV lines. Their bodies become cold and stiff and their tongues protrude from their mouths as their faces and bodies begin to discolor. The parents were horrified and I was in shock. Our attending physician was great. She said reassuringly to both the parents and to me, 'That's perfectly normal.' It really helped me to see the attending crying during the process. It made the nurses think that it was all right to be sad and it showed the parents that the doctors cared. As the baby gasped for each breath and the parents screamed hysterically I listened periodically for a heart rate until her heart stopped beating and the doctor confirmed her death.

"After babies die we nurses do the postmortem care. We dress them up to make them look alive. We have makeup and special clothes and blankets. We take pictures and make a memory kit for the parents. After she died and the parents stepped out of the room I realized that after working sixteen hours and being emotionally and physically drained I didn't have enough left in me to do the post-mortem care. Fortunately, her other primary nurse from the day shift was called and came in to help. After we were done taking pictures, bathing her, and doing footprints, handprints, and obtaining a lock of hair, we dressed her in a hospital-issued T-shirt, wrapped her in hospital blankets, and put her in a body bag. The feeling of putting a baby into a body bag, which is similar to a giant-sized ziplock, is unnerving. At that point, as I tried to understand the overwhelming event I'd just experienced, I wondered if I could continue in this profession.

"According to protocol, the nurse calls the transportation service and they come with a fishing-tackle box and take the baby to the morgue, but for dignity's sake we put her in the bottom drawer of a bassinet and took her down. That was the first time either of us had been to the morgue, which was also a strange experience. To pick up the baby that you'd once held in your arms and who'd looked back at you so lovingly and place her on a cold steel shelf marked 'for babies only' was excruciating. We walked back to the unit solemnly, neither of us saying a word.

"I'd been on for twenty hours and had cried through the whole experience. Finally I went home and slept. My husband found me crying in my sleep. He said, 'You've got to quit!' I took a week off and went to her funeral. It helped me to do that and to talk to her family. They kept thanking us over and over again. It was hard to know how I should behave. They invited the other primary nurse and me to go to the grave site. During the service the parents said a lot of nice things about the nurses. They recognized that although we weren't biologically related to the baby we, too, had formed an attachment to her and had bonded with her. They appreciated that we'd experienced parts of her life, both good and bad, that no one else had. That helped. In some sense I think they were giving us permission to be sad and to grieve with them.

"After her death I was an absolute wreck. I was so overwhelmed, but I knew I wanted to go back to work and that I didn't want to take my husband's advice and simply give up. She'd been my primary baby for the entire four months of her life and I would miss her dearly, but I simply had to move on. After a week off I decided that the best thing I could do was to return to work. The first night I went to a delivery of triplets. Two of the babies died and I had to do the postmortem care along with a colleague. Surprised and shocked, I was again unnerved and wondered how I'd deal with this situation so soon after her death. With much relief I found that it was easier because I hadn't bonded to the two babies that had died."

Katie's story illustrates several ways of dealing with the deaths of children: joining the family in the grieving process for their child; returning to work despite her grief; and learning that patients' deaths did not affect her as deeply if she were not emotionally attached to them. The first two coping strategies, joining the family in its grief and returning to work (or "getting back on the horse that threw you") are positive and healthy adaptations to loss. The third, not attaching to the patients one cares for, is potentially riskier. It decreases the caregiver's conscious pain, but if carried too far it can lead to emotional withdrawal, mechanical care-giving, and eventual burnout.

In this book I have attempted to understand how medical and nursing professionals cope as a part of their personal and professional lives with the deaths of children, and with the grief of the families of those children. I have based it on a series of individual interviews that I conducted with the members of a pediatric hospital's medical and nursing staff, individuals who work in the intensive care unit, the hematology-oncology unit, and the neonatal intensive care unit. These are the places in the pediatric hospital, along with the emergency room, where children are most likely to die and where caregivers have the most experience in dealing with children's deaths. The interviews were guided by a detailed, semi-structured questionnaire that I developed to learn more about the participants' education, training, and on-the-job experiences with children's deaths, their emotional reactions to those deaths, and their styles for coping personally and professionally with the strong feelings and painful questions aroused by them (Appendix A). I also tried to learn as much as I could about each individual's personal and family background and how they and those around them had coped with the dying and deaths of others.

The children's hospital from which the participants were drawn is located in Portland, Oregon, and is part of the Oregon Health and Science University. Its residents and faculty attended medical schools and, in the case of the faculty, were trained all around the country—although there is, perhaps, a slight West Coast predominance. They are, in my view, representative of pediatric specialists and residents in the United States. The nurses are more likely to have gone to nursing school in Oregon and adjoining states and thus may reflect a regional bias in their training and experience. The cultural milieu of the hospital is probably more informal than in many other parts of the country, in keeping with the relatively relaxed atmosphere of the Pacific Northwest. It is certainly less formal and hierarchical than hospitals where I trained and worked in Boston and Houston.

Over the years in which I conducted the interviews, it frequently occurred to me that there were other groups of people involved with dying children and their families whose stories I might also have included. The hospital's chaplains, Child Life workers, social workers, volunteers, and ward administrative staff also play important roles in the lives and deaths of children treated in the pediatric hospital, and their stories and reflections also deserve to be told. However, I decided to limit the book's focus to those who actually bear the responsibility for children's treatment, the hospital's doctors

11

and nurses. Not that their stories are more important than the others, but their grieving is complicated by the fact that they must live with the consequences of their decision-making, entangling grief with guilt and self-reproach.

The book is set out in three parts to reflect the professional disciplines of those I interviewed, beginning with the experiences of pediatric residents, followed by those of the hospital's attending physicians, and concluding with the reflections of the nurses. For those unfamiliar with the hierarchy of teaching hospitals, pediatric residents are physicians-in-training. After completing medical school, physicians who choose to enter pediatrics complete three years of full-time residency training. The hospital's attending physicians supervise their work, which is largely in-hospital. The attendings, or attending physicians, are the hospital's senior doctors, who have completed their residency training and any additional subspecialty fellowship training, such as neonatology or hematology-oncology. The medical staff members of the teaching hospital where I conducted my research were employed either by the university's Department of Pediatrics or by a large managed-care company, while the nurses were employed by the hospital. Nurses, although they carry out treatments prescribed by physicians, have their own distinct professional identity and licensure and follow a separate chain of command.

I chose to begin the book with the experiences of pediatric residents because they, along with recent nursing graduates, are the newest members of the health-care team and have had the least time to develop psychological defenses to deal with the tragedy of children's deaths. Their perspectives are thus fresher and more akin to those of the layperson confronted by death than are those of the more experienced caregivers. The recollections of the attending physicians and nurses reflect the effects of time and experience on the evolution of coping strategies, which ideally become more flexible and functional, allowing the person to grieve the loss of a child without becoming paralyzed or incapable of investing emotion in subsequent children. Separating the nurses' from the physicians' stories helps to illustrate the differences and similarities in their ways of responding to children's deaths.

The chapters, each focusing on one individual, are organized in the same manner, with numbered sections that begin with the participants' first professional experiences of a child's death. The second section reflects their family and religious backgrounds, their early experiences with death, and the strategies they developed as young people to deal with dying and death. The third section recounts their reasons for entering medicine or nursing, their present satisfaction with their career choice, and their educational, training, and on-the-job preparation for dealing with patients' deaths. In the fourth section they reflect on their abilities to cope with the deaths of children, and in the fifth about how working with dying children affects their views of their own and their family members' mortality. Section six examines those factors that contribute to "good" and "bad" deaths of children; in section seven, participants evaluate their professional colleagues' abilities to cope with children's deaths.

During the interviews I wrote down the participants' responses as they spoke, much as I would do in a clinical interview, and later typed up my notes. I then asked each person to review the transcript of his or her interview and to make whatever additions, deletions, and corrections they chose. I did this to assure that everyone was comfortable with the contents of the interview and to offer them an opportunity to add further thoughts. Most people made few if any changes, but several rewrote portions of their interviews or added new material. These thoughtful reflections sometimes lacked the "bite" of conversational responses, but in work like this that involves a partnership between writer and subject, I believe that it is important for the participants to have control over the final version of their remarks.

The professional literature addressing physicians' and nurses' emotional reactions to the deaths of their child patients suggests that caring for dying children and their families is one of the most difficult areas in medical and nursing practice (Appendix B). While nurses and physicians do grieve the deaths of their child patients, their ways of experiencing and processing their grief vary both individually and between professional groups. There appears to be a tendency for physicians to deal with their grief intellectually and in isolation, while nurses seem to experience their grief more directly and emotionally and to find support for their grieving among their peers. Many factors, however, may modify an individual's reactions to the death of a child patient, either by intensifying or minimizing his or her conscious experience of grief. Identification and empathy with the patient and family, for example, increase the conscious experience of grief, while denial and repression put it "out of mind" and diminish it, at least for the near term.

Healthy grieving for a dying child is necessary for nurses and physicians, but their grieving process differs in fundamental ways from that of parents and other family members. Societal expectations for grieving family members are relaxed during the time of acute mourning and no one expects them to continue to function at their highest level. Grieving nurses and physicians, on the other hand, must immediately turn their attention to the care of other patients and may find that they will soon have new patients to mourn. Thus their grieving process is a delicate balance between allowing themselves to experience feelings of loss and keeping their emotions sufficiently under control so that they do not compromise their function or lose the ability to reinvest their professional energies in other patients and families. Over time, this cycle of repeated grieving while continuing to perform one's professional role may exert a heavy toll physically, emotionally, occupationally, and socially. Professionals must find ways to put aside their grief until they can find an appropriate manner, time, and place to experience it, such as at a memorial service, a funeral, a quiet moment at home, or at a movie theater during a sad film. They must also strive to develop a balance in their personal and professional lives so that they are able to remain both functional and responsive as human beings.

The anthropologist Ernest Becker (1973) suggests that humans, as the only living things capable of thinking of themselves as objects, are also the only animals that can imagine their own deaths. To keep from being paralyzed by this knowledge people must exercise denial and repression. While the "death anxiety" engendered by the realization that we, too, will die is not completely repressed, great variation is found in our individual capacities to tolerate it.

Following Becker, Liechty (2000) characterizes the three major defensive reactions of health-care personnel to death anxiety as the "professional," "not me," and "messianic." Those with "professional" defensive reactions abstract the illness from the person and treat it, the disease, and not the whole human being. "That's an interesting case," "He's a chronic schizophrenic," or "Don't you wish that were your liver" are examples of this type of defense. "Not me" defenses are characterized by an empathic disconnect between patient and physician or nurse, acting to distance the patient to the point where one no longer identifies with his or her suffering. As the Fat Man in Shem's *The House of God* puts it, "The patient is the one with the disease" (1978, p. 420). The "messianic" defensive reaction involves complete identification with the patient's pain, the assumption of it as one's own, and resultant attempts to fix it. The boundaries between caregiver and patient are lost, and saving the patient's life becomes an almost holy quest.

In the interviews that follow we will find examples of all of these defensive reactions, sometimes in the same person. With time, experience, and personal growth the reactions often evolved into what I would consider a healthier defensive style, one in which you are able to share the pain of another without becoming so overwhelmed by it that you either cannot function or lose the ability to distinguish the sufferer's pain from your own.

It was my expectation that an individual's ways of coping with the deaths of children would have more to do with his or her early life experiences and unconscious ego-defense mechanisms than with any didactic teaching or on-the-job training during or after medical or nursing school. I anticipated that more resilient and emotionally sturdy people would cope more effectively with children's deaths than those who overly personalized their professional experiences, much as I had done early in my training, or those who extinguished any conscious experience of their grief. I also expected that those who were new to the field, residents and younger nurses, would have the most difficulty in coping with children's deaths and would be the most overwhelmed by them. No amount of education and training can fully prepare young physicians and nurses for the experiences and emotions they will encounter when treating dying children and their families. Only when you actually bear the responsibility for patients' care can you appreciate the deeply challenging effects of their deaths on your personal and professional identities.

The study's results tended to support and expand these initial hypotheses. The deaths that most affected, and to some extent traumatized, both new and experienced practitioners were those that occurred early in their careers when they were more vulnerable and less well defended psychologically. Their coping strategies for dealing with patients' deaths were largely influenced by "what you bring to the table," although observations of their colleagues' styles and their own subsequent life experiences might modify these strategies, usually in a healthier and more functional direction. Medical and nursing training generally did not play a major role in the development of participants' coping strategies, primarily because formal instruction about dealing with death took place in the early, nonclinical years of school before they had begun to experience patient deaths on the wards. Coping with children's deaths could be facilitated by collegial and familial support and made more difficult by overidentification with the child and/or the family. While children's deaths did not usually influence the participants' conscious fears for their own mortality, they did heighten their concerns about the vulnerability of their children and family members. They also increased their awareness of the fragility of life; "anything can happen at any time." "Good" deaths for children were characterized by parental, child, and medical team acceptance of death, time to say good-bye, and adequate use of pain-control medications. "Bad" deaths were acute, unexpected, and unaccepted, with discord between parents and the medical staff and continuation of treatment beyond the point where a reasonable person might expect recovery. Finally, participants tended to evaluate their colleagues' strengths and weaknesses in light of their own. People who behaved more like the participants did were generally admired, while those with different coping styles were often felt to be either too close or too distant.

During the years in which I conducted the interviews two important events occurred that are reflected in several of the narratives. The first was the suicide of an attending physician who worked in the Neonatal Intensive Care Unit. Her death had a devastating impact on her colleagues and was very troubling for the pediatric residents, who were at that stage in their careers when one works to craft a professional identity. They struggled to understand how a senior physician, who seemingly had it made from a professional standpoint, could take her own life. In the course of meetings held to discuss the suicide, several residents expressed the perception that their own unhappiness and concerns about their training and work lives were not being addressed, much as they imagined those of the dead woman might have been neglected.

The second major event in the hospital's life was a nursing strike. It sharply divided the nursing staff into those who observed the strike and those who chose to work despite it. The strike also created tensions between physicians, many of whom opposed the strike because of its perceived effects on patient care, and the nurses who went on strike. Over the months it took to resolve the workplace issues that had led to the strike and to get the nurses back to work many bitter and angry feelings were generated, which at some level persist to the present day.

During the period of time in which I was reviewing the copyedited text of this book I experienced a potentially life-threatening illness, developing a deep-vein thrombosis (blood clot) in my left leg and a resultant pulmonary embolus (a blood clot that travels to the lungs) that necessitated a brief hospitalization and anticoagulation (blood thinning) treatment. Interestingly, my denial almost prevented me from seeking medical care for my painful, swollen left leg and the acute onset of shortness of breath because I attributed the former to a running injury and the latter to bronchitis, failing to make the deduction that they were related phenomena.

The most unsettling experience during my hospitalization was having a young medical intern ask me if I were "a full code," that is, did I want people to put a breathing tube down my throat and attempt to resuscitate me if my heart and/or lungs should suddenly stop working. Not being a "full code" would imply that I already had a life-ending illness and a low quality of life and that resuscitation would only serve to prolong the inevitable. I was so stunned by her question that I could not think of a reply. Did she, I wondered, know something about my medical condition that I did not? Had I, in the space of a few hours, been transformed from a healthy, functional professional into a "gomer," defined by Shem in *The House of God* as "a human being who has lost—often through age—what goes into being a human being" (p. 424)? Finally I asked what she thought. "I don't know," she replied. In the course of a single day I had gone from being a professor in a medical school to being a patient in our university hospital who, in the judgment of at least one young health care professional, might no longer be worth making any extra effort to keep alive.

During my recovery, as I dealt psychologically with a heightened awareness of the fragility of life, I found it difficult to return to work on this manuscript that focuses on coping with death. However, the experience did reemphasize for me several of the points that I hope reading these intensely personal narratives will convey. Each of us, patient, parent, doctor, or nurse, is at all times only a step away from death. If we share nothing else, we are united in the fear of our inevitable mortality. In caring for the dying and their loved ones we as physicians and nurses must find a way to maintain the empathy and compassion that we would want to receive in our own dying process. We must explore and understand our fear of death so that denial and repression do not cause us to withdraw the human warmth that should surround and comfort the dying and their families. I hope that reading this book, and reflecting on the honest and heartfelt stories told by its participants, will help those new to the medical and nursing professions, as well as those who have been in practice for years, to hold onto or reawaken that passion to treat the whole human being that enlivens and sustains the art of healing.

PART I

RESIDENTS

R esidents, along with recent nursing school graduates, are the newest members of the pediatric health-care team and are often the most vulnerable to the intense, grinding, and sometimes terrifying experiences of critical care. Despite four years of medical school, two of which are spent on the wards assisting in the care of patients, the reality of bearing responsibility for patients and being transformed from observers into participants makes a profound difference in their experience of patients', their patients', dying and deaths.

Long hours, exhaustion, and the relative inaccessibility of friends and family, who are often separated by time and distance, add to the potentially traumatic effects on residents when children are dying. Because the hierarchical nature of university teaching hospitals distances them from the attending physicians, and interdisciplinary issues may separate them from the nurses, the residents are usually one another's best sources of comfort and understanding. The presence of many more women in medicine, and especially in pediatrics, appears to me to have improved the quality of resident-to-resident support and done much to erode the sometimes abusive, macho atmosphere in which many older physicians trained. Vestiges of the "suck it up and move on" mentality, however, still remain among senior attendings and can reduce the likelihood that residents will turn to them for help. This is reinforced by the residents' frequent perception that the attendings are assessing them, writing evaluations for their files, and judging their suitability as future practitioners.

Some residents have already begun their families by the time they enter training and have children of their own. Their spouses may also be in residency training or working full time and this, combined with the residents' long hours and nights on-call, may make them relatively unavailable as sources of support. Residents with children identify them as a source of strength and comfort after long hours in the hospital, but they also recognize that their children may contribute to overidentification with their child patients because of similarities in age, gender, appearance, or behavior. One resident commented to me that whenever she walked through the pediatric intensive care unit she would have to steel herself against the sight of the children's little toes sticking out from under their blankets, because they were always so perfect and reminded her of her own child.

While the attending physicians and experienced nurses have selected intensive care or hematology-oncology as their areas of specialization, the residents are still generalists and many have not developed the psychological defense mechanisms that allow specialized practitioners to deal with children's deaths as a part of their routine. After training, people who are unable or unwilling to deal with dying children usually opt for other areas of practice in which such experiences rarely or never occur. The residents, however, have not yet been able to choose what branch of pediatrics suits them best. Despite this, they will be exposed during their residency to more deaths than most will encounter at any other time during their careers. Because they are relatively unprepared to encounter dying children, the shock and pain of their initial encounters with death are often quite disorganizing. As one attending put it, "they're like deer caught in the headlights."

"The patient dies and that's it, next patient!"

Christie has found that her son's difficult birth and the deep love
she feels for him have made dealing with the deaths of children
very painful. Her work with dying children has intensified her concerns about his well-being to an at times almost unbearable
degree. Witnessing the death of a child that reminds her of her
son stimulates a powerful maternal need to be home with him, to
hug him, and to treasure his life. While she knows that she cannot protect him from everything, after an especially difficult death
her protectiveness is heightened for the next few days. She believes
that she and her resident colleagues could do a much better job
of helping dying children and their families to cope with death
if they were not so overworked, exhausted, and inhibited by the
presence of attending physicians whose approaches to children's
deaths often differ greatly from their own.

I

"The first child I cared for who died was in the ICU during the third
month of my residency. He was brain dead and had been beaten up
by someone. He was the same age as my son. Around the same time
another child was brought in. He'd been in a car accident and died.
Both deaths hit me hard. I wanted to assign blame. It was easier
because I could blame the parents, but harder because they walked
out fine and their children were dead. I was angry with them. They
were given the responsibility of caring for children and they didn't.
   "After the child that was abused died I cried and cried for three
days in a row. Now that I have a child I'm more vulnerable, but pro-

fessionally, I have no choice; there are other children to care for. The family of the child that died in the car accident decided that he could be an organ donor. I had no idea what that meant. The child remained in the PICU for another twenty-four hours and was kept on machines until they could harvest his organs. It was so hard! I had to walk by because there were patients on either side that I was caring for. He was dead and his parents were gone and grieving. What would I do if it were my child knowing that he'd have to be in the ICU after his death? Would I stay or go? It raised questions about organ donation. I always wanted to be an organ donor, but learning about the process made me wonder. It was so distressing! We usually try to make children better, but he was dead and there were all those machines working. It was disheartening to go by the room. I felt hopeless and helpless. I tried to focus on the people that were being helped by the organ donation. How did the parents decide to leave? He'd still be there for another day. I felt bad for them and for his little brother. 'Good-bye, we're going forever.' He looked so alive because all his injuries were internal. It was like in the movie *Coma*.

"I coped with it by turning my feelings off at work. I also talked with a nurse when I was on call about the abused child that died. Rather than blaming or being angry she focused on the child's spirit giving the father's spirit more strength. She wanted to help the person who had murdered his own child.

"I'm less angry now. I wanted to remember those dead children, to honor them by keeping them alive in me, but to forget the details. I kind of accepted their deaths as part of this job I've chosen. I've tried to feel and hope for the abuser.

"Subsequent deaths haven't been so devastating. I'd been through it and cared for a couple of children that died. It's not easy to care for a child that dies, but each death eases the overall difficulty of it. Children die. It's very sad, but despite all of our efforts they die. Sometimes someone is to blame and sometimes not. It's a numbing experience. With most of the other children I've cared for that died there was a little relief because they had long-term problems and had struggled so hard for a long time. They weren't as sudden as those first two and that made it easier. The deaths were hard on everyone, but maybe better for the children. It also made me more aware of exploring end-of-life issues with parents. What's the best thing: more experimental treatment; another bone marrow transplant? Or stopping the medications and helping the child to enjoy something like a day outside of the hospital, a trip.

"I haven't yet been so involved in a patient's care that I've felt something I did caused the death. It feels a bit like a failure when a child dies. We don't know enough to prevent or cure what the child died of. Children are supposed to live and it's hard to have them die. Our job is to keep children healthy and safe and then they die. I think of the parents. I can't imagine my child dying. I feel so much for them since I've had a child. It's really hard if they're around his age. I lose it! It makes me more nervous about him. Then I try not to go overboard. I can't keep him one hundred percent safe, but for a few days after a child dies I'm extra protective of him."

II

Christie's father worked in sales and then as a distributor and manufacturer's representative in the electronics industry. Her mother worked as an elementary school librarian and a secretary and then did administrative and clerical work for a bank and a children's hospital.

"My dad had quite a temper and he and my mother fought a lot. It was more relaxed when he wasn't there. He traveled a lot for work. I always felt closer to my mother. I was the youngest and the only girl, dad's little sweetheart. It was a nice relationship in that way and I felt close to him intermittently, but there was also a lot of anxiety. I felt that I wasn't quite up to par with his expectations."

Her parents separated twice, first when she was in the third grade and then again when she was in the seventh grade. She recalls feeling "quite glad when they separated. Most of my friends' parents were divorced and I thought that I'd be part of the in-crowd. The main factor was that it was so much more relaxed! I didn't have that queasy feeling that he'd explode at any minute. When they separated in the seventh grade I didn't want to visit him.

"My father's family came from Mexico. He was born in the United States, but many of his siblings were born in Mexico. He grew up Roman Catholic, but never practiced as an adult. My mother was Anglo and grew up in the Lutheran church. We attended a Baptist church initially, then a Presbyterian church. We went to church, but without my dad, and church was not a major factor in our lives. We didn't talk about religion at home.

"A lot of my father's beliefs were more Latino, but we grew up in an Anglo style. We lived in the suburbs and were an average suburban white family. I was attracted to my father's Latino background. His father decided that the family should assimilate in the United States and my father grew up removed from Mexican culture. Some Latino attitudes, like the role of the man in the family, persisted. I regretted the absence of Latino ethnicity when I was a child. I remember a couple of Latino children in my class. They celebrated their cultural holidays and I felt that we should be doing that, too.

"My Latino ethnicity didn't affect me most of the time. I was just another white kid in the suburbs. There were only a few minority students in my school and I didn't look Latino. It was a little hard for me because my last name was Latino, and that caused tension as other children or neighbors would say prejudiced things about Mexican culture. I found that distressing. And there were also a few Latinos who were into Hispanic power and I sometimes felt a little lost."

Death was discussed "pretty openly" in her family. "A lot of people died. My father was the youngest of twelve children and we had a lot of older relatives. The youngest death I remember was when I was six years old. People died throughout my life and my parents didn't keep it a secret, but we didn't have any big talks about it."

She isn't sure what her parents' views of death were. "People just died. There weren't any religious overtones and it was pretty matter-of-fact. 'He died.' My mother might have said something about the spirit or the soul; 'They're gone and we remember them.' That was all. People were dying every year and we hardly ever talked about. That's interesting in itself!

"After death people went to heaven. No one went to hell. It was a little confusing. I'd see the body lowered into the ground, but heaven was up there. Why were they down there? I don't recall any discussions about it. The Presbyterian church taught that a member of the church who accepted Jesus Christ had a joyous reunion with God and everlasting life with Him."

As a child "I had some concept of heaven. Everyone was up there somewhere having a party. In the fourth grade my puppy died. I think that someone suggested the idea of a dog heaven and I carried that idea over to people. I remember that one or two weeks after he died the veterinarian's office called. I thought they'd called to say that they'd made a mistake and he was still alive!"

The first death Christie recalls occurred when she was six. "A paternal uncle died. I had great memories of him although I'm not sure if it's what I remembered or what my father told me about him. I remember missing him, but I didn't attend the funeral. I felt a little sad. He had an infectious laugh. I was close to his daughter, who was fifteen years older than I was, and I thought about how his death would be for her. I think of him now and then whenever I think of people that have died or when I see my cousin.

"When I was fifteen a good friend of mine died while my parents were out of town. A drunk driver killed her. Three months later my mother's father died and a year and a half after that my father's mother. I just realized now that all those deaths occurred at around the same time. My friend's death was awful. Two weeks before it happened I'd had a dream that my best friend had died. I told her and we talked about it. Then a couple of weeks later this other girl died. It was on a Friday night and three of my girlfriends and I were out driving around, going to the mall, and drinking. We were driving up a road toward a main busy street and a place where we all hung out. An accident had just occurred. There was a crushed

27

motorcycle and ambulances over in the field. We said, 'That's bad,' but we didn't know that it was one of our best friends. She was on a motorcycle with another friend, who was driving. The drunk driver that killed her was a guy who had graduated from our high school. The next morning another friend came over and asked if I'd heard about Diane. That's when I realized that the accident we'd seen was hers. It was awful, the worst thing. We'd just met her after our junior high schools merged. She was a vivacious, happy person. I sat opposite her in class and when I went to school on Monday her chair was empty. The funeral was two days later. It was overwhelming. She was very popular and there were so many people. We talked about the accident, about her, and about how awful it all was. A few years ago I found an article that I'd saved about her. It made me very sad and I wondered what she would have become. What a waste!

"Her death didn't make us stop drinking and driving. I had no thoughts of my own mortality. I was a typical teenager! Now I realize that I was really lucky. We did some pretty stupid things in high school. She wasn't doing anything wrong or dumb. She'd been very involved in her church and I remember in the memorial service a lot of talk about her being with God in a better place. Looking back I think that she would have been all right with her death because of her beliefs. I also remember thinking that the drunk driver should be locked up and the key thrown away!

"My mother's father died at three or four A.M. on New Year's Day. It had just turned 1979. I was with a church youth group in a cabin in the mountains for New Year's. We'd stayed up late and I went to sleep in a sleeping bag with everyone around. Suddenly I shot up from a dead sleep thinking about my grandfather. The next morning I thought 'That was weird.' I went home that afternoon. I remember getting out of the car, feeling happy, saying good-bye, and walking into the house. There was an eerie feeling in the house and I was nervous. I walked in and things got quiet. Everyone was talking softly and it was so obvious that something awful had happened. I saw a vacuum cleaner in the middle of the floor. My mother would never leave a vacuum cleaner out. I knew that something was wrong. I asked, 'Where's Mom?' I was closer to her than anyone else in the family and I thought that something had happened to her. My father said, 'Sweetheart, your grandfather died.' Initially it was a relief that it was he and not my mother. She'd already gone to Nebraska where my grandparents lived.

"I adored my grandfather, except he never wanted my mother to marry my father because he was prejudiced. He used to say to me, 'You're all right for a little spic.' I remember visiting them in Nebraska and having a ball. I went every couple of years and I thought that he was neat. I missed him and still do. He was fun. He cleaned the bank and used to take us with him. We'd run around changing the calendars on the desks. I remember being sad, missing him, and being sad for my grandmother. She had a hard time. They'd been married for fifty years. She had to move because she couldn't afford the house and she didn't seem to know what to do. She was never quite the same again. I used to talk with him after he died. I'd think of him and tell him what I was doing. Now I talk to my grandmother. She died two years ago. That was awful! I may start crying now. I was very close to her and loved her. She made quilts. When her grandchildren got married she gave them one. She said to me, 'I don't know if you'll ever get married' and gave me a quilt. This was several years before I met my husband. She was so excited when I did get married. She and my husband had a special relationship. A few years ago I called to tell her that I was pregnant. I think she was happier than anyone! She'd given up on me marrying or having children. I'd picked out her husband's name for the baby if it were a boy. The night that I went into labor she had a stroke. My mother called to tell me. The next day Grandma wasn't doing well. My mother was struggling about whether to be with her mother or me and finally went to be with her. I called my grandmother at the hospital, but she wasn't responsive. I told her that we were going to name the boy after my grandfather.

"Two days later my son was born and the circumstances were awful. I needed an emergency C-section. His heart rate dropped and he had to be intubated. I was in the hospital, my baby was in the NICU, my mother was in Nebraska, and my grandmother had had a stroke and was unresponsive. Three days later I had a dream. My grandmother and my favorite aunt, who had died a few weeks after my wedding, were walking toward me. There was a little baby boy between them and me. They picked up the baby and walked away with him. I said, 'You can't take my baby!' I woke up and went to the NICU. From then on he got stronger and stronger and my grandmother got weaker and weaker. She died two weeks later. I believe that she'd heard me tell her that I'd named my son after my grandfather. I believe there was a connection. She gave him strength and gave him to me. As she gave him her strength she became weaker. He's two now and doing fine.

"I talk to her when I'm sad and miss her. I think of her when my husband uses the rolling pin she gave him or when my son does something that would make her laugh or cry. I miss her. I used to call her when I wanted to tell her something. I called her and wrote her a lot. I got close to her after graduating from college and realizing what a neat person she was."

III

"I used to work as a writer and editor for a healthcare publication. I thought it was interesting and decided that I wanted to be an orthopedic surgeon. It made so much sense. You could do something. I'd had knee surgery myself. However, I decided not to do orthopedics because of the life style and the long residency. Primary care also seemed more important to me. There was more that I could do to help someone other than just fix the knee. I got interested in working with an underserved population. And I like children. They're honest, brave, and up-front. Everything is an adventure for them!"

Thinking about her present level of career satisfaction she rolled her eyes. "I struggle with it. If I can focus on the time after my residency I'm satisfied, but right now I'm not so satisfied. I like the patients in my continuity clinic. I overheard one of my patient's mothers say, 'Dr. E. is the best doctor!' She looks at me as her child's pediatrician. Everywhere else the attendings are in charge. The negative parts of the job are not sleeping, not seeing my family, working too hard, worrying that I'll make a mistake because I'm tired and busy, and not having time to relate to people. I don't have time to learn what I need to know. I don't have a life! I forgot my nephew's birthday. That's so unlike me. I hate it! This isn't me. I lose connection with my friends. It's a job you could spend all of your time doing.

"My long-term interest is in hematology-oncology, but I don't think I want to do more training or live in a big city. I want to go back home and be closer to my family. I'll probably do general pediatrics on a part-time basis. What I get from my clinic now is what keeps me going."

"Nothing in medical school can really prepare you to deal with patients' deaths. I had a positive experience with a dying patient as a third-year medical student. I was doing a rural rotation and he was an eighty-four-year-old man with an abdominal aortic aneurysm. He knew that he had it, but chose not to do anything about it even though he knew it would probably kill him. He said, 'I've lived a wonderful life and I have a great family. I don't want to go through all of that.' He died three days later. His wife was so distraught. She understood what he wanted, but she had a hard time with it. She said, 'I have to go with what he thinks.' He handled it so well and so did she. We provided comfort care. Their children came. I got to be there with them in the hospital for twelve hours. It felt like a fun family gathering. They were telling jokes and watching a football game. When I came back to the hospital he'd gone to sleep. Thirty minutes later his daughter came out and said, 'We need your help. I think he's dead.' I didn't have a stethoscope so I felt the pulse. There wasn't a pulse so I yelled for a stethoscope. He'd died. It was peaceful and the family was all there. He was a nice funny man. It showed me that death could be all right. His daughter came up to me and said, 'Thank you so much. You've done a lot for our family.' I had the time to be there with them. Now I don't have any time.

"In medical school we had a course that included many sessions on death and dying. It was in the winter, rainy and gloomy, terrible timing. Residents, attendings, and older medical students came and talked about their experiences with dying patients. That was good. We got to hear peoples' real experiences. It made it seem less far away and removed having other medical students talk about it. We also had classes about discussing end-of-life care with families. It seemed very superficial at the time because you weren't actually caring for a dying patient. They did try. They made us think about things. It would've helped to work with dying patients as they die and to interact with the family like at a hospice.

"It's harder with children than with adults to say that we need to stop and let this patient die. We're inherently more reluctant to say that it's all right for a child to die or to stop and say 'What are we doing?' 'Are we helping this patient and this family?' 'Is there really a chance that the patient can get better?' I see so much of the opposite, like using new experimental treatments for cancer. It's frustrating. In the N I C U everything is done to save these little preemies. One baby was trying to die and we weren't letting it. It's hard and frustrating and there's no time to deal with stuff. The patient dies and that's it, next patient! There's always so much to do and no time to do a real debriefing. People would be willing to talk, but there's no time. I remember one baby. I was so impressed with the attending. I respected the way that she handled the baby's death. One of the residents' wives was pregnant and here's this baby dying. The resident was having a hard time thinking of his new baby. She was great with him.

"It would be good if there were a special conference for people on rotations where children are likely to die, the P I C U , N I C U , and hematology-oncology. It's distressing to me that there's such a division between the residents and the nurses. Sometimes there's a lot of animosity. A group of people from different disciplines would help us to see that these deaths affect everyone. We could share the experiences together. That nurse I mentioned had so much experience and had amazing insights into children's deaths. She was at peace with it. She wasn't angry at the father for the abuse."

IV

Christie feels that she is "getting better every day" at coping with the deaths of patients. "A recent death in my family helped. My niece, the child of my brother and sister-in-law, died in utero. They didn't do early chromosome testing and in the last two months of the pregnancy they found out that they had a child with Down Syndrome. The baby had lots of anomalies and died in the eighth month of pregnancy so they had to go through with a regular delivery. They had a memorial service. It was awful! To think that such a tiny young thing could die, but her life would have been so hard with all her problems. It made me more empathic with families and gave me another experience with a child's death. I don't know if it's harder to have a patient or a family member die. Experience helps. Remember that boy who died because his father beat him? I get angry and still have a hard time with that. I cope with it by crying the next time I'm alone and by hugging my son. Other children that die with something preventable, a freak accident or disease, are harder to deal with. I cry and hug my son. I know that child could be mine. Any time I care for a dying child around my son's age it's *really* hard! I had a very difficult delivery. It was terrifying, but he did fine! I can sometimes tell parents in the N I C U that I know it's hard to have a baby here because I had one here, too.

"I'm getting better at knowing that there are things that are out of our control. My job is not always to save a life. Making things better can sometimes mean that a child is going to die. I can't change all of those situations. In addition to the tragedy there's another part. The child's suffering will end. I'm better now at seeing beyond the tragedy. I've seen that in conversations with parents. They say 'I don't know how you can deal with this, it's so tragic.' They can only see the tragedy. I've seen myself grow in seeing beyond the death and tragedy, but they can't.

"Yes, I get angry, but I don't think it helps. It makes it easier for me, but as the P I C U nurse said, 'What does it help?' I can be angry with the abusive father, with the father who drives too fast, or with the mother who takes drugs, but that energy could be directed elsewhere and perhaps help. That nurse was so helpful and I think of her often. I look at what she did for me in a five- or ten-minute talk. She is spreading so much good and my anger doesn't help. I'm also pretty emotional about things. I can get completely overwhelmed. 'This poor little person; how can he die?' Having my own son makes it harder.

"It helps me to cope with the death of a child if I feel that I've done something to help the child or the family along the way. It makes it more difficult if I feel that I haven't been able to do anything to help. There are a few people who give me support, people who've had more experience with children's deaths. They also have helping, nurturing personalities. They're calming and empathic. They don't give answers or say much. They just acknowledge that it's hard. They've been there and know that it'll always be hard. There are a few people that I could call at any time and get help with a child's death. Just talking about it helps. I don't like being the only one dealing with it. It helps knowing that they've been through it before and understand."

Her husband does not provide much support. "He tries hard, but I need to talk to someone who knows what it's like. It's hard for people to relate to our work. He sees it as one hundred percent awful. 'If I did that I'd go crazy.' One of my friends says, 'I don't know why you chose that field.'"

V

Her own mortality "never enters my mind, but I do think about my son. It's too painful to think about. He needs to be grown and settled when I die! Long ago I used to imagine that I'd die in a plane crash. Then I was in one, a two-seater, and I didn't die. So I think that it can't happen again. I picture myself being an old person when I die. If I die at one hundred, my son will be sixty-five. I want to have everything done. I have so many things to do in my life. I want to travel and to have time with my child and husband. I also want to have a good effect on people's lives and to read and write more. It's especially difficult when I'm caring for a child with cancer or a traumatic injury. I think of him whenever anything bad happens to a child or even when I hear about it on the news. He has brought so much joy to my life!

"Driving home thinking about a child's death I'll start crying. Sometimes it's related to an experience that I've just had and sometimes it's an extension to thinking of my son. What would I do if he dies? I go home, stand in his room, and kiss him. That reassures me. His birth experience was bad. Sometimes I rationalize and think, 'He's had his bad experience.' I know that it's not rational, but it helps anyway."

Christie copes with her death anxiety and her anxiety about the possible death of her son by utilizing denial and magical thinking. "Despite all the death around me I never think of my own death"—"I can't die in a plane crash because I've already been in a plane crash and survived"—"Nothing can happen to my son because he has had his bad experience." Recognizing that her thinking is not logical, she still finds comfort in irrational beliefs that sustain her in a place where other innocent children suffer and die each day.

VI

A "good death" for a child depends on the situation. "If it's a traumatic injury the best thing is that the child is in the P I C U and everything is being done. If the child has a terminal illness and has been dying for a long time, and the child knows he's dying, then being in the P I C U and having everything done is the worst possible outcome. At the beginning after a diagnosis of cancer or another life-threatening illness end-of-life issues have to be addressed. If the child and the family decide never to give up, to try every experimental treatment, then it's all right. However, if the child doesn't want that and is tired and wants to be home then she should be in a comfortable setting and all right with what's happening.

"One of the worst deaths I experienced was a child in the PICU. She knew that she was going to die, but the father denied to the end that she was dying. I think that she wouldn't have wanted to die as she did. She did it for her father because he couldn't accept her death. She was robbed of a good death because she was so focused on what he wanted. It always bothers me when the child is being strong for her parents. The doctors need to help. We have to say that the condition could end up in death. It has to be addressed from the beginning. We have to decide together with the family and the child what a good death would be. The child should get two votes and everyone else one vote! Children know when they're not all right. A friend of mine had a child, a nineteen-year-old, who was very ill. They tried lots of things. Finally she said, 'This isn't working. I'm going to die and I don't want to die here feeling miserable. I want to go home.' She went home and her family and friends came. There was a two-day vigil and she died. For her, dying in the hospital would have been the worst thing.

"I think children understand more about death than we ever give them credit for. Under four years of age they probably don't have a concept of death. I've seen very insightful seven-year-olds. Most get to the point of knowing that they're dying. Early on in the process all the professionals have to agree that it's a terminal illness. The doctors and the parents have a responsibility to be honest with each other and with the child. Then if things go badly it's not the beginning of the discussion of 'What are we going to do?' If everyone is talking about it along the way it makes it a lot easier. The things that interfere with the process are physician and parent denial. Doctors want to save lives and keep trying. That's admirable, but they also have to address the possibility of the child dying. Doctors aren't good at dealing with death. They view it as a failure. I once asked an experienced hematology-oncology doctor if her work is depressing. She said, 'Success is doing what's best for the child and helping him with life or death.'"

VII

Christie's residency colleagues, like her, are not well prepared to cope with the deaths of their child patients. "There's not a forum or time to talk about it with them. People in my class amaze me and I'm so honored to be with them. Most are so empathic and able to help others going through a hard time with a child's death. It's hard for them because of time constraints. It's hard to care for yourself. The problem is the system. It doesn't allow people to work through children's deaths. None of us is good at saying 'What can I do better for the child, the family, and myself?' There was a boy that died in the P I C U. There were ten other patients and I was the only resident. I had to care for the other children. It gets you through, but if you don't pay attention to patients' deaths and their effects on you it may explode or implode. When we get together as residents I want to have fun and get to know them as individuals. 'Tell me about your vacation, not your dying patients.'

"A couple of people I know are able to focus on ensuring the least amount of suffering for the child. They're able to deal with the child's life while he's alive and try to help with that rather than just keeping the child alive. It may be asking an attending about D N R (do not resuscitate) orders or approaching the child about his death. They act on something that will help the child while he's alive. That helps them to cope. 'I made a difference. I helped that child.' As residents it's harder for us to advocate for the child.

"We'd be good at helping children cope with their deaths, but we're supervised by attendings that aren't. I've sensed a resistance in them to end-of-life issues, and that puts the residents in a tough place. Many are of a similar mind that every child shouldn't die in the P I C U with full support. They acknowledge that sometimes death is all right and that it's important to determine what a good death for a child would be.

"I feel limited by what the attending says and does. Most of my experiences with dying children have been with children that I didn't know well. I think it's a strength that I consciously think about the issue and believe that we should deal with it rather than dismissing it or thinking that it doesn't need to be dealt with. My problem is inexperience and not knowing what to do. Maybe I could help a child to start talking about dying, but I don't know what I'd say. I might flail."

2

"They came into the hospital with a daughter and they left with a small blue box of her stuff."

Anne learned from her close-knit, religious family to talk openly about her feelings. In medical school she was encouraged to talk about her emotional reactions to patients' deaths. However, her experience as a resident has taught her something different. While she can discuss her feelings openly with her resident colleagues, she perceives that her attending physicians do not encourage or approve of such openness. She believes that they will think she is weak and a whiner if she talks about her feelings. She also believes that they do not reach out to residents who are having trouble dealing with the difficult emotions stirred up by their medical training. Instead, she thinks that they judge such residents as not being strong enough. It is Anne's opinion that parents and children would want their doctors to be sensitive. However, her observations during training suggest that her teachers view such sensitivity quite negatively.

I

Anne first experienced a child patient's death "on my first day on the wards and my second month of training. A patient came in early in the morning from an outside clinic. She had a fever and a purple rash. My job was to take a brief history, do a physical exam, and then admit her to the intensive care unit. About six and a half hours after she was admitted she died. It was very striking. I talked with her parents and told them how sorry I was. I saw them leaving later that day. They came in with a daughter and they left with a small blue box of her stuff. It was horrible and really upsetting. She'd been well the day before. It made me realize that anything can happen at any time. Anyone can get sick. It made me think of my own mortality. It made me realize how fragile we all are and how changed her parents' lives would be."

After the patient's death "I talked to everyone I worked with, with her other caregivers, and with my husband. There was an article about her death in the newspaper. I clipped it out and put it on the refrigerator. I put it there to remember her. It's still there. I felt that I couldn't save her, but I could save her memory and think about her family.

"I hope that her death makes me more sensitive to listening to what parents are telling me. If they think their child needs to be seen you should bring the child in. I tried to learn something practical from her death."

The deaths of subsequent children have not affected her as much. "I haven't saved the news clippings about other deaths I've been involved with. I don't remember the names of all the other children who've died. When she died I was an intern, it was my first death, and I was so scared. Later I became a little more used to it. Her death was so unexpected. With other deaths the children have often been sick for a long time. Sometimes it's almost a relief when they die. But her death was different. It wasn't a relief. She hadn't suffered for years like some others have."

She copes with the deaths of child patients by "trying to help the family understand what happened. I can't take away the pain, but I try to be sensitive about what happened. Taking care of me comes later. Talking with people involved in the case helps. I talk with my husband. I tell him someone died and describe my feelings without sharing the details of the case. Talking helps me the most. It's like a release to explain my feelings to someone else. It's all going around in my head. It helps to put it in words and clarify my feelings. Then eventually you get sick of talking about it. At that point I'm done and I want to move on. Talking about the event helps me to figure out my feelings. The first question is, Could I have done anything differently? Even if you withdrew support, was it done right, was it ethical? If you feel comfortable with yourself that you did what you could, you can cope better."

If she were to make a mistake that caused the death of a child "it would be really hard. You'd need to talk to a counselor and talk with the hospital attorney. If you think there may be a lawsuit you'd have to inform people. My father is a lawyer and I've asked him for legal advice about cases. In one case I thought someone else had done something wrong. You could tell what I thought from reading my notes in the chart. If my notes had disappeared it might have looked like I hadn't done the right thing. In the midst of dealing with your own grief you have to think of your responsibility. Our society is litigious. If I made a mistake and there was a bad outcome it would be really hard. I'd take it really hard. I'd have to get professional counseling. You could lose your license and your whole career over something like that. Hopefully someone would catch your mistake.

"Sometimes we're on call and we're sleepy. I remember once that a nurse came and woke me up about a patient. I couldn't recall who it was, but I got up and followed her down the hall anyway, too embarrassed to ask her whom the patient was. Then I finally woke up and remembered.

"We review problem cases formally in M and M [morbidity and mortality] conferences, but you can't really talk with your colleagues about screwing up because that could come back to haunt you. People are pretty frank, but no one will admit their guilt in front of other people. If something bad happens everyone covers their butt.

"Our goal is to save lives, to make lives better. People expect doctors to know and do everything. If you can't make a diagnosis the parents get upset. I remember one case when I was covering for another resident. During the night one of her patients had a crisis. He'd been doing well earlier in the evening, but by the time I was called things had changed dramatically. I ran to the ward and the patient looked terrible. There wasn't a heartbeat. It was the most terrifying moment of my life. The family, the nurses, and the intern were all looking at me and I had to tell them that there was no heartbeat. The family was screaming, 'What have you done to our child?' It was so terrifying. I thought that I'd get in trouble. Even though I'd called an attending for help earlier I thought that maybe I hadn't called the right person. I was afraid I'd lose my license. I was afraid I'd be sued. I was also upset because the patient had gotten so sick. It was really upsetting. I was senior resident on the ward and I didn't want a child's heart stopping on my watch. It was like your worst nightmare come true. I had a feeling of dread as if my own heart had stopped beating.

"Afterwards I talked with every resident I could. I probably talked with more people than I should have. I did it before the hospital administration could tell me not to. I justified it to myself by saying that I wanted to teach people something. 'Even though you're told not to go over an attending's head, if you're concerned about a patient you should do it.' I talked about it nonstop. Then the hospital started having meetings 'to help people cope.' But I think they were really trying to find out what had happened so they could protect themselves. I also talked with my family about it and got their emotional support. The talking helped me a lot. I thought, 'Now everyone understands and I can move on.'

"Whenever I hear the name of the attending I called I feel angry. I feel fear when I think of the child's heart stopping. I feel sad for the child's family. I remember how abandoned I felt then. It was scary. If I think about it enough it's still upsetting. I'm still intimidated by some attendings, but if I'm worried about a child I know that I've got to have a thick skin. I can't worry about what they think of me. I just have to call them. I keep reminding myself that what is most important is the child's well-being. I know you've got to play a game of respect and that you catch more flies with honey, but you can't always make people happy if you're going to call them at night.

"Personally I find the death of a child very sad. I picture myself in the parents' position. I grieve. I dump a lot on my husband, a lot of my feelings. It was more of a problem when I was an intern. I think he got tired of listening to it. It wasn't fair to him and so we talked about it. I decided that maybe I should talk with my professional friends about my feelings. We came to an understanding. He's still very supportive, but I try not to bring everything home. We've been married for six years and I'm proud that we didn't let medical school and medical training come between us."

II

Anne's mother and father are both Mormons, but her mother was much more devout. Most of her father's family had left the church and he did not consider himself religious. Her mother's family was very militant about their religion and looked down on Anne because she, like her father, left the church in her early teens. Her younger brother and his wife were also quite religious and "have strong opinions about my not being like them."

The tension between Anne and her brother came to a head when she went off to medical school. She left Utah and went to the East Coast for both college and medical school. "In Utah people treat you differently if you're not religious. I didn't want to live there." When she went to medical school her boyfriend, now her husband, moved with her and they lived together. "We wouldn't have done that at home. Our families wouldn't have approved. My brother was working for the Church. He wrote me a letter saying that it was against God's teaching and that I was breaking the law of chastity. The Church would condemn my behavior. It hurt my feelings a lot because I'd supported him emotionally in his work for the Church. I stopped writing because I was mad and what he said was insulting. We haven't been close since then."

She thinks that her strong religious heritage is "interesting, but I don't agree with the Church's teaching. In my neighborhood back home people weren't nice to me. I'd invite them to my birthday parties, but they wouldn't invite me. My sister thought it was because my dad wasn't religious. Or maybe it was because I was smarter than they were. They weren't nice to me even though I was going to church. I felt hurt and left out. I wanted to achieve to show them. I can do better and be better than you people who live in their parents' basements. I also worked hard because I'm a woman. In my religious tradition females aren't encouraged to succeed. Women are supposed to marry and stay at home. I'm as smart as any man!

"My religious heritage made me want to be my own person and to make decisions for myself. Even though it was not the teaching of the Church my mother encouraged me to study and to have a profession. She saw people getting divorced and the women had no skills to support themselves. I stopped going to church when I was twelve or thirteen. I had some battles with my mother, but not as bad as my sister had the year before. I didn't want to go to church because it made you feel bad about yourself. It said that you're a sinner and imperfect. I'm a perfectionist. I'm hard enough on myself and I didn't need the Church criticizing me as well. I wanted the Church to make me feel good about myself. So at that point I started distancing myself from the Church and from Utah. I still have morals and standards. The Church taught me that. However, mine aren't as strict. I drink alcohol and I lived with my husband before we got married. I was baptized, but I wasn't married in the Church. My husband is also very anti-Church."

Her family was "fairly open" about death. "My paternal grandfather died when I was ten. It was really hard on everyone, but it was especially hard on my father. We talked about my grandfather. He was a decent person. He was the kindest, most accepting and open of our four grandparents. We talked about how we'd miss him and tried to remember what he was like.

"My parents were very frank with me about death. Their friend's son committed suicide. My dad brought it up with me because he wanted to talk with me about it. He said, 'We'd never want you to do that. You can always come to me for help. We can always work things out no matter how sad you are.' I was sixteen and a freshman in college living in a sorority house. I think he was concerned about my being so young and living away from home. I don't think he was worried that I might be depressed. He has struggled with depression all his adult life. I've worried that he might commit suicide, but he wouldn't because he's too logical. He has made changes in his life. He has known others who committed suicide. One of his clients was a shoplifter and a shopaholic. She charged too much and accumulated huge debts. She embezzled to pay the debts and then killed herself. He and I talked about it. He wished that he could have helped her more.

"I think my father has thought about suicide. He told my sister that he had and my sister told me. She became depressed earlier in her life than I did. I didn't experience it until I was in residency. It took a long time for me to recognize it. Other people noticed something was wrong. Rather than tell me they wrote me a bad evaluation saying that I complained too much. It's in my permanent record."

Anne's parents differed in their views about what happens to people after they die. "My mother took the Church's view. There's a heaven and an apocalypse. After you die you go to a waiting place. When Christ comes he decides who will go to heaven and who will burn. My father wasn't sure what happens. He thought that people were either happier after they died or entered nothingness. He's read a lot about Eastern religions. When my cat died they reassured me that I'd see him again. My mom told me that I'd see him in heaven. She said, 'He's happy there and free of pain.'"

She learned to cope with the deaths of others by "talking about the death in our immediate family. My parents were reflective. They told us how important we are to them and how important the person who died was. They were pretty open about death. They thought that talking about it was the best strategy. A man in my dad's office died of a heart attack. He talked about it and cried.

"An aunt who was close to my parents died when I was in medical school. She lived near us, and her family used to vacation with us. It was really hard on me. I couldn't attend the funeral because of exams. That was hard for my family. Then I got married two weeks after her death and that cast a pall over the wedding, especially for my mother. She was very emotional and had trouble coping with her sister's death. She took out her feelings on my husband. She wanted people to pay attention to her even though it was my day. We got married back east and very few people came to the wedding. Then we took our honeymoon with both sets of parents. That was a mistake! My husband wanted my attention and my parents wanted my attention. They felt that he was taking me away from them. My husband and my parents didn't get along very well for a long time after that. When we got home my father called and yelled at my husband, telling him off. He said that he hadn't treated my mom right. I was really caught in the middle. I wanted to make up with my parents, but I also had to support my husband. Since then I've managed to bring my parents and my husband back together. I say good things to them about him."

The best way to cope with death is "to talk and be open about it. It isn't a sign of weakness. That's a problem in medicine. You're supposed to be strong and not bothered by death. You just keep going. After the suicide of a faculty member we all said that we'd help each other if we were down, but no one helped me or came to me. The faculty didn't want to hear that I was depressed and they didn't help me. Instead they called me a whiner. When I mentioned it to one attending he changed the subject and walked away. After finding out what they'd written in my record I decided that I wouldn't say anything more.

"There's one colleague I can really talk to. She helped me to see that I was depressed. At the meeting about the faculty member's suicide she brought up what I wanted to say. She said that she was angry because people were saying things about feelings, but no one really does that. If you do they think you're weak."

III

Anne chose medicine because "I was interested in science and wanted to work with people. I probably went into pediatrics because I'm sensitive and wanted to be with sensitive people. I also enjoy working with children more than with adults. It's so hard to make changes in adults' lifestyles.

"Residency has been frustrating. If the entire career were like residency I don't think that many people would stay with it. It's an abusive system. They expect you to work a lot of hours with no sleep and no one gives you a break. You're expected to perform even if you were on call the night before. Sometimes residents show up trying to look a little grungy, wearing their scrubs and not combing their hair to let the faculty know that they've been up all night, but they don't notice. One time I was doing a couple of rotations at once. My clinic was overbooked and I didn't have the time to do a dictation [a recorded message of clinical care that is later typed up for signature by the physician]. I'd been up all night, but the guy from the other service didn't care. He just wanted his dictation. Another example is that you have to take admissions the day after you've been on call. You don't get to sleep when you're on call and you may be there until six o'clock the next day."

The positive side of training has been "working with children, seeing their different stages of development, and feeling that you can make a difference. Children rebound more quickly and you get feedback. You give an antibiotic and they often get better really fast. My special interest is in working with babies. They grow on a daily basis, I like doing procedures, and I'm interested in genetics and the physiology of the newborn."

On the negative side is "child abuse. It's more prevalent than I'd ever dreamed. People do things to their children that I wouldn't think of doing. There are ignorant parents who don't care to read to their children. They don't realize how formative those early years are. It's frustrating to see how some people parent. I hope that I can make a difference. So many people raise their children in a way that makes me sad."

In the future she plans to work in a neonatal intensive care unit and do research. "It's nice to have a balance between clinical work and research. I'd also like to get involved in community education, preventing premature babies. One of the good things about medicine is that you're always learning. On the other hand, you can never feel that you've mastered the field."

"In medical school they had a few lectures about death and in our small groups we dealt with death and dying. It wasn't in a clinical setting where deaths really occurred. One day during the time my aunt was dying we were talking about dealing with dying patients. I thought of my aunt and of not being at the funeral. I got emotional, cried, and had to walk out. I was embarrassed to cry. Fortunately I had a sensitive mentor. He was an older, semiretired doctor. Afterward he was helpful. He wanted to talk about it.

"Sitting and talking about death in medical school is different than dealing with it as a resident. In medical school they told us to talk about it. As a resident you just move on and don't talk about it. Maybe now they're training a generation of doctors who can talk about their patients' deaths. If someone has been through something rough they need to give you a break and talk to you about how you're doing. Maybe the person supervising you could ask how you're doing. Instead it's what went wrong and what could we do differently. You need to be objective to learn and need to be able to distance yourself, but at some point you have to face what happened. If the death is a sensitive issue for the hospital they don't want you to talk about it."

IV

Even though talking about a difficult case or a child's death is a good way for Anne to cope with her feelings, there are constraints within the system that make it difficult for her. "I complain to my colleagues and I cry with them, but then there's the problem of confidentiality. You're not supposed to talk about it. Anyone you talk to can get subpoenaed. And it makes you look weak. We don't talk to the attendings. You're supposed to be strong, invincible, and they're evaluating you. We're women in medicine and we have to show the men that we aren't bowled over by death."

She thinks that there should be more communication between the residents and the attending physicians, but she does not see a way to make it happen. "They're evaluating you. They expect you to keep working no matter what happens." Reflecting for a moment, she tried to understand how things might appear from the attendings' perspective. "One night a premature infant I'd been caring for died. The next morning one of the nurses came up to me crying and said that she wanted to talk about the death. I experienced it as a criticism. She said that I'd walked away from the bedside. All I was doing was going to wake up the attending that was sleeping ten feet away, but at just that moment the baby arrested and the nurse had to try to resuscitate it herself. I'd have been able to talk to her about her feelings if I hadn't felt so criticized. Maybe the attendings feel they're being criticized. Maybe that's why communication breaks down between hierarchical levels.

"The residents are very supportive of one another. We're all in the same boat. We try not to abuse each other. We may get grumpy, but the residents are prepared to be sensitive to one another. We all get pretty emotional about death. We're prepared to talk with each other, but we find it difficult. When a patient dies we let each other know by email."

After a patient dies, the help residents receive from their supervisors "depends on the attending. Some are less sensitive in general, not just about death, but about everything. They don't help you at all. If a parent is emotional and irrational and you're having trouble dealing with him or her, some attending physicians don't have the skills themselves and won't help you. There was one incident in which the attending refused to help me with an upset mom after her child died. When the mom finally talked to the attending she gave negative feedback about me, but he never said anything. Then he wrote me up accusing me of being a poor communicator! I talked with the residency-training director and he was really nice and supportive. He let me tear up the attending's letter myself.

"I'm more willing than most to talk about things that bother me. I talk with my husband and my friends. Not about confidential stuff, but about how I feel. I'm sensitive. My parents said that maybe I'm too sensitive. That's why it hurts to be called a poor communicator. I may take death and dying harder than others do. Whenever my parents said anything critical I'd get all upset. Sometimes I don't let things roll off my back too well. I've had a hard time dealing with that in my profession. I want my evaluations to be stellar! To get into medical school I had to have perfect As, then to get a good residency I had to have perfect evaluations. Bad evaluations hurt my feelings. It was especially bad when I was depressed. They don't love me here the way they did in medical school. I'm working my butt off here, but where's the positive feedback? I'm sensitive and a good communicator. When I have time I have the desire and the ability to talk to people about death. I think most people would want a doctor who is sensitive."

V

The experience of residency and the deaths of child patients have made Anne more aware of her own mortality. "I try to appreciate things more. I've opened up communications with my parents because of my experiences in residency of how short life can be. I appreciate my own health and realize how lucky we are not to have had deaths within our own family. I appreciate that my parents are still around. When I was in medical school I used to like telling them things that would shock them. Later on I talked with them about my experiences because I needed someone to talk to. Also, having seen how other people raise their children I appreciate the way my parents raised me."

VI

A "good" death is one that is "pain free, usually with drugs. The family gets to say good-bye before the child dies. The parents realize it's inevitable and they accept it. That's rare, but it's better if they can at least be at ease with what has happened. They're comfortable with the decisions that have been made. They realize that there's no hope and they want their child to be comfortable. It's also good if the parents don't insist on putting the child through heroic measures. Sometimes parents want to continue treating the child when the doctors don't. They're not ready to let go."

A bad death is when children have to "suffer, when their pain isn't addressed, or when they're put through a long series of procedures, especially if we know it isn't profitable, but the parents just won't let go." Other examples of bad deaths are "a child we could have helped if he'd been brought in sooner" or a case in which "child abuse has led to death. Those deaths are so useless.

"People often don't explain to children who are going into a hospital that they're not going to die. Children who can talk worry about it more than they say and more than the adults around them will acknowledge.

"I don't talk with children about death. I don't know what words work best. I've only been on the medical side. It's not really a resident's role. It's more for the attendings to do." She acknowledged, however, that the attendings rarely do it. She remembered "a clinic patient in clinic that was terminally ill. The nurse and I contacted the 'Make A Wish Foundation.' She went to Disneyland. It was very rewarding for me. It made me feel better about dealing with her death. Her family was very grateful. It was a poor family. No one had ever told them about Social Security. I talked about it with them, helped them with the paperwork, got their records together, and helped to get them some money. I felt like I was really able to make a difference for them."

Children have at times asked her if they are going to die. "Usually they're afraid of what is happening to them at the time. I try to say something positive like, 'We're doing all we can to help. Don't worry.' I don't have any experience sitting down and saying, 'You'll die eventually.' I don't want to take away their hope. I've often talked to the parents of premature infants and told them what they can expect. We have morbidity and mortality tables that tell what kinds of problems they can expect and the odds on their surviving at different birth weights. If a mother wants to know we bring out the numbers. I've had a lot of talks about that with the mothers of premature infants. I'm pretty good at it, providing appropriate information that they can use. I try to explain things in terms they understand."

Parents sometimes ask if their children are going to die. "You never really know. I try to be honest. I say, 'No one knows. We're doing all we can.' I try to give them hope. Some of them fixate on God intervening. In those cases I say, 'God will decide. No one knows what God will do.' Those cases are almost easier because the parents realize that not everything is in our control."

Talking to parents after their children have died is very difficult. "Those are hard conversations to have. I try to involve the attendings. It's emotionally hard. You don't want to think of a child dying. It's hard to see the parents' grief. It's especially hard if there's a language barrier and it's even worse if it's on the phone with an interpreter."

VII

"One faculty member committed suicide recently. She wasn't coping well with something. I compared myself with her. I decided that if what I'm doing is too much for me then I'll do something else. I can always go into private practice, even though that's looked down on in academics, and work half-time if I need to save my marriage or myself.

"I think the residents cope well. We complain a lot to each other and we whine a lot. That's how we cope and it helps. We feel better afterwards. I think, 'I'm suffering, but so are they.' When we're together outside of the hospital that's all we do, we complain. The attendings don't talk to us much about their feelings; they're a different caste level. It seems like they have it all together. Then one of them kills herself. But it seems like they're coping well."

Her resident colleagues are "pretty good" about talking with dying children "when they have the time, like the child in my clinic. On the ward they don't have the time. They can't sit around and hold patients' hands." She then interjected how much she had hated the movie Wit. "It portrayed the doctors in such a negative manner. They were uncaring, cold researchers. All they cared about was experimenting on their patients. Maybe I was like that when I was on hematology-oncology, but that was because of the pressures of the job, not because I'm an unfeeling, uncaring person. That movie really touched a nerve. It isn't my fault that I'm so busy. It's not because I'm a jerk!"

3

"What prevents us from being 'midwives of death,' something that has always been the physician's role?"

Interested in social activism, Ashley entered medical school and pediatric training hoping to work in an underserved or international setting. The rigorous demands of residency, however, forced her to focus on the biological rather than the psychosocial aspects of medical care and left her with a feeling of disappointment in herself and her training. She knows that if she became more personally involved with patients and their families she could have a positive impact on them and that the interactions would be important for her. What stops her from opening up emotional topics are the pressures of time and work. There is always so much to do, and her primary goal is to "get the work done and get out of here." Now that she is in part-time private practice she has been able to find the time and internal space to really listen to her patients and their parents.

I

Ashley's first experience of a child's death "was a two-and-a-half year old boy, a hematology-oncology patient. I knew him well. It was hard because of his up-and-down course. One doctor said that we should do a bone marrow transplant and that got the mother's hopes up. Then when he died you wished that you could have worked harder. He declined very quickly, fluctuating between a full code and a D N R. The day before he died, his mother decided that he wouldn't be going for another procedure. She didn't want him intubated. She'd suddenly seen something in him and knew that he'd die. The next day he kept deteriorating. We'd have intubated him, but because of her decision we could take the monitors away and get the family around. It was time for him to go. His death was positive and his mother was ready.

"That child had changed the mother's life. She'd been using drugs, but when he came she stopped. She thought of him as her angel and then he passed away. I went to the funeral service and I could see him in her eyes. It was very moving. The father was a wreck. The nurses and doctors were cynical about him because he never came around. The mother, on the other hand, had a lot of sorrow, but she was the strong one. It was a hard experience. It was sad and painful to go to the service, but I felt that I needed to go. I was grateful for the extra moments I'd spent with him and frustrated that I hadn't spent more time and that I'd held back.

"It helped to go to the service because it was a good place to be sad. It was impossible not to feel sad. There was music, photos, and lots of people telling stories about him. Seeing his mother and how strong she was it seemed like his short life had been very meaningful because it had turned her life around."

That first death "made me try harder to reach out to families and patients and allow them to see my feelings about a sad situation. Before, I held back and felt badly about it. Now I'm more likely to be personal with the patients. You realize that beneath the veneer of professionalism it's about people's lives. It's not a professional issue, but a personal one. We're there for the most difficult part of people's lives and we see them at their most vulnerable. It's a mistake to gloss over that. It's hard, as a resident, because you're at risk of the family thinking that you're not the real doctor, that you're young, inexperienced, and haven't had children. That makes you feel more pressured to be 'professional.'"

Compared to that first death, subsequent deaths of children have not affected Ashley as deeply. "I knew that little boy the best. I haven't gone to any funeral services since then. I'm not sure if subsequent deaths were really that different. My behavior changed, but I don't know if the children or the parents' experience of me was different. Different deaths affect you differently depending on how well you knew the patient and the family. Subsequent deaths haven't felt any less painful. I do delete emails that I receive about the deaths of children more easily now. In my intern year I'd get the emails and not know what to do with them. Should I save them in a folder? Now I don't worry about saving them.

"I've coped with the deaths of subsequent children by becoming more interested in the dying process, in how the child experiences it, and how the families seem to know when it's going to happen. Increasingly I believe that children and families know. It seems that the parents change their plan of treatment and shortly after that the child dies. The child doesn't seem to be there anymore, like his spirit is gone—like he's checked out. I think the parents pick up on that."

The most difficult aspect about a child's death is "thinking that I could have done something differently. However, I haven't had many experiences in which I've felt that the treatment has failed the patient or that I've missed something and that's why the patient died. It's all murky for me whether these issues are professional or personal. We spend so much of our lives in the hospital with these patients. It's hard to separate professional and personal when you're a resident. We sleep here, eat here, have all of our friends here, and it's our community. For some of the children and parents who are here a lot we become their family. Then it's personal.

"When a child is dying you see his family members and friends. I get to know them better and you get to know the child better. There are more pictures around of the family, the house, and the dog. As the time comes closer everyone tries to do things, to have this person visit or to do that thing, all the things that are at the core of who the child is. Then the child dies and I realize that I never knew him. I feel that I didn't have enough time to know him or for him to know me and for me to give on a personal level. Do I draw back? I must, but I always feel that I pull back because I don't want to intrude. That's what I think I'm doing, why I'm not giving more of myself personally."

"My family spoke openly about death after it happened. We were taught to cope with death by talking about it and crying if you felt sad. We remembered the dead person, drew pictures for him, and wrote him a letter. As a child I believed in heaven, but I had some doubts. 'How does everyone fit?' However, I did believe that you kept going.

"When I was eleven my father's father died suddenly. It was the first time I'd seen my father cry. I was really sad at the funeral. I kind of liked the experience of funerals because people talked about the person who had died. I liked the experience of laughing and crying at the same time. Those early losses and my family's openness helped me to be good at telling people how I feel. I tell people that I love them and to take care of themselves. When I say good-bye to someone I think, 'maybe I'll never see her again.'

"My parents believed in an afterlife and that people would meet others they knew there. I went to a Roman Catholic school for two years. One teacher said that we shouldn't cry when people die because we're just feeling sorry for ourselves. They were better off. That made a big impression on me. I repeated it to my mother when her father died the next year. My mother was always changing her mind about religion and exploring other options. One year she was very Catholic and the next we went hiking instead of going to church. However, we always believed in an afterlife. After people died their souls left their bodies. The person that we'd known wasn't there anymore. The body was like a guitar case. When the person died, the music was gone."

Ashley modeled her early strategies for coping with death after the words of her teacher. "I thought that it was all right to be sad, but that you should keep your sadness to yourself. I didn't accept for my own life what the teacher said about heaven being a better place. I wanted to live forever! I didn't think that I'd be better off dead."

Growing up, her primary experiences with death were those of her paternal and maternal grandfathers and her paternal uncle. "My maternal grandfather had colon cancer. I didn't cry very much after his death even though I loved him. A few months earlier my brother and I went to see him in the hospital. He was cachectic and looked like he was about to die. My brother and I got into an argument about who hated school more. Later I had a lot of guilt for arguing about such a dumb thing the last time I was with my grandfather. He had hospice care and died at home. My mother was there with him when he died. The sunlight was shining on his face and she knew that he was dead. It was a nice memory for her. She thinks that he comes as a ghost sometimes. He was musical, played the piano by ear, and liked to sing and dance a lot. She does, too. When she plays music she thinks that his spirit comes by her.

"When I was twenty-three and taking pre-medical classes my father's brother died. He was only forty-six and it was unexpected, a sudden myocardial infarction. It was a sad, sad thing. He had two young children and he and his wife were quite close. My grandmother was very sad to lose a son. My father felt bad. I remember him saying, 'I keep thinking that maybe it should have been me.' He got depressed, started jogging, stopped eating fat and cholesterol, and got really skinny. That's when I began to be concerned about health matters.

"My paternal grandfather was strict, had high expectations, and wanted me to do well and succeed. I felt sad because I couldn't show him that I'd done well. We were supposed to go to Europe together. After his death there was a sense that things weren't complete between us. I wish that he could see me now. I just visited his house. My grandmother is in great health. If he were still there would he be more involved in our world?"

III

"I was attracted to medicine because you're able to help people in a concrete way. I'm also interested in international work and thought that I'd have more opportunities to do that in medicine. I liked my early rotations on pediatrics and thought the pediatricians had more social activism and liberalism, two interests of mine. I hoped they'd inspire me and keep those interests going. I was also interested in psychiatry and the opportunity to manage behavioral problems."

Ashley believes she chose a good residency program but adds, "I'm not sure that I can satisfy my interest in social issues. We work a lot of hours and are very task- and learning-oriented. There's less time and interest in family dynamics and the issues of poverty and behavior. We're stuck in the biological instead of the biopsychosocial model. The things I enjoy most are a barrier to getting work done and having my own life. Ultimately, I'd like to have more flexibility in what I do and the population I work with. I'd like to work in underserved areas and spend some time abroad. I recognize the uniqueness of the way in which we're invited into people's lives, and when I'm not exhausted or stressed I realize what a privilege it is.

"We're too busy. There's not much time for the human side. Most of my fellow pediatric residents went into the field to help people and to work with the whole family. These days it's hard to do that. You're too busy. You don't have time to explore the other issues in children's lives, the psychosocial aspects. That's especially true on the hematology-oncology service. You're so busy and it's hard to make contact. You breeze in and out of people's rooms, where parents are facing the possible death of their child. It's distressing and I don't like it."

In the future she wants to practice general pediatrics. "Hopefully I'll find a niche in an underserved population or a psychosocially challenging population. I can't take the yuppie parents. I feel like saying, 'Get a grip! In developing countries a five-year-old sibling raises the younger children and they do all right. Get a grip!' They have too much time and money. I also get tired of telling parents to have their children wear bicycle helmets. It seems so trivial in a worldwide perspective."

Ashley is "very satisfied" with her medical school preparation for dealing with the deaths of patients. "My school was particularly good at it. I saw more deaths as a medical student than I have thus far in residency. We met in small groups and discussed support systems, our concepts of death, and our belief-systems around death. We talked a lot about physician-assisted suicide and ethics. We weren't taught about how to cope with the deaths of our patients. Our teachers were empathic in saying how difficult it can be. As a student on the medical service I had a lot of patients that died. I had more time and worked with two dying adults intensively, got to know them fairly well, and watched them die. One man I remember especially. It was as if he'd just decided to die. Then there was an old woman. She was all dressed up like a queen and her husband and sons were with her. She got sicker and sicker and then had surgery to remove a clot. I went to see her in the SICU [Surgical Intensive Care Unit] and asked the resident where she was. He said, 'Over there.' I looked over and she was being coded!

"Part of my decision to go into pediatrics had to do with those people I met in medical school, old people that seemed to die alone. Fifty years ago they were like me, looking forward to their lives and going out dancing. In pediatrics it's not as heartbreaking. It's more comforting because there's usually someone there."

She wishes that she had been taught "how to talk with parents about the deaths of their children. As a resident I often feel that they don't want me around. All you can say is 'I'm so sorry.' It would be good to be reminded that at some point you're just another person and that you can step out of your medical role. When I've gone by and said how sorry I am that their child has gotten sicker, the parents respond very positively."

IV

"I don't think that I'm well prepared to cope with the deaths of children. The majority of patients I've cared for on the hematology-oncology service have died. You feel almost distant and you can't believe that you feel that way. Then you feel like you're cold. 'I've been with all of those dead patients and I'm not sobbing.' Then at another time a child is dying in front of you, the parents are sad, and you're crying with them. I'm not very prepared to talk with children about dying, but I've become interested in it. One patient came in on Thursday and died on Monday. The attending said to the mother, 'I'm not sure when he'll die, but it'll be soon.' The mother said, 'If it's going to be that quick I shouldn't take him home. I'd have a dead boy and then what would I do?' The child had seemed out of it, but when he heard her say that he moaned and opened his eyes. The attending took the mother out into the hall and asked, 'Have you told him that he's dying?' She said, 'I'm not sure. I've talked about heaven.' The parents looked at one another, horrified that they hadn't talked with their son about dying. It was remarkable how the child responded. When the doctor said the word 'dying' he moved a bit and there was a flicker in his eyes. When the mother talked about having a dead boy he moaned, seemed to be trying to wake up, and moved his eyes. It was so sad and awful. I've been told that hearing is one of the last senses to go.

"Intermittently I've done well coping with children's deaths. I'm not afraid of dealing with people and don't mind being nearby when a patient is dying. I can comfortably interact with a dying patient. However, I fluctuate in terms of whether or not I take the time to acknowledge the situation with the parents. Sometimes I'm intimidated when I hear that a child is dying and I think, 'They won't want me there.' Holding back is a weakness. Sometimes I think that the family doesn't want to see me. I'm not the attending. Some families have seen so many nurses and residents that they don't really know you. When you know the child and the family and have a connection then it's easier to be involved. Sometimes I'm afraid that if I get involved they'll turn a cold shoulder to me."

After a child dies, it helps "to talk with the other residents that knew the patient, to reminisce about her as a real person and child, to see her positives and negatives, and to realize that it's all a part of who she was. It can hinder your ability to cope with a child's death if you keep on walking by and don't take a minute to think about the child and about your interactions with her, to see what the child meant to the world and to her family. When I do that I don't feel resolved or good about myself."

Her colleagues provide one another with "as much support as you ask for. We work so closely together and they're wonderful people for the most part. We have so many experiences in common. The problem with being a resident is that you just keep going and don't ask for help when you need it. Professionally it would be helpful to have more [Morbidity and Mortality conferences]. We don't have them very often, only in the NICU [Neonatal Intensive Care Unit]. They provide learning and closure. You know how something happened. There was a hematology-oncology memorial service for all the children that died that year. It's the only time in the year that we do something like that and it only happens for the hematology-oncology patients. It's nice to have a time to remember.

"Friends outside of medicine are more shocked than supportive. They think that what you're dealing with on a day-to-day basis is awful! They'll say things like, 'The most stressful thing I did today was to figure out what flight to take to Chicago.' My husband is in medicine so he gets it, but we're both in residency training and have enough of the hospital. We wanted our life together to be separate from that. I don't think that people outside of this world can really understand what it's like. Everything about it is so heavy."

V

The deaths of child patients remind Ashley "that anything can happen at any time. The visions we have of living to be one hundred years old may just be fantasies. You see pictures of children before they were sick. Before you meet them they looked like anyone else on the street. Most of my colleagues that have children think more about the mortality of their children than about their own mortality.

"I think about the mortality of my family members more frequently than the average person. Whenever someone leaves after a visit I wonder if it's the last time I'll see him or her again. My mother and

brother were here last weekend. I don't want to have regrets that I
didn't say what I wanted to say. I'm aware that anything can happen. I'm amazed that nothing has happened yet! You feel like you're
living a lucky life, but will you stay lucky?" The effect of such
thoughts is "in a way more positive than negative. I'm not fearful
about losing the people I love. Instead, I try to value them.

"I don't think about my mortality very often because I still kind
of think that I'll live to be old." Thoughts about dying "make me
sad. I have good friends, a husband, and family. I think about how
they'd be affected and how sad they'd be. It also makes me sad
because I love life. Heaven doesn't sound that interesting."

VI

A "good death" is one that is "painless and the child is surrounded
by people she loves and that love her. There's no fear." A "bad death"
is "the opposite of those things. I don't know what I think about
sudden death. It seems unfair. The six-year-old child of a family
friend died on a soccer field. He just dropped dead. His life was cut
short and there weren't any final words."

She believes that children "understand more than we used to think
about their own deaths. When they're told that it's all right to go,
they tend to pass. Do you remember that hematology-oncology
patient we talked about earlier? When we talked about his death
he stirred. He hadn't realized that this was it. When he heard it, he
seemed to accept it and died that afternoon.

"Parents and siblings should be part of the dying process so that
everyone is at peace with the situation and no one feels anxious about
it. It's also important that dying children understand what's going
to happen. We should talk with them. We should let them know
what's going on and explain what will happen to them. They pick
up on the vibes around them. Their fantasies are often scarier than
the reality of what they're going to experience, like the grim reaper
coming and taking them away.

"I don't think I've been as helpful to terminally ill children as I'd like to be. I could be. It's frustrating because helping a dying patient come to grips with his own death is an inspiring experience. Doctors are expected to be a part of the birth process. We should also be midwives of the dying process. However, we've ceded that role to others because of a lack of time and because we're afraid of the experience. One of the attending physicians on the hematology-oncology service is wonderful with dying patients. He's an inspiration. Others just breeze by.

"I'm not afraid to talk about death. The problem is time. I don't manage it well. As a resident I didn't find time in the day to do those things. If I had I'd have felt better about my residency experience, but in the moment you're more focused on getting things done and getting out of here. Whenever I took the time to talk with patients about dying I felt better about myself, but the Child Life people are around and they've got the time to develop relationships with the children and their families. As a resident you're always blowing in and out. The patients and families have more contact with the attendings or Child Life. I don't think the Child Life people are too keen on having us involved. They see it as their turf." [Child Life is a therapeutic discipline that works within pediatric hospitals to help children and their parents adjust to the experience of the child's hospitalization and illness.]

On reflection Ashley is not sure if she ever spoke with a dying child about his or her death. "I've taken on the role of assessing their pain and anxiety and how I can help them with medications." She has talked with the parents of terminally children. "They ask clinical questions. 'When will it happen? What will happen?' They ask about medications and treating the child's symptoms. Some parents are very fearful and don't want to be in the way. Sometimes you need to put your arm around them and bring them to the child. You have to touch the child and show them that they can touch the child, too."

When parents ask her questions about their child's impending death she feels "helpless. I try to answer their questions clinically, but the details and timing of a patient's death can be unpredictable.

It's hard to know how messy things may or may not get close to the end."

VII

"Each of the residents has a different way of coping. Some cry at the moment and cry with the family. Others don't do that. I'm not sure how well prepared the other residents are, but they have coping skills that came from somewhere and that are probably totally different from what they learned in medical school. People seem to rely most on what they've learned in their lives about how to cope. The strongest ones are those that can be human, crying with the family and hugging them, but in a contained way. Some attendings have that skill and others don't. Some residents want to be in another field because of the deaths and the weight of the responsibility. I think it's better to figure out what happened and see if there's something to learn.

"The only time the residents don't cope well is when they see death as a professional failure—like they're not good doctors. Some cry more and some go to more services. The people who have the most trouble coping are those who don't think about the child or the sadness of the death, but more about how they've failed. We're in training. We'd be awful if we didn't take any responsibility for our actions, but we're part of a team. As we go through residency we're self-centered. That's why patients' deaths can be so confusing. You're just trying to preserve yourself. It's hard on your health, your personal life, and your mood. It's you against the residency.

"My colleagues really care. They love some of the children and have developed relationships with them. They're part of the loving energy that can surround dying children. However, we're not trained to know what to say and when to start talking about the issues related to dying. Many children aren't terminal for that long. We treat, treat, and treat and then the treatment fails and there's not much time left before the child dies. During the treatment we're doctors committed to saving the patient's life, and talking about death seems contradictory to that. When the child is terminal, none of us has time to sit down and talk. You can't turn your pager off!

"We don't talk about children's deaths that much. All the images and memories are there, but we don't talk about them. They're powerful and they don't go away. Before medical school I worked in a psychiatric residential treatment center and got to know the patients well. I never forget them. When I think about the children I've cared for here that have died I think of what might have been and about how their families' lives were affected by their deaths.

"What is it that keeps us from taking on the role of 'midwives of death' that has traditionally been a physician's role? What have we given up and why? It's definitely to the detriment of the patients, the physicians as people, and their souls.

"I didn't finish my residency feeling triumphant. It was more of a letdown. I didn't feel that I honored the things I should have honored, like working with patients and families around dying and in the psychosocial arena. Those are the things that you don't want to touch because they'll take hours to sort out. For a person like me, who was always interested in those things, it was depressing to see how resistant I'd become to opening those boxes. Now that I'm in practice I understand more about why I felt let down and was so disappointed with myself. I work part-time and have time to listen. I have the 'inner space' you need to have to be a listener."

4

"What could you say? It wasn't all right.
Her beautiful only child was going to die."

Jane had worked for several years as a teacher, but after her brother's suicide, that became a major element in her choice of medicine as a career. She was attracted to the field, in part, by the opportunity to work with patients' families around the tragic illnesses and deaths of their loved ones. Her training, with its focus on the technical aspects of patient care, has been somewhat disappointing from an emotional standpoint, but she hopes eventually to find a career path that will let her focus more on the interactive rather than the strictly biological and scientific aspects of medicine.

I

"My first experience of a child's death was during my pediatric clinical clerkship in medical school. It was a small unit and we knew all the patients well. The child was a preteen with cancer. He was just getting comfort care. One night he died. I came in the next morning. The family and staff were sitting on the floor talking and crying, working through the death. We gave them space. I remember how sad they were. I wasn't directly involved, but I wrote about it in my residency application. I felt pretty sad about it. Ironically, a friend of mine had just had a baby and I went to visit her right afterward. It was nice to see an active, healthy newborn. It made me feel better. I let myself think about it and feel sad. I thought the staff handled it well and honored the parents' emotions. It was a good experience. It gave me an example of an appropriate way to handle feelings without dwelling on them and letting them drag you down.

"I haven't had that many deaths yet, as a resident. There was a child on hematology-oncology. He was very young and had a large, difficult family. They went to the press a lot when they were unhappy with the care they were receiving. They accused people of prejudice. When he was dying the whole family was around. There was lots of confusion and concerns. The family was pretty emotive.

"The next one was a cardiac surgery patient in the PICU. He was a four-year-old from Russia with Down syndrome. We had to convince the family to have surgery. Then he had trouble. One night he got septic and died. I was off that night, and the next day everything was very somber and the curtains were drawn. I was told he'd died and I burst into tears. I went into the room and looked at him. Then the day started. It was devastating for me because the family wasn't there and I couldn't talk with them. I saw them a week later and noticed the look in their eyes. I had constantly told them that he'd be okay, but then he died. They didn't want to see me. They seemed distant and a little cold. I could understand that. I felt terrible and withdrew from my patients for a while.

"Recently there was a three-year-old that died. I took care of him from diagnosis to death. I got to know the mother and the child well. He went downhill and died. During his last hospitalization the family asked about me a lot. I was able to go visit him and spend time with him and his mother. I went to his service. It was very nice and his mother coped well. She was sad and angry, but it was a wonderful service and I had a good encounter with her. It was really sad for me after he died. I burst into tears and had a tough day the next day. You're so tired and have few resources to cope. My good experiences around death have to do with open emotions and honesty, not pretending and not denying.

"I cope best by letting myself be sad and talking with others. After the death of the child in the PICU when the parents were so upset, I felt sad and guilty that I'd said it would be all right but it wasn't. Maybe I shouldn't have been so optimistic, but I was honest with them. In medicine you have to learn to say that you don't know if it'll be all right. I eventually found a middle ground. Now I allow myself to be emotional, but I stand back a little further and things don't go quite as deep or to the core. I'm sad when a child dies, but it breaks my heart to see the parents. It relates directly to my parents' loss of my brother.

"After a death I wonder if we made the right decisions, did the right things, and advocated appropriately for the child. As interns we're not so instrumental and the attendings usually make the critical decisions. However, a good friend of mine was caring for the three-year-old when he died and she went through a lot. She was concerned that she hadn't pushed for comfort care as opposed to aggressive treatment. It's good to know that you've done everything up to a point, but then to let the children die comfortably. People fight so hard for children here. Many children die in the P I C U with tubes down their throats."

Having moved from another part of the country, Jane misses the support of old friends. "Here in a new place with new friends and having just broken up with a close partner I really miss hugs and someone to be with. When the three-year-old died I called an old friend who's also an intern, and mentioned the death to her. You just want someone to put her arms around you. I kind of wish my mom were here to wrap me up and make me feel comfortable and safe."

II

"My family dealt with death pretty openly. I have a memory from when I was about twelve or thirteen years old. My mother's father had died and she had picked me up at junior high school in the middle of the day. She was in tears. I knew that he'd been ill, but his death was unexpected. What I remember is that there was a lot of sadness, but no one became distraught or hardened by the experience. There was a funeral with an open casket. It was the first time I'd seen a dead person and it was an odd feeling. Later there was a wake with his friends. He was buried in a beautiful cemetery at the foot of the mountains. It was nice. Everyone said a few words at the burial service except for me. I wanted to speak, but I was too shy.

"My family didn't talk about heaven. As a child I had a sense that dead people went somewhere peaceful and that it was safe. My memories of religion were of traveling in Nepal and other parts of Asia and visiting monasteries and temples. It was holy, quiet, and peaceful. Maybe that's where I got the idea of what it's like after death. I didn't get any formal teaching about it. I developed my own views based on gleanings from several religions. Basically, I thought that when people died their bodies stopped working, and I was comfortable with the idea that they were going to a more peaceful place.

"I learned from my family that it was okay to be sad and to cry after a person dies. My mother was very emotional, but not in a fall-apart way. Tears and affection were all right. My father was more stoical. As an adult I've seen him become more emotional, but in my childhood I only saw him cry once or twice. His mother died when he was young and his father was a tough man. The most my father would do was to admit that things were sad and upsetting.

"I remember a little boy dying of leukemia when I was in elementary school. I didn't know him, but it was a big deal. The whole community was sad, and I remember feeling sad for his family. Every time we drove by their house, even years later, I can remember feeling sad for them. When I was twelve or thirteen a TV actor I liked accidentally shot himself. I don't remember his name or the name of the program, but I used to watch it a lot. I felt very upset and remember thinking for the first time how tragic and awful accidental death is."

The most painful and powerful death in Jane's life was the suicide of her younger brother at the age of twenty-five. He had developed symptoms of schizophrenia during his first year in college. "There was a lot of trauma and drama. He was in [a well-known psychiatric hospital] several times. Each time he was hospitalized he progressed from a locked unit to spending more and more time outside of the hospital, but he'd eventually relapse. He had a long history of denial, cheeking his medications and escaping from the hospital. One day he left the hospital to pick up some eyeglasses, took the subway downtown, and jumped off a bridge. He was missing for a few days before people learned what had happened."

Crying, she continued, "My brother's death totally broke my heart. We'd talked in the family about the possibility of him committing suicide someday. It was very hard. I thought that we were a perfect, normal family before he became ill. We did have some experience with mental illness, because my maternal grandmother had bipolar disorder. It was a total shock when he died even though we'd known it might happen. Over the previous six months he'd distanced himself from the family. That made it harder, the guilt. I reached out to him at times and pulled back at others. I wasn't sure when it was right to do either. Shortly before his death I started pulling back. I was writing to him but not calling. I wasn't sure if my contact benefited him or upset him more. I'd been seeing a psychiatrist for about a year at the time. The therapy was mostly about my brother. I'd just seen the psychiatrist the day I learned about my brother's death. I'd left his office, stopped at the grocery store, and was looking forward to going out to the theater that night. When I pulled into the driveway at home, my mother's cousin was there. We went inside and as we walked upstairs I began to sense what he was going to tell me. I sat down on the bed and he said, 'Your brother's dead.'

"I coped with his death by working through it. I'm still working through it. I was in a post-baccalaureate pre-medicine program at the time. I kept seeing the psychiatrist and the treatment helped. I also dealt with it a lot by myself, crying alone. The feelings and thoughts were always with me and I didn't want to burden others. One day I cried all day long. I went to my mother's cousin's house, but they weren't there. My boyfriend was away. I resorted to exercise, and especially dance, to cope with the sadness of his loss. I still cope with it in the same way. I feel the sadness more when I'm tired and of course now I'm tired all the time.

"I'd talked with him about his illness, and after he died I read his journals. My parents had moved abroad a few months before his death. The doctor had told them, 'You've to get on with your own lives.' They rented out our house so I had to go over and clean out his things. We divided up his clothes and I put his journals and paintings in storage. My parents came home and we had a big service for him at the museum where my mother had worked. There was a lot of talking. I talked with his psychiatrist a lot. For years I've wanted to talk with her again, to understand her perspective on his death. She told me that he was psychotic a lot of the time. I tried to see him in a new light. I tried to hold on, not to who he'd been, but to who he'd become.

"I feel that I've blocked out a lot of my memories of our youth together. Plus my family is spread out now. I've never been back to the place where we lived. It's still rented out so someday we'll all have to go back. Up until a little while ago I struggled every day to cope with his death. I began to feel better over time, letting go of him to some extent and becoming more settled and happy with my own life. Then I moved out here and have again become more vulnerable to my feelings about his loss. I wouldn't be in medicine if it weren't for his illness. I was teaching French and history and working with troubled kids at the time he died. My brother had several psychiatrists. Those that were incompetent made me want to become a doctor, the psychiatrists who didn't believe in using medication even when he was psychotic. I've thought some about becoming a psychiatrist, but it's too close to home. My clinical rotations on psychiatry were painful. It was just too close."

Jane had several other experiences with death before entering medicine. "A close friend from high school committed suicide in college. She shot herself in the head. The senior resident in my dormitory came to my room and said, 'Your friend Emily tried to kill herself. She's dead.' I ran screaming down the hall! I was in shock and denial. I'd spoken with her just before coming back to school. I had no inkling there was anything wrong. I'd told her how much I liked school and there she was with all that sadness and I never knew it. She was Jewish. They have lovely traditions around death and after she died we sat Shiva.

"I had another high school friend I wasn't as close to that died in a small plane crash when she was twenty-four. She died together with her husband and father. They had a huge traditional church service and funeral.

"Then there was my best friend in high school, Jill. Her best friend in college was killed skiing at the age of twenty-five. We'd all done things together and been quite close. It was awful! I remember saying out loud, 'When is all this dying going to stop?' It was hard for me, but even harder for Jill. I wanted to be there for her."

All those deaths of people her age "just didn't make sense. In my life I've always had this idea that whatever happens, happens for a reason. There must be a reason. Something good has to come out of bad events. I've wondered why I've been spared. It doesn't make sense to me. How's it decided who dies and who lives? I still think about it a lot. I've tried to develop a greater appreciation for life. I'm alive and they're not and I should take advantage of life and live each day to the fullest. Now when I'm working so hard it's easy to forget to live life to the fullest. To deal with my feelings I dance. My dancing is very spiritual and improvisational. That's where I go to let go, to heal myself, and to think about the people I've lost. I think about my brother, the friends I've lost, or a patient I've cared for the night before. I use it to process my feelings and thoughts. I use symbolic movements. I feel freedom and relief. Sometimes I dance alone and at other times I go to classes where there are dozens of others like me dancing from the bottom of their souls."

III

Jane was drawn to medicine because it was a way to help people and because of her brother's illness. "Some of his doctors weren't so good. We need good people to talk to the families and help them to understand." She enjoys medicine because "there's human contact and it incorporates so many disciplines. You can choose a specialty or do general work. You can take it anywhere in the world.

It's something that's needed. Stuck in the mire of internship you have trouble remembering that!

"I've always worked with children. At fifteen I was a camp counselor and really liked it. I like the combination of well-child care and taking care of children who are very sick. In internal medicine you deal with elderly people. They're so ill and it's very sad. Often they're alone. Children have so much resilience. When they feel better they jump up and down in the crib! Their family is around them. They give you a big smile. When they're really sick or dying it's harder, but the joy outweighs the sadness.

"I've never doubted my choice of pediatrics. I'm so thrilled to be doing it. I've had my bad moments like when the children are really sick or dying. Those are the main things that have upset me this year. Sometimes I'll run to the bathroom, sit down on the floor, and cry.

"I used to think that after training I'd do general pediatrics in a small town in Colorado, but over the last few years I've recognized how important city life is to me because of the culture, dance, and personal factors. Now I think of doing community-based clinical work with adolescents. I'm also interested in international relief or refugee work, but I'd have to consider safety and personal factors."

Medical school did little to prepare Jane to cope with the death of patients. "I did go to New York for a palliative-care rotation and the issue was addressed much more there around individual patients." She wishes that there were more opportunities in medical school to discuss personal coping around patient deaths, "but it's so hard to get people together and talk about dying. Everyone is so busy."

In her residency training, her only formal experiences of talking about how to cope personally with the deaths of patients have come in meetings with an individual faculty member who has a special interest in the area and in one discussion with her resident group. "When you're on-service it depends on the attending and how busy he or she is. It's not great, but there's a core group trying to improve the situation. I definitely talk about it with my fellow interns. We talk about how hard it was and how sad. It's easier to share work-related emotions than personal feelings because I'm afraid to be judged about those.

"We're so busy. There's no official time for anything. When a faculty member committed suicide earlier this year we all met and talked. It seemed like a good thing and I'm glad the department did it. There's one attending who's able to cry with patients and yet be professional. Then there's another who's so removed that he doesn't show any feelings."

IV

Her own ability to cope with the deaths of patients "depends." "When someone is chronically ill and you've cared for him over time and he's having a hard time adjusting to his illness, you sometimes come to the realization that death might be a relief to him or to his family. There was a nine-year-old child; he was very nice, very sick, and had a lovely family. He got a transplant and died recently. I remember the family in the room. It was sad and stressful but also energizing because of the family. A couple of weeks later I was walking down the street and saw a family with children. They were happy and just walking down the street. It was them! I was glad for them that they could be back to normal without losing their sadness. It was a positive death.

"I'm still working on how to cope with patients' deaths. There's nothing you can say. You can be there and hold their hand. You can say it'll be all right when it won't be. I have good rapport with people. I can sit in silence and listen and let them talk. I'm good at distracting children and making them laugh, but my experience is limited. There was another nine-year-old who had an awkward gait for about a week. Her CT scan showed a huge tumor. It was inoperable and she only had six months to live. Her mother, family, and friends were there. They spent a day or two in the hallway, crying. I was walking down the hall and saw the mother with her parents. They asked her, 'What can we do?' She said, 'Go back in the room, be with her, she's going to die.' The mother was standing in the hallway and I put my arm around her. What can you say? It wasn't all right. Her beautiful only child was going to die. I said, 'Your family is wonderful. You're surrounded by wonderful people.' She thanked me and cried. Then I had to leave her standing there in the hallway."

V

"Every death makes me realize that life is short. It's good to be reminded of that when I'm working so hard. I'm lucky enough to still be alive." The deaths of patients make her think of the mortality of her own family members. "It scares me. It brings the realization closer that I could lose them at any time. In medical school when we were learning about chronic illnesses that people get as they age I worried about my parents. They're so far away." She also thinks of her own mortality, especially when going to a patient's funeral. "I wonder who'd show up at my funeral and what they'd think or say. Those are pretty selfish thoughts. I think some people would miss me and be sad. My family would be sad. But I don't think about it in much detail."

VI

A "good death" is one in which "the child is comfortable and in an environment where she or the family wants her to be. There's time for people to say good-bye and time to accept the death even if they can't make sense of it. There are people around who care about them and are supportive. It's a sunny day with a blue sky. It's amazing how much children know, understand, and accept, if they have peace—even that three-year-old who died. He seemed calm at the end. He told his mother he loved her and then he died. You get to a point when people have the realization that it's inevitable and they want to take care of those they love. The mother of the three-year-old had a horrible life doing drugs, but she had cleaned herself up before his birth. After his death she said that it would dishonor his memory if she went back to that." A "bad death," by contrast, is one of "pain, chaos, and being in the hospital. The family and caregivers are angry and bitter. It's a rainy day."

Terminally ill children understand "more than we realize. They have an innate understanding that we don't foster or help them to express because of our extreme efforts to fight their illness. They need to have hope and not give up. Children are very wise. I've seen some of them behave in wise ways. They have a basic understanding of physicality and emotion. Children say things the way they are. It's only later that you learn to deny, manipulate, experience your feelings as inappropriate, and take medications to cover up. Everything gets more complicated. As a child, things aren't so complex; they're more basic and innate." She believes that there should be "an appropriate amount of honesty and communication" with terminally ill children about their illnesses. She also recognizes that it is difficult to find the line between fighting a child's illness and helping them to die. "I hope to learn about that. Every case is different. It's about what is best for the child, and that's often a gray area."

Thus far in her career Jane has had relatively little experience talking with terminally ill children about dying. "I don't know much about that yet. Our treatment is pretty aggressive and the residents don't have much say. Yet we're the ones who are around when children spiral down and die." She sees herself as "being there for the parents and making myself available. I'm as open and as honest as I can be. I'm receptive to them. I think they know that I care and that matters a lot. I think parents are comfortable with me. Sometimes I don't feel that I can answer all their questions or tell them what they want to hear. I'm afraid that if I'm too emotionally involved I'll get too upset. My initial encounters with the families are often at night when I'm on call. I don't know them that well and don't know what to say. I can sit in silence and be there for them. When I was in the NICU one of the patient's parents called every day, but never asked how the child was. I found that I had to say, 'He may die' and told her she needed to come in. He died at two months of age. I held the baby while he died and I couldn't help crying. I wasn't just mourning that baby but all the others I've cared for and wondered about. He looked peaceful in my arms with his little arms crossed and all the tubes out. He looked comfortable, and I felt guilty as if I'd been torturing him."

VII

Other interns cope with patient deaths "pretty well. We each have different ways to approach things. Two guys will do it differently than two girls. People will admit to someone they're close to that they feel sad." The attendings "run the full spectrum. There's one senior doctor, a great guy, who feels deeply. A patient of ours died and I called him. He was quite sad and shared a few thoughts about it. Others are a little gruff. They say it's sad, but they don't get emotional about it. Others are like fighters and don't want to let the children die.

"Several of my colleagues build very good relationships with the families. They let themselves get close without falling apart. They also have good relationships with individual patients. There's no one that's so defended that . . . well, maybe there are a couple. They're more scientific and don't want to get close because they can't. Some have stronger personalities. They're willing to fight the idea of letting someone go, but ultimately their hearts are in the right place. They do the right thing.

"Everyone has his or her own personality and reactions. Some talk and cry with you, others say it sucks. One or two say 'I don't let myself get that involved and upset.' I think that's based on their cultural traditions, religious beliefs, and past experiences. You get used to people being sick and dying. How many people go to work where people die every day? It's important to learn from each experience. Our program's pretty big, spread out, and academically oriented. We find comfort from our fellow residents, not from the attendings. I don't feel comfortable being emotional around them because they're judging me. The one time I showed emotion with an attending I felt really uncomfortable having him know that I was upset. Later in the week he approached me and wanted to know how I was. He said that I seemed to be working slowly on the rotation and that he'd decided that I work slowly when I'm sad. But when you're at work you're working. You can't take two hours off to cry!"

5

"I can't remember a time that we got together and talked about our feelings. Men don't do that."

Jack has adopted an outwardly stoic approach to tragic events. He tries to keep a professional distance from his dying patients and their parents, but finds that in unguarded moments when he is alone and watching television the repressed sadness will suddenly well up within him. He disagrees with those of his resident colleagues who feel that one should be emotionally open with patients, believing instead that a physician's job is to advise and consult, not to embrace the tragedies of patients' and families' lives. His struggle to remain in control may reflect his identification with his mother and with an early experience with his father after the death of his paternal grandmother. He recalls his father being so upset by her death that he was unable to work and spent a week crying about her loss, until his wife told him that enough was enough and that he had to pull himself together.

I

Jack was an intern when his first child patient died. "It was a PICU patient, a little girl. I'd been caring for her for a month. After I left the service she went somewhere else for ECMO [Extra-Corporeal Membrane Oxygenation] and died during it. No one really knew what was going on. It was primarily a lung problem, but people couldn't pin it down. She kept getting worse and worse. She kept me up every night that I was on call. Her mother and father were very nice, but they were always in your face wanting to know what you were doing and why.

"I kept wondering about what I'd done or not done, especially with fluid management. Did I overload the child or dry her out? Would that have made a difference? At first I felt that I should have done better or done more. Other people said, 'You did the best you could,' but I kept wondering, 'Did I push her over the edge to the point that she began to spiral down?'

"I wasn't on the service when she died and so her death was more of a peripheral event to me. Mostly I questioned myself because we didn't know the answers about what illness she had. It was the family's first and only child, too, and that made it hard. Last month on hematology-oncology several children died. I questioned myself a lot regarding decisions I made about their fluid status. I'm afraid that I'll do the wrong thing. I guess it's fear. With the deaths of subsequent children, I've questioned myself less than I did with that first one because I feel that I've done all that I could. You still feel bad if you're on call when they die.

"My primary experiences thus far have been with terminal children, not with sudden deaths. They're children with bad diseases who are really sick and most of them die. The hardest thing is trying to decide at what point you should try to talk with the parents about when to stop. It always seems to happen in the middle of the night. There was one child who had bad leukemia. The PICU didn't want to take her because they felt she was terminal and that it would be futile. The family was Spanish-speaking and I was on the phone with them speaking with the interpreter. Culturally and linguistically, it was hard to get the message across. I asked them, 'Where do you want to go from here?' They kept saying, 'Do what you think is best. We don't want to hamper your decision-making.' It was hard to make them see that we wanted their help in making the decision. Day after day we say to parents, 'We'll do this or that,' but with the death issue we want the parents' input."

From a personal perspective the most difficult aspect of a patient's death is that "the parents have just lost their child. What's it like to go home after the death and see the child's room? The child will never be there again. It must be devastating. However, we don't talk about it much with each other. My colleagues seem to do well. They all keep up a very professional outlook. When we do discuss patients' deaths we talk about their medical care. I can't remember a time that we got together and talked about our feelings. Men don't do that."

II

Jack is a Korean American. His father visited the United States in 1960 as a member of the Korean Olympic speed-skating team, liked the country, and decided he wanted to live here someday. When Jack was two years old, his father immigrated to the U.S. on a temporary visa and a year later brought his wife, Jack, and Jack's older brother to join him. The family remained here for three more years but had to move to Canada because they were unable to acquire permanent residency status in the United States. There his father worked as a pipe welder and his mother as a clerk-typist. When Jack was fifteen the family moved to Texas, where Jack completed high school. He attended college and medical school in the Pacific Northwest, where his parents and brother now live in a town close to where Jack works. His father makes iron gates and air-conditioning ducts, and his brother, who is married and has a child, is a patent attorney.

Growing up as a Korean in Canada was difficult. "Other children made fun of me because of my ethnicity. There weren't other Asians in my grade school and only a few in my high school. It was hard. I asked my mother, 'Why am I different from the other children?' She told me about Korea's long cultural history and said that it was good to be Korean, but the teasing still hurt. Eventually, it died down.

"I've incorporated the way my parents brought me up with strong family values and ties even when I can't stand my relatives. I still think that a father should be stern and in charge. I believe in corporal punishment. I identify with my Korean heritage, but in college the Koreans were too extreme. They grouped together, saw themselves as 'true Koreans,' and were cliquish—so I hung out by myself. I also believe that education is important, but I'm not sure that's ethnic."

Death was discussed "pretty openly" in Jack's family. "If a person died they talked about it, about how the person had died and their feelings about him. Death was a part of life. You discussed it and then moved on. When my father's mother died he was devastated. It was the first time I'd ever seen him cry. He blubbered for a while, at least a week, crying constantly and didn't go to work or do anything. Initially my mother was supportive, but after a while she said, 'That's enough!' That made him angry!

"When I was eight or nine I had this sudden realization that I was mortal and that life would end. I couldn't get the thought out of my mind. It kept me up at night. I told my mother and she told me to read the Bible. Her belief was that there's a soul and that it goes on, I'm not sure how. I still struggle with the question of what happens when you die. The thought of being around forever is unthinkable and yet you don't want this life to end. It's not as disturbing to me now as it was then. Sometimes I lie there pondering, kind of like a panic attack, a negative feeling. You're gone, but where are you? Am I just a bunch of signals and pathways in my brain? Is that it? As a kid I thought about it a lot, but never came up with a good conclusion about what happens. I still haven't. Seeing children die I'm more objective. I think less about the mind of the child and more about systems and failures of systems in the child's body.

"I never had anyone close to me die. I had classmates who committed suicide, but no close family members died. My maternal great-grandmother died when I was eleven. I felt sad and my mother was very sad. She'd raised her from the age of fourteen. I only met her once in Korea, but my mother had stories about her. My paternal grandmother died when I was fourteen. She was someone I didn't know very well, but it was weird seeing my father mourning. I'd never seen him do anything like that before. He wasn't as strong and as stoic as he seemed.

"I knew two guys from high school who committed suicide in college. One hung himself in the shower, the other shot himself. I didn't know them well and didn't get along with them. I felt bad, maybe a little guilty because they'd irritated me and I wasn't nice to them. Their deaths didn't affect me a lot. Every once in a while I think of them."

III

Jack first became interested in medicine "watching NOVA. There was a special on heart transplants. I wanted to do something like that. I liked interacting with people. After college I got into research and liked that, too. Then I heard of the MD/PhD program. I never had a great epiphany like, 'Wow, medicine is what I want to do!' It was just a professional field that seemed attractive. In medical school I liked it and did well. I decided on pediatrics near the end of my third year because I had the most fun with the residents and attendings on pediatrics. I also liked the fact that children got better faster than adults did, and they're cute!

"Overall I'm satisfied with my choice of profession, although it depends on the day. I like ward medicine, the interaction with patients, caring for sick children, and I like the faculty and the other residents. I enjoyed my ICU rotation, but I hated the emergency room, the speed at which you have to go, and seeing patients who aren't really sick but just want something. It's like a really fast-paced clinic. You think, 'Well, the child might be sick. If he gets worse he'll come back.' That's not as satisfying as really knowing what you're treating. I also don't like clinic medicine, seeing children who aren't really that sick, trying to reassure parents, and the fast pace." In the future he hopes to do hematology-oncology. "I had a good time there during my fourth-year medical student rotation. There's lots of translational medicine" [medicine that applies basic science discoveries to clinical care].

In medical school "they tried to go into death and dying. A lot of it was a joke. We role-played, doing things like telling your best friend that he's dying. You can't keep a straight face! In the end you have to experience it. In my third year very few of my patients died.

The worst one was a psychiatric patient. I felt really bad about him. He was an intravenous drug user with out-of-control insulin-dependent diabetes. He was in for a heroin detoxification and had abscesses and hepatitis. We got lots of consults and really tuned him up! He was very appreciative. He told me that he worried about the place where he lived, 'Heroin Alley.' He was afraid that when he went back there he'd get strung out again. The day before his discharge he wanted to talk to me, but I was too busy. He was discharged home and two days later he was found dead in his room. No one knows why. There was an autopsy and it said that he died of hepatitis, but it just didn't make sense. I felt really bad. Did he do something crazy? Did we discharge him too early? Did he really not want to go back to where he lived? Was he in despair? He had insulin and could have given himself too much. I didn't have a big outpouring of emotion. I thought about it, felt bad, and then got so busy that I forgot about it. I'll probably always remember his death. It was my first one in school and I really felt like I was caring for him. He looked so good and then two days later he was found dead in his room! It was so inexplicable. We had a morbidity and mortality conference and decided that maybe he didn't understand his insulin regimen."

During residency Jack has had no formal training about how to deal with patient deaths. "When a chronic patient dies they send out an e-mail and tell you about the memorial service. I don't think that it's really possible to teach someone how to deal with patients' deaths, although it's always good to hear how other people have dealt with it.

"If things are really bothering me I can talk to my family. I usually keep things inside and then every so often I have a meltdown and feel really sad. It usually happens when I'm watching television, or movies like Awakenings, with Robert De Niro and Robin Williams. There was one scene in which one of the characters was getting sick again and the main character was having a hard time with it. Another example is a film in which Peter Falk plays an old man who's bringing up his grandson. The scene that got to me was about the grandfather's death. Things like that often happen near the end of a bad month. I get sad and then I'm fine. I almost never talk with friends or residents about it. It doesn't seem like a topic for discussion. I worry that they'll think I'm a blubbering idiot. It's not done." Was Jack thinking of his father's "blubbering" and of his mother's annoyance at this flaw in his stoic facade?

"Everyone here seems very open. If you're having trouble you can talk with anybody, including the chairman of the department or the training director. It's nice to hear or read about how other people deal with things so you know that you're not alone, that not everyone is stoic. It's an illustration of the different ways that people deal with death. I'd feel uncomfortable if it happened one-on-one, like another resident telling me his or her personal experience. I'd feel like I was sharing too much information. When people do share their experiences and feelings in an open forum I feel uncomfortable. It's not something I talk with people about. I sometimes think, 'Get a grip! It's not the end of the world; it's the profession you chose.' In medical school we had discussions about it. 'If patients and families cry should you cry, too?' Most of the men thought, 'No, you're the professional, be stoic.' The women said, 'No, you should cry with your patient.'"

IV

"When there's a death I think about the entire situation. I try to review the care we provided, what happened, my decisions, the impact on the family, and then resolve it and move on. I don't think about deaths much afterward except for the mystery ones where you don't know why the child died.

"Some children that die I think about longer than I should. I keep revisiting my decision-making and the impact of the death on the family. I try not to get too involved personally with the families. I feel that professionally I shouldn't become their friend. That would make it harder. I have a close friend who gets very attached to her patients and when they die she loses control for a few days.

"Sometimes there's too much collegial support! They're always willing to listen. Sometimes they just keep asking and asking. My reaction is 'Enough already! It's over!' I have a few close friends that I talk to, but after that I don't need to keep talking. After a patient dies some of my colleagues keep asking, 'How're you doing?' Maybe they need to leave me alone a little bit. It gets overwhelming. Some people like a forum to talk about things. It helps to bring out a lot of feelings. I've never done well in such settings. I'd prefer going to a bar with a couple of friends. When we talk it's not about how we feel, but about the decisions that were made and what could have been done differently.

"After a child dies most of my colleagues say, 'You did everything you could,' but sometimes there are things that I could have done differently. It would be good if they were a bit more critical rather than supportive and if they'd hash it out more. If they did I might feel attacked, but since I have a good relationship with them I think I'd see them as helping. When that first patient of mine died, the PICU attending and I discussed the case and he brought up things that I hadn't thought of. That helped a lot and it stuck out in my mind."

V

Jack tries not to think about his own mortality. "When I do I wonder, 'Why am I doing all this work when I could be out enjoying myself rather than being tired, beating myself up, and being yelled at?'" He also tries not to think about the mortality of his family members. "Doing internal medicine as a medical student made my family's mortality closer. I'd think, 'Wow, they're my parents' age!' Seeing children dying is different. I have a young nephew. When I see newly diagnosed cancer it's unnerving to think that the child was healthy before he was diagnosed. I think of my nephew—but then I think, 'It couldn't happen to him.'

"As my parents get older I think about their mortality more. At dinner with my parents there are things that my mother cooks that no one else can cook. I sometimes think, 'There will be a time when

I'll never have this again, when I'll not have these people that I've known all my life.' They're healthy, so I don't think about it a lot. It frightens me when I do think about it. It's frightening to think that they'll be gone. Then I think that there will be a time when I'm gone, too. It's better not to think about it. It's pretty frightening, the finality of it all. Once you're gone, you're gone. There's no coming back. It's too big to think about. I used to believe that there was an afterlife. Maybe I still do, but it doesn't make sense to me. Even if there is an afterlife there has to be some finality to that, too. If it goes on, where does it go? It's incomprehensible!"

Jack's death anxiety is quite high. When he realized as a child that he, too, was mortal he was unable to sleep and turned to his mother for help. Now that he is on his own, he tries to keep thoughts of death out of his conscious mind. With patients he focuses on "failing systems" rather than the child as a whole. He is uncomfortable with colleagues who are open with their feelings around the death of a child, believing that they are behaving "unprofessionally." Yet in quiet, solitary moments while watching a movie in which people die his feelings rush to the surface and he breaks down in tears.

VI

A "good death" for Jack is one in which "the child doesn't get coded and goes peacefully and quietly. When a child codes it's such a flail! It's not a pretty picture. Another part of a 'good death' is when the patient has enough time to die and time for the family to say good-bye. If there's no time to say good-bye it's so hard for the family. I hate codes! In the end there's this lump of a child with lines everywhere and intubated. The family can't talk to him and he's as good as dead. We're keeping the system alive until it fails. Of course, if they code and do well that's a different story."

"Bad deaths" are "codes and the unexpected ones when the child is hit by a car, comes to the PICU, and never regains consciousness. With the chronic ones you know it's the end and you have time to come to grips with it."

How much terminally ill children understand about their death "depends on their age. The younger children don't have a good grasp on it, but teenagers do. With chronically ill younger children it's very hard. I'm not sure they have the awareness to understand what their death means. For them, talking with other children in the same situation might help. I don't know how well that would work with teenagers. With them it might be better to do it one-on-one."

He does not believe that "residents have enough exposure to help dying kids with their deaths. We're still too busy learning and taking care of little things in the hospital. Our role is to explain to the parents what's going on. The attendings are more likely to talk with the child. A lot depends on the child's age. They say less to the little children and more to teenagers. I had one parent who got mad because we talked with the patient, an eighteen-year-old, and the rest of the family about his death. He'd wanted to do it himself. We're trained not to beat around the bush and sugarcoat things. Sometimes we don't take into account the family dynamics."

Jack has heard residents talking with terminally ill children about their deaths "a few times. They sit there and talk with them and take the time to sit and listen. It's hard for residents to find the time to do that. There's so much to do so we shy away from it. Our initial role is to treat and cure. When death comes we get everything done and try to leave. That's changing. People are getting into palliative aspects of care, but in general we shy away from those issues.

"I hardly spend any time with dying children and their parents sitting and talking. I'm so busy as a resident. I shy away from the rooms where there are children that may die in a day or two. My excuse is that I'm giving the family time to say good-bye. I do well being with the families and explaining the medical aspects to them. The attendings will say something and then have to leave and the family will ask me to explain what they've just said. Sometimes they yell at me and take out their frustrations. It seems to help them. It's easier for the families to yell at the residents than at the attendings. I don't take it personally. They're just angry at the situation, not at you as an individual.

"I don't talk to children about death very much. I'm not sure if it's their age or my trying to put up a wall. It comes back to not being too personally involved with the patient. In the book *The House of God*, it's the patient that has the disease not you. You can't get so involved with the illness that you feel you're the one that's sick.

"Often the child is intubated and there's no way for him to talk to me. Usually it's an acute event or they're spiraling down and we're dealing with the family, not the child. With the family I say, 'Your child is most likely going to die.' Parents ask if the child will suffer. I try to explain that we do our best to make sure that the child doesn't and what we do does make it appear that the child is suffering less. That reassures the parents."

VII

Jack is not sure if it represents a strength or a weakness in his colleagues, but he has noticed that "when they talk with one another about patients' deaths all of a sudden they feel better." He himself tries to be "more objective about it. I try not to think of the patient's social role or how the family will react. I don't want to be too emotional. That would be especially hard in hematology-oncology."

Some of his colleagues "get too attached. When a patient dies they're too emotionally involved. A friend of mine and I discussed how involved you should be. Some say that you should show support and cry with the family. My feeling is that you shouldn't show emotion on the surface. You're not a part of the family and not a friend. You're there to advise and to take care of the patient. Many people feel differently than I do and say, 'I think you can show caring and concern without losing your professionalism.'"

PART II

ATTENDING PHYSICIANS

Attending physicians are the hospital's senior doctors. They have worked in their specialties for many years, often for decades, and have well-developed strategies for coping with the deaths of children. In situations where cure is no longer possible they have learned through experience and the examples of others to focus their energies on providing palliative end-of-life care for the patient and the family.

The care of a dying child is focused on ensuring that the child is comfortable and pain-free. If he or she is alert and old enough to understand what is happening, it may also mean helping the child to prepare for and come to some degree of peace with death.

The care of the parents of a dying child requires the physician to help them survive intact through one of the most devastating of life's experiences, the loss of a child. It also means helping them manage their feelings so that they can help their child through the dying process. In many respects, these latter tasks require more sensitivity, experience, and emotional stability from physicians than does caring for the dying child. The excruciating pain of losing a child summons up parental psychological defenses of denial, repression, and projection that complicate the physician's work and can make him or her feel attacked, powerless, frustrated, and angry. These feelings may lead the doctor to withdraw physically and emotionally from the dying child's care, including returning to the room only to address mechanical concerns like medication dosages or respirator settings and leaving the nurses to cope with the parents' grief and anger. Ultimately, the physician's goal is to engage and guide the parents to an understanding that their child is going to die and that they must shift their energies from rescuing the child to helping him transition as painlessly as possible through the dying process. Some families, and especially those that are more dysfunctional, can make this transition difficult and at times impossible. They may press for cure when it is no longer possible and make the child suffer through needless medical treatments. They may make the child feel responsible for their emotions rather than supporting the child's feelings. They may challenge and dispute every decision and fire any doctor who does not agree with them. They may hide from the child the fact that he or she is dying until it is too late for the child to say good-bye. And in the end the child will still die but probably have a more painful and emotionally tumultuous death than need have been, a death that brings no one comfort or resolution.

There is no "bright line" that identifies the point at which cure-oriented treatment stops and dying-oriented palliative care begins. Physicians and nurses will often disagree among themselves about when it is time to stop working for cure, and this may lead to both immediate and retrospective concerns that one has either gone too far or not gone far enough in actively treating the child's disease. Parents, distraught at the prospect of losing their child, may pressure the team to try just one more treatment or to consult with another expert before letting go. As the tensions around these difficult decisions mount it becomes increasingly challenging for everyone involved to think clearly and objectively about what is going on and about what is best for the child and the family.

Despite their experience and knowledge, the attending physicians do not emerge unscathed from the process of helping dying children and their parents to confront and endure this final stage of the life cycle. Each brings his or her particular vulnerabilities to the work. Having one's own children often increases a physician's sensitivity to the deaths of child patients, especially if the patients call them to mind. Similar facial features, personality characteristics, names, and ages sometimes bring to a physician's attention in a sudden and startling manner the fact that this could be his or her son or daughter dying.

Identification with the child's parents also makes caring for the child and family a much more emotionally charged experience. Several of the attending physicians commented on the difficulties of working with the dying children of "PLU's"—people like us—well-educated, successful professionals. To experience the suffering of people with whom they could easily identify challenged their abilities to keep their emotional responses in check. Yet they realized that those breathtaking, often instantaneous identifications with the child and/or its parents and the feelings they provoked must be put away and dealt with later. Otherwise the physician would become too disabled by emotions to function effectively.

Where do all those suppressed and repressed feelings go? How do they affect the physicians who experience them? How do they affect their relationships with the people they love? Colleagues, friends, and family members may provide some support and understanding, but the pace of work in a children's hospital is very fast and there is seldom time to mourn and discuss one's feelings about a child's death. As a result, the feelings of the physicians tended to come out during very private moments when they were alone with their emotions and did not have to explain why they were upset. An attending on the hematology-oncology service told me, "We oncologists tend to cry a lot at movies," and a pediatric intensivist said, "Sometimes I go on vacation and spend the first three or four days crying."

Their feelings may also be worked out in other more indirect and sometimes destructive ways. Some physicians may feel overcome with guilt after the death of a child and have to await the postmortem pathology report or a case discussion to persuade themselves that the child's death was not their fault. Others may "flog" (aggressively treat a child beyond the point where reason would indicate little promise of a cure) in order to convince themselves that they have done all they could. Still others may become withdrawn, depressed, or irritable or feel burned-out after a string of deaths and begin to believe that they can no longer continue in such an emotionally demanding field. This, in turn, may lead a physician to consider a change in specialty within medicine, to choose a new career, or to retire early. Most of the attending physicians I talked with did not see themselves remaining in clinical roles in intensive care or hematology-oncology for their entire careers. The work was simply too demanding—both physically and emotionally.

6

"It's my job to get families through
the worst time in their lives."

Al is a forty-seven-year-old physician who worked in the Pediatric Intensive Care Unit until illness forced him to choose another career path. For many years he coped with the deaths of children by "not remembering," repressing the painful memories of the tragedies he had witnessed. Following the deaths of his parents and the psychotherapy he undertook to deal with his feelings, his capacity to repress diminished, and he became more aware of and interested in his emotional reactions to children's deaths. Like many other senior physicians and nurses, one of his adaptive coping strategies for dealing with the deaths of children has been to focus much of his attention on the children's parents and on helping them through the exquisitely painful process of losing a child.

I

"The first kid I cared for who died was a teenage Japanese girl with leukemia. I was on call and was told to be with her. She was very pretty. She bled out. She was D N R and knew that she was going to die. She was scared and I was scared. There was no debriefing afterward, and I don't know why she died. I remember the contrast between how pretty she was and how ugly her death was." He does not recall how he coped with her death. "If I don't like something, I don't remember it. My wife says that it's more of a curse than a gift. I'm sure I cried a little. I've never forgotten that experience. I coped with it by putting it away.

"Thinking about all the children who've died since then, there have been so many I don't remember them all. I do remember a few. I think about what I didn't know then or what I might have missed. I was oblivious to it, the tragedy of someone dying that young. I wonder if twenty years later that girl would have died. I wonder what comes after death. Nobody knows. It's hard for me to believe that 'you' just stop, whatever it is that makes 'you,' you. My father thought there was nothing after death. I get annoyed with religions pretending they have an answer, but I know they're comforting for most people."

Al's reactions to the deaths of child patients were "directly proportional to how well I knew the family. After I had children of my own, deaths affected me if the patients were the same ages and gender as my children. I remember a bunch of wonderful families. It was terrible to get them through it even if the death was expected. I also remember one situation that was actually funny! The patient was a boy from the hematology-oncology service. He knew that he was going to die and he wanted to be in his favorite clothes, so the family dressed him up, including his baseball cap. After his death the family asked for the death certificate so they could take him home. They didn't want to go through the lobby so we put him on a gurney with a sheet over him still wearing his baseball cap. We took him to the loading dock in the back of the hospital and the family drove the car around. His older brother was driving. It was a 1982 LeSabre sedan, beat up and souped-up a little. I couldn't figure out how to work the lift to get the gurney down so the family did it. Then they opened the car door, took the sheet off, and put him in the front seat wearing his favorite T-shirt and baseball cap. His mother was in the front and his brother was in the back. They started joking about it. The brother said, 'Can I pick up his arm and have him wave?' Then they took off. They said, 'He would've wanted it this way. He was making jokes the day he died.'

"How I coped depended on the situation. There have been so many deaths, hundreds. I concentrated on getting the family through it and didn't deal emotionally with what was happening. There were a few situations where I got to know the families well and got attached to them. Those were harder. However, by the time I walked out the door to go home I'd tucked my feelings away."

Initially Al coped with the pain of children's deaths by "forgetting" or repressing his feelings and the memory of the child's death. Identification with the parents or child bridged the empathic gap between Al and those he cared for and made the deaths and losses more painful for him. Interestingly, as he described the effects of identification with the patient or the parents Al unconsciously shifted away from the pain of those memories to a funny story about the boy in the baseball cap. This unconscious transition suggests that it is still difficult for him to tolerate painful feelings and that he protects himself from them by the use of humor.

Professionally, the most difficult aspect of coping with the death of a child "was getting the family to understand that their child was going to die and that since it was inevitable, there was a good and a bad way to die. I tried to get them to choose the way that was easiest for the child and for them. Sometimes it just wasn't possible. Emotionally, psychologically, or intellectually, they just didn't get it or they didn't get it for religious reasons. They'd say, 'No, there's going to be a miracle, don't take him off the ventilator.' I'd tell them, 'If there's going to be a miracle it can happen off the ventilator as well as on it!' I once worked with the psychotic father of a three-month-old who had a cardiac arrest. The child was lying there stiff as a board, with his back arched and only his heels and head touching the bed. The father said that he wanted to give the child some beer to make him pee. 'It makes me pee,' he said. Those kinds of crazy reactions are pretty common. A friend of mine is a critical care physician back East. He once had an anencephalic baby whose parents insisted that everything be done to keep the child alive despite its having no brain. That baby was in the unit for eight months! Professionally, it's frustrating to see families not able to come to an understanding and put an end to the child's suffering."

Personally, the deaths of child patients trouble Al because of "the lack of fairness. Why should a child have to die? How fair is that?

When my parents died it wasn't good either, but they were in their eighties."

Families' denial of the fact that their child was going to die frustrated Al because it kept him from being able to help the child and family experience a "good" death. This made it more difficult for him to cope with the dying process, because it blocked his ability to channel his pain into assisting the child and family. The caregiver's coping process is intimately and reciprocally connected with the coping process of the family. It is a dance in which each partner must adapt to the movements of the other. If that does not happen, the end result will be a death that is more painful and less satisfactory for all concerned.

II

Al grew up in the Northeast where his father owned a small construction company and his mother was occupied with home duties. His great-grandparents were Jews from Russia and two of his grandparents were born there. All were raised in conservative, traditional households. He experienced his family's ethnic and religious background as "an annoyance. I never liked it. They made me go to Hebrew school. I was making straight As in public school but flunked Hebrew school. The classes were terrible! In temple I sat with my mother and the other children. The service was in Hebrew and I didn't understand it. When I got older I had a Bar Mitzvah. I couldn't stand it, but I did it out of respect for my father. I made a deal with my parents that after the Bar Mitzvah I wouldn't have to go to temple again. Before the Bar Mitzvah the cantor called my parents and said, 'He'll never be ready.' My father asked me, 'Are you going to do this?' I said, 'Yes, just tell them to leave me alone.' They did and I memorized my verses the night before the service. That was the last time I was in a synagogue prior to my father's death."

Within his family, death was discussed "almost not at all. My mother, who was very overprotective, consciously kept me from it.

My parents married late in life and had me when they were older. I had very few relatives and most of my parents' families were dead before I was born. I never went to a funeral and the only sick person I ever saw was my mother's sister.

"My father never talked about his father, but he did have a few stories about his mother. For him 'going on and on' was two sentences! Before he died my father showed me where his parents were buried. His father died when my dad was twenty-five. He never got on with his father. His father wasn't very nice, wasn't home much, and was very strict. My father wasn't that upset when his father died. However, he worshipped his mother."

Death "was bad, not a good thing to happen. They never talked about it. The inference was, 'don't discuss it; ignore it.' I initially thought that dead people either went to heaven or hell. Then when I was nine or ten I asked my father what Jewish people think. He told me they don't know. I couldn't imagine anyone going to hell. Heaven didn't make any sense either. As I got older I hoped that something good would happen, but my concern was that there was nothing. That was my father's concern when he was dying, that there was nothing. If someone died there was the expectation that you'd awkwardly say you were sorry, if you said anything. My struggle was wanting to say I was sorry but not knowing how to."

The deaths Al experienced as a child were those of his maternal grandfather when he was eight, his maternal grandmother when he was ten, a paternal aunt when he was twelve, and a maternal aunt when he was sixteen. "I didn't have any pets growing up except that my mother accidentally put the goldfish in the disposal. She was an Edith Bunker type. I remember the white porcelain sink and the goldfish going down. It was terrible! I remember crying.

"I was too little to remember my grandfather's death. I only knew my grandmother when she was sick with cancer. I remember knocking her wig off once and that her apartment didn't smell good. My father's sister Claudia was a wonderful woman. She was a big, heavy, happy person who lived in a great old house. She was very nice. She never had children because her husband didn't want any. I was very upset when she died. I saw her in the hospital. She was quite jaundiced. I didn't understand it. I don't remember feeling much of anything at the time. It was the same with my mother's sister Mary. I knew her very well. We went to her house for the holidays. She was very attractive. She had diabetes and went blind. One day she vomited and died. I'm sure I felt bad, but I have no specific memories of how I felt. I'm aware of my feelings at the time, but then I put them somewhere and they're gone. I forget about them and move on to other things. My father was just like I am and so is my oldest daughter. If there's something really, really bad, my daughter and I giggle. There are only two incidents that I couldn't put away like that: the death of the first child I cared for and my parents' deaths."

Al's coping style of "not remembering anything unpleasant" (repression) developed long before he entered medical school or residency. It was a strategy he learned from his father and one that has, apparently, been adopted by his oldest daughter. While these coping strategies that we learn "at our parents' knee" are not immutable, they change very slowly, and often we do not even notice them until a decisive event, psychotherapy, or the passage of time and the growth of insight bring them into conscious awareness.

III

Al was an English major in college. "My goal was to be an English teacher and coach basketball. Between my sophomore and junior years I was at home and helped my favorite English teacher and basketball coach to move. Afterward I was talking with him and told him that I wanted to be like him. 'Are you nuts? I barely make enough to live on. This life sucks. Don't do it. Go be a doctor!' One of my best friend's fathers was a doctor, so I asked him about it. He said, 'Where else can you be altruistic and get paid for it?' So I decided to become a doctor. I changed majors to biological sciences and then applied to medical school.

"I chose pediatrics because it's easier to deal with a baby with a diaper full of poop than an old lady with a diaper full of poop. I initially ranked internal medicine higher because of the intellectual experience. I loved my pediatric internship and loved the ICU. I was drawn to the ICU because it was exciting. It was like a physiology lab and things happened right away. Most children got better or died. It was clean. Not many chronically ill children came out. In general pediatrics the parents are annoying and runny noses and earaches are boring. I liked oncology, but it was too depressing."

A year and a half ago Al had to give up his work in the PICU for health reasons. "Up until then I was very satisfied with my career choice. I'd accomplished a lot of my academic goals. The physiology is clear-cut, but exciting. The procedures were fun to do and I was very good at doing them. Running an arrest is a tremendous rush. The thing I miss most is going in at two A.M., taking a kid who is crashing and burning, pulling him together, then sitting around afterward talking about how we'd done such a good job in a calm, controlled fashion and everyone felt good about it. I miss helping families get through the process. I got to like that later after the clinical work became routine. I liked helping families get through the hospitalization, especially if the child died. I was really good at that. As I learn about my personality type I realize that it's directly related to my ability to compartmentalize. I was able to help the family focus on letting their child die rather than rehashing failed treatments. You can't ignore it when a child dies. Helping the family through it is very satisfying."

The worst parts of his job were "the children dying, the hours, and being away from my family." In the future he hopes to work as a department chair or stay in administration and research. "I have to do one of those things because of my physical limitations. I don't have a choice. Research has always made the job interesting."

He recalls his medical school preparation for coping with the deaths of patients as "very inadequate. We didn't have any special courses or talks. The only thing I remember is being overwhelmed on neurology when I diagnosed an adult as having ALS [amyotrophic lateral sclerosis or Lou Gehrig's Disease]. It was horrible that you were giving someone notice that his life was going to end in a couple of years." Al believes that medical students should "have doctors come and discuss their experiences with them and should read Kübler-Ross." (Elisabeth Kübler-Ross's book, On Death and Dying, proposed five psychological stages through which dying people pass and had a powerful influence on contemporary thinking about the dying process.) "Even better would be to have patients' families come in and talk about their family member's death and how they experienced health-care professionals around it. My mother died in a hospice. The people they sent out were poorly educated.

"Short of a psychoanalysis, my personality is such that you could have lectured me until doomsday and it wouldn't have helped. I saw things as black and white. Subtle discussions wouldn't have helped. Today I could go in and talk about death and how I cope with it. It's interesting to look at the medical students who've experienced death in their families versus those who haven't. A death in my family was one of the things that opened me up."

As a fellow on cardiology, "I was on one night. There was a thirty or thirty-five-year-old woman with Eisenmenger's syndrome [a form of congenital heart disease in which the pulmonary vasculature is obstructed, leading to unoxygenated blood being pumped from the right to the left atrium and resulting in cyanosis]. She was sitting on a bedpan straining at stool and keeled over and died. Her husband was there. We couldn't resuscitate her. She was older than I was, but I was caring for her. From then on there were people dying left and right. I remember a couple of things. On Friday afternoons we had 'vent rounds' in the ICU. I was new. I thought they were 'ventilator rounds,' but when I walked into the room there was a psychiatrist and the nurses and doctors were talking about their feelings. I thought, 'What the hell is this?' and got up and left. Most of what I learned was from watching my mentors speak with the families of children who were dying, what they said, how they said it, and the family's reaction. That was the best learning experience

I had. There is only about a 5 percent mortality in the P I C U . Most patients do well.

"As an attending I was on my own. After five years of training I had enough experience; I had two children of my own and I began to know what to do. I'd see a child my daughter's age and think about losing my own child. I put myself in the parents' place. I developed a style that was related to my own psychopathology. I believe that it's an advantage in my field. I'm able to cut to the chase and make things simple for families. They're so overwhelmed that they can't focus and will latch onto anything. My job is to get them through this episode, which is the worst time in their lives. No matter what I say or do they won't feel good, but I can help them to get through it intact. I have a simplified way of explaining things and helping them to make choices. I don't ask open-ended questions or offer choices. I help them to feel in control of an out-of-control situation."

Al's description of his development as a physician illustrates one of the challenges in educating medical caregivers about coping with death. You cannot learn something before you are ready to learn it. Al's early ability to repress his feelings was so complete that discussing emotions was a waste of time until his parents' deaths "opened him up." However, he was able to learn by observing his mentors. This suggests that learning to cope with children's deaths can occur in different ways and that educational approaches must be oriented to the strengths and weaknesses of each individual.

IV

"I think I cope with kids' deaths better than anyone else in the hospital except for a few people. One of them is a chaplain. The families and nurses love him. He has a very gentle, but pragmatic approach. My strengths are being able to guide the families through the dying process and to help them focus on what needs to be done." His weakness is "not dealing with the emotional aspects. I'm not sure if it's actually a weakness. If I were capable of being sucked into the emotional morass with the family I couldn't be objective with them and help them to understand how children die. If we can't keep the child alive then we have to help him to die with his parents there and assure the family that he's not suffering. You don't want to draw it out or prolong it. You wouldn't want to do that for your own child. There's one exception to that. I've kept children alive until their family gets there.

"I can tell when children are entering the dying process. Once they start, the end result is that they're going to die. At that point there's nothing else that we can do. We need to switch modes from trying to save life into one of care and comfort, especially of the family. We make sure they understand the finality of the dying process. Sometimes I'll say, 'He's not here, he's already gone.' I'm good at explaining the concept of brain death. It's not intuitive to most people."

Three things helped Al to cope with children's deaths. "First, if they died well, with no pain and suffering and I got the family through in as good a shape as possible by having them be there when the child died, allowing them to hold him, and giving them enough time to be with him. Second, being able to put it away by the time I got home. Third, my family: I lose myself in my family. The children need help with their homework. They're completely oblivious to my work world."

Getting too close to a patient's family made it more difficult. "Then it was more like with that first patient. I can't forget that. It was such a shock.

"I got very little support from my physician colleagues. The nurses looked to me more to give support than to get it. Once in a while I'd get teary-eyed. That blew them out of the water! I didn't ask for much. I'm not set up that way. I never solicit help. My wife asks me, 'How do you do it?' I say, 'I don't think about it!' Now after seventeen years of marriage she believes me."

He does not think he needed any further support from his colleagues. "It was too late for me. There are things that could be done for younger people so that they're not so overwhelmed. Forced counseling or discussions would be good or a discussion of the different ways to cope."

V

"I'm scared to death about my children dying. When a child died who was the same age and gender as one of them I'd think about it. When my children get sick I always think of the worst thing first like meningococcemia."

He does not think about his children's mortality often, but "I think of my parents' all the time. I also think more often about my wife's and my own deaths. A slightly older colleague died today and that made me think about being on the downward slope of the age curve. I have some medical problems and I get up in pain every day now. What will it be like in thirty years? It's very depressing to think about the deaths of my parents, especially my father's death, and when I think of them I feel tremendous loss and sadness. I worry about my mother-in-law who is seventy-five and how her death will affect everyone. Then it's my generation's turn. I don't worry quite so much about that yet.

"I thought of my own mortality today! Up until three years ago I didn't think about it often. After my father died I thought about it more and now that I have a chronic illness I think about it a lot more. Last year at this time I was being worked up for diplopia [double vision]. They were concerned that it might be A L S. I had an E M G [electromyelogram] and it was very painful. You're worried about dying and you're having a really painful test! I know that my chronic pain won't get any better. It'll never go away and it'll probably get worse. On the other hand that's the way it is. I'm less worried about dying than about how uncomfortable it'll be. I'm most concerned about the years leading up to it, the decrease in function and the pain. My mother took a year to die and she didn't die well. My father was pretty good until the last three months of his life and then he couldn't do much. Those last three months were terrible."

Al's defensive reaction to his death anxiety, a nearly total and complete repression of any experience that might touch on his mortality, worked very effectively until his parents died and he was threatened with the prospect of an incurable disease. Those experiences overwhelmed his defenses and opened him up to a deeply painful but ultimately enlightening encounter with the sadness of loss that surrounds everything mortal. While he continues to repress painful feelings, he is available now in a way that he was not before. His humanity and vulnerability are there for others and for him to explore.

VI

A "good death" is one in which "the family is present. They understand that the child will die. The child is adequately medicated so that there's no pain and she's not aware. The death is quick and it doesn't drag on. The health-care team is all on the same page. I've come close to performing active euthanasia, but in a legal and ethical manner acceptable in the United States. If a child is going to die, the parents don't want the death to drag on, and so many ICU physicians use drugs for dying patients that have 'wanted' side effects. I'd give the child a cocktail of Pentothal [a barbiturate] that acts as a sedative and relieves pain but also ensures that she won't take any agonal or ineffective breaths that would prolong her suffering. Otherwise children would gasp for a few minutes to a few hours after removal from life support. Is that unethical? Is that euthanasia? I don't believe so."

A "bad death" is when "the family doesn't understand or accept it, or where there is disagreement among the health-care professionals. Consultants, and especially hematology-oncology people, sometimes disagree with the discontinuation of life support. I also worked with one newly 'reborn' Christian physician who tried to resuscitate a child for twenty minutes *after* the child was pronounced dead!"

He believes older children have a "very high degree" of understanding about their own deaths. "I had one patient, a sixteen-year-old with end-stage cardiac disease. His parents wouldn't leave the room. We all knew he'd die soon, but he didn't want to die in front of his family. He encouraged them to go to lunch. After they left he died. He knew they couldn't handle watching him die."

Many people I interviewed commented on children trying to spare their parents the pain of watching them die or waiting to die until the parents, in some way, gave them permission to do so. While it cannot be proven, their reflections suggest that for some children, at least, dying is in part an active process that involves at some level a choice and a conscious letting go.

As for helping children cope with their deaths, "I'm not sure that it's a problem in the PICU. Those who are going to die there, die of their acute illness despite active treatment or have a head injury and never wake up. Child Life prepares children with cancer. At my end it's a nonissue. I don't know about children who die on the floor or at home. I've had more deaths than anyone here because of the context of my work, probably five to six hundred children over the course of the past eighteen years.

"The Child Life people I've met do great work with the siblings and parents. The nursing staff also does very good work. Unfortunately, the residents and the medical students aren't that helpful. That's because of their inexperience. When a child patient dies, they need nurturing and care themselves! Some of the attendings are good and some aren't. Those from hematology-oncology and cardiology do well. In eighteen years I've only seen one primary care doctor who came into the PICU when his patient died. Primary care doctors never talk with parents about the child's shortened life expectancy or the fact that she's going to die. This leads the parents to have unrealistic expectations when the inevitable happens.

"Working in the Intensive Care Unit breeds sensitivity and knowledge, not so much about helping the children but about getting their families through it. Our patients usually weren't conscious before they died. We made sure they had adequate analgesia. If we did get a verbal patient, it was very hard to deal with because we didn't have much experience with patients like that. It was also difficult if we'd gotten to know the patients' families well before the child's death and had become attached to them. That happens with 'frequent flyers,' children who have multiple operations. Emotionally those deaths were very hard. For the younger doctors and nurses those deaths are devastating. You can tell by the look on their faces. It's like a deer caught in the headlights."

Given the physical condition of most of the patients he treated, Al believes that giving them psychological help is "often not applicable." As for helping them to avoid pain and suffering from a neurological perspective, "I was their best friend. I made sure they didn't feel any pain. I looked for an autonomic response. I pinched them hard. If there wasn't a change in their pulse and blood pressure, then I knew their brain wasn't experiencing pain. I taught that to the residents.

"I don't think I ever told a child that he or she was dying. If they were semiconscious I let the family be with them. I always told the families and I let them communicate what they wanted in their own way. I do remember a couple of children asking, 'Am I going to die?' I can't remember exactly what I said. One of them was a teenager so I probably said, 'Yes, maybe today, maybe tomorrow, maybe a long time from now.' He said, 'What's a long time?' I said, 'A few weeks, a few months, nobody really knows.' He was a sharp boy. I was taken aback by his question. No child had ever asked me that before. My immediate thought was, 'I don't want to be here!' I imagine that the oncologists have a lot more experience answering that kind of question."

Al was much more adept at discussing the deaths of children with parents. "I don't think there's anything I haven't been asked before: 'Who, what, when, where, why, why, why, why? Is there anything you can do? Is there anything that somebody can do? Why my child?' However, people who ask those questions are in the minority. By the time I saw them the majority of parents had worked through their denial already. Acceptance comes pretty quickly and then grief starts. I told them they had to be strong to get their child through it. Most focused on that as a coping mechanism. They pushed aside their feelings and those of other family members and focused on the child.

"About 20 percent got hysterical, angry, and had the 'whys?' I've had drunken parents and a psychotic parent. I've had parents who started partying almost immediately after their child died. But the overwhelming majority was there for their children. When I identified parents who needed help, I told them to be absolutely certain that they got counseling. I would give a family member my card and ask them to call so I could help them. I remember my father's death. It was a black hole and I can't recall any of the details. If someone gave me advice I don't remember it. That's why I gave parents my card, in case there were questions later."

Parents who asked "normal questions or if they repeated questions once or twice, that was all right; that was part of my job. The ones who asked over and over again, who couldn't understand what was going to happen, those were incredibly taxing and I sometimes felt angry with them. I rarely showed it, but I'd sometimes cut them off. I'd say, 'I've already explained that. You already know that.' If the parents were psychotic or drunk, I just stayed away. I felt sorry for the nurses because they couldn't walk away. If it was a dysfunctional family it was a dysfunctional death."

VII

His colleagues' abilities to cope with patients' deaths "depended on their subspecialty. The ones in which children die—critical care, hematology-oncology, pulmonary—do better than other subspecialties. I can count on the fingers of one hand the number of times a general pediatrician has come to a child's death. And when they do, they say nothing. I've never seen a general pediatrician discuss the prognosis for children that we know are going to die or that are going to be developmentally delayed. Never! The parents are really underserved by them. Only one or two percent of the parents of those children know that their children have shortened life-expectancies. No one tells the family. They have no idea until the child dies at eleven or twelve. General pediatricians are very poorly prepared to deal with death. They don't have to do it that often.

"My critical-care colleagues have the experience and understand the physiology of dying. They know when a person is going to die. They've dealt with the gamut of parental personality types, religious, drunk, educated, uneducated, angry, or accepting. The longer you work in the ICU the more you see. It's directly proportional to how long they've been practicing critical-care medicine. The longer the better, although doing it for too long can be overwhelming and lead to burnout, especially for the nurses. They're with the patient for ten to twelve hours at a time. They get the questions the family doesn't ask me. I developed tremendous respect for all they do to help the families of dying children. One thing I was taught is that after the child dies, you should help the nurse clean up the patient and the bed. I try to teach our junior faculty that.

"I don't remember any of my colleagues saying 'I can't take it anymore, I won't do this for a living,' but I've never actually talked to them about it. I don't know what they did after I went home. I can remember nurses crying. I'd put my arm around them, but there weren't any follow-up conversations. I didn't pay that much attention to the residents because they were constantly changing. I did pay attention to the nurses I worked with every day. Their biggest strength is that they have each other to talk to. I know they talk about patients' deaths much more than the doctors do. It's the nurses who go to the funerals. It's probably related to how well they get to know the families. They're at the bedside eight or nine hours a day. They really talk and get to know them."

He emphasized one final point. "My reaction to the deaths of my parents was a hundred million times stronger than my reactions to the deaths of the children I cared for. Not that those deaths weren't important, but it's the difference between one's own incredible grief and empathy and sympathy for somebody else."

The pain experienced by parents at the loss of their child is orders of magnitude greater than the pain experienced by the child's doctors and nurses. While this book explores the grieving of the professionals involved in children's medical care, it is important to emphasize that the key participants in a child's deaths are the child and his or her parents and family members.

7

"Coping with death is a process; you find your own way."

Lee, a thirty-nine-year-old pediatric intensivist, modeled her coping strategies after those of her father, whose role within their family was to keep things together and to rescue those who were weak. Growing up, she was expected to deal with and solve problems, not to be overwhelmed and emotional like her mother and sister. As an intensivist in a pediatric teaching hospital she continues to function as a bulwark of strength for those around her. Under her competent and masterful facade, however, she is a sensitive person who functions best in a highly structured environment. The death of her mother, with whom she had an intense, conflictual relationship, was devastating for her and highlighted her vulnerability in dealing with the loss of important people in her life. Within her professional milieu, her brilliance and well-developed coping mechanisms mask her underlying sensitivity, which she guards tenaciously. Only when she is alone do the grief and sadness she experiences in her work come to the surface and temporarily overwhelm her defenses.

I

Lee's first experience of a child patient's death occurred on the last day of her internship. "There was a little girl about five or six years old who was admitted to the floor for croup. We residents were across the street at our end-of-the-year banquet. While we were there, she aspirated a hotdog and asphyxiated. She developed severe ARDS [acute respiratory distress syndrome] and went on ECMO in the

PICU. The PICU fellows cared for her because she was on ECMO. I was a resident in the PICU during the first month of my second year and helped with her care. It went on for two or three weeks. When we saw that she wasn't going to survive, we took her off ECMO and she became the residents' patient again. The second night off ECMO she was doing worse and worse. The fellow wasn't helping me to try to make her better. He thought she was going to die. I was getting increasingly frantic. I called the attending to try to get help and she came in. I remember being upset and frustrated that I couldn't make the child better. It hadn't been made clear to me that she would get worse and die and that we would just let it happen.

"It was a very sad and tragic situation. The fellow who intubated her had a hard time doing it. I had tremendous respect for him. He was smart and a very good doctor. I felt bad for him because he felt responsible. It highlighted for me that sometimes things don't go well and you're responsible. It was a very busy month and I just kept on going. I remember thinking that it was unfair to give up on her. I didn't know the scientific literature then about the decision that was being made. It would have helped if the people in charge had spelled out their reasoning to the rest of us involved in her care.

"I'm not sure if her death still affects me. In general I feel that I wasn't given a lot of guidance in my training by my teachers. They left a lot for me to figure out on my own. You can't spoon-feed it. You have to learn about it on your own. Now I try to be clear with the residents about what our expectations are when a patient is going to die, what we can and can't do. Each death is different and individual. Some are harder and some are easier. With some I'm more involved than with others. I don't think of that first death as a turning point. I see it all as part of a continuum."

II

Lee's family consisted of her mother, father, and a sister who is two years her junior. Her parents divorced when she was twelve, and they both remarried when she was fourteen. She lived with her mother and stepfather until she left for college, and they subsequently divorced when she was nineteen. "Have you ever read *The Drama of the Gifted Child*? It's about the children of narcissistic parents and how they cope and survive. That's my life story."

She does not recall how she responded to her parents' divorce. "My father says that, typically, my sister cried and I said, 'What'll we do for dinner tonight?' or something equally banal. I don't recall my emotional response. I thought it was a good idea because they fought all the time. My father stayed pretty involved. He came over and took us out to dinner. The divorce wasn't that difficult. It was his remarriage that was difficult. His new wife had a family. Then he and she had a child together, and I felt that I wasn't an important part of his life anymore. I felt abandoned. I didn't feel unhappy and I'm not sure how I coped with it at the time. Later I coped by getting involved in a long-term relationship with an older man."

Her mother was often ill during the years before her parents' divorce. "She was an alcoholic and was hospitalized several times for gastrointestinal complaints, including a perforated ulcer." Lee did not recall her emotional reaction to being separated from her mother. "Either I didn't have a reaction or I don't remember it. My father was very involved in our upbringing. I don't recall any problems. I was the oldest child and filled in for her. My mother was a very narcissistic woman. My father was warmer and a more emotional person. He says that she was wonderful with us when we were very young. Based on my reaction to her death I believe that was true. However, my memory of her during the years when I was growing up is that she wasn't a warm, emotional person."

Her mother's death "was much more difficult than I'd thought it would be. She was brilliant, attractive, and difficult. We had a bad relationship when I was a teenager, although it got better as I got older. Being with her wasn't enjoyable for me. I learned about her death when I was on service in the hospital. My mother hadn't shown up for work for a few days. That was completely unlike her. My sister went to her house and called the police, who found her dead.

She was presumed to have died of an arrhythmia. I went to my mother's home and my sister and I did the whole funeral thing. We got her a casket, had a funeral, and cleaned out her house. It was much more painful than I would have imagined. Because of our difficult relationship I hadn't expected that it would be so hard when she died. I was shocked by my response. It was like a physical pain. It was very painful and very sad. I felt sad for her that she'd had a lot of emotional problems and a lot of problems with her upbringing. She'd worked hard and hadn't had the opportunity to enjoy her life. Now she never would. She was fifty-nine and close to retirement. Now she wouldn't be able to retire and have fun. In her house I found a portrait of her in her wedding dress. I remember seeing it and sobbing. It was like all the crappy part of our relationship and the difficulty dealing with her became irrelevant. She was my mother. She was probably a very good mother when I was young. A bond had formed before the other stuff happened. It was still there.

"My sister had an even harder time with her death. She had a lot of guilt. She has three children and lived near my mother. Because my mother was such a pain in the ass, she didn't include her in her life as much as my mother would have liked.

"I wasn't a good daughter and she wasn't a good mother. I had moments of guilt, but it wasn't pervasive. Viewing her at the funeral home was an incredibly emotional, painful experience. I did the eulogy. I have horrendous stage fright about public speaking. I get nervous at faculty meetings. When I have to give talks I take propranolol, but I didn't have any with me at the funeral. Just before giving the eulogy, I went into the bathroom to calm down. I looked in the mirror and I saw my mother. I said to myself, 'You can do it' and I wasn't nervous at all. I talked about who she was. You could view her through the categories of the people in her life—her friends at work, her personal friends, people at AA, the men in her life, her daughters, and her grandchildren. I went through those categories and what they meant to her and what she was to them and how they saw her. I was glad I could do it. It sort of fit with what happens in our family. My sister is a more emotional person. I hold it together and do what needs to be done. The eulogy seemed to separate me from my grieving for her because it was like me being an adult. Grieving for her was more like me being a child.

"There's a Tracy Chapman song that still makes me cry. I took the tape from her car. It's called 'The Promise,' and it has words like 'Will you remember me, will you hold me close, will you wait for me?' I play it a lot when I drive to work. During the first couple of months after she died I started sobbing whenever I heard it. Now it still makes me cry but less so than before. It's about someone you love being gone and wanting to be reunited with them when you die. I think about reunion. Now when I think about her I feel sad and I cry. After I cry I feel better. If I'm at work I just put the sadness away."

After her mother's death, "I was struck by how caring the residents and nurses were. They were very kind and expressed their condolences. I really appreciated it. I tend to be independent and don't like getting help from people. I was surprised that I could accept it. I appreciated people saying something and acknowledging her death. I'd come back from her funeral and gone right to work. I felt pretty shell-shocked and couldn't focus worth a damn. I told the staff that I could only concentrate for about five minutes at a time. They were really nice about it."

The earliest death Lee can remember is that of Robert Kennedy in 1968. "I was five or six then. My mother, sister, and I were in our first house watching TV in the den. I remember seeing a train coming into a station and my mom crying. I don't think I understood it at the time. I knew something big and sad had happened. It was a little bit scary to see her crying. She wasn't someone who cried. My mother's father died when I was eight years old. I didn't know him. The only thing I remember is that my mother went back for the funeral even though she was terrified of flying. My father's father died when I was ten or eleven. I was sad. I knew him and remembered him as a person. He was a big guy and had had several bad strokes. I remember him sitting in his chair and my helping him put his socks on. He was legendary in our family's folklore. He was a minister in a small town, a big deal, imposing and overbearing.

"My father's mother and my mother's mother died within two months of each other, about one month before I was married. I think about my dad's mom's funeral occasionally. The memory is still very vivid. She was a warm, loving grandmother. She had cancer and was about eighty-five when she died. She was incredibly active, a musician who taught music in the schools. Even when she was retired and arthritic she still played for the old peoples' groups. In her retirement home she had a friend who played the piano, and she played the organ. She died in March. The previous November my father had told me that she was getting worse, and he and I went to visit. We stayed with her for four or five days. As I was leaving I gave her a hug and said good-bye. We both realized that it was really good-bye. It was very sad. At the viewing in the funeral home they played a tape that she and her friend had made. She improvised and it was a different style of playing. The whole thing was kind of spooky. My father talked at the funeral. We followed the Danish tradition and, as they lowered the coffin, we began to sing traditional songs. It was really difficult. She was buried at her husband's first church. My cousins were the pallbearers. We stood there crying and singing old Danish songs. It was rainy and the wind was blowing. It was touching, the continuity of the family, our heritage, and all the people who had known them."

Lee's ideas about what happens after death "went through phases. As an early adolescent I was interested in different religions, reincarnation, whatever was out there. Then I went through a year or so of being an active Christian and going to church with friends. I was sort of an explorer of alternative religions. My most pervasive thought was that some sort of spiritual entity continues afterward. We don't know what it is. We don't have the ability to know. That's still what I think."

Coping with death was based around "the theme of not being a burden to others. If you were upset, fine, but don't be a pain in the ass about it; keep it to yourself. In my father's family he was the oldest. His role was to take care of things, to rescue the females in the family, to say the eulogy at his parents' funerals, to be the strong one. Everybody has his or her grief. You do, too, but you don't let yourself fall apart and become a burden to others. I modeled my coping style after my father's."

This coping strategy of taking charge and not allowing herself to fall apart works very well for Lee as an intensivist in a teaching hospital, where she supports residents, medical students, and nurses. Her colleagues refer to her as "The Rock" and marvel at her ability to keep going no matter what is happening, but she hints at the fact that in addition to rescuing others there is a part of her that would at times like to be rescued. How she meets this need in her personal life is not clear, but it does illustrate an important point about caregivers in medicine. One of the motivations for caregiving is the wish that "others would do unto you as you have done unto them."

While her conscious identification is with her father, at a deeper, more emotional level she is also like her mother, vulnerable and strongly affected by separation and loss. As she looked at her mother's picture in her wedding dress, feelings overwhelmed her; and when she looked in the mirror at the funeral home, she saw her mother in herself.

III

No one in Lee's family had ever been a physician. "I was a good student in a public high school and the expectation was that smart people went into either medicine or law. When I was thirteen a friend of my mother's and I were in a car accident. I hurt my back and she was almost killed. She was in the hospital for months and then stayed with us after she got out. I was really attached to her and took care of her. My mother got a little jealous and made her leave.

"In college I majored first in math then in biology. I saw myself more as a science person and I got the very strong impression from my professors that medicine is a trade and that a real scientist gets a PhD. I guess I sort of fell into medicine. I applied to medical school, got in, and then had to decide if I'd do it. It wasn't a very well thought out decision. It seemed like the thing to do. I liked science and had taken anthropology courses. Medicine seemed to offer a more holistic approach to science than a basic science career.

"I never thought that I'd do pediatrics. I chose it as my first clinical rotation because I didn't think that I'd like it, but I loved inpatient pediatrics. I looked forward to going to work and was sad on the weekends when I didn't get to go in. I liked inpatient medicine, caring for sick patients, and having multiple patients at once. I liked going to rounds, interacting with the nurses, talking with the consultants, and trying to figure out what was wrong. I liked pediatricians more than internists. And children are more honest patients than adults are. They have less baggage and you're dealing more with the disease process."

She has mixed feelings about her career choice. "I love the medicine. I had a romanticized view of medicine that I still feel. I feel privileged to be able to do it. It's remarkable to do critical care, to use what I know to make children better. When it works it thrills me. I'm less happy with the mechanics of medicine, administration, meetings, regulations, and constraints. I'm not sure that there's anything else I'd rather be doing, although I'd like to be doing a little less of what I do. It's physically fatiguing."

In medical school she learned about death from Elisabeth Kübler-Ross. "We got her spiel and read her stuff. I remember classes focusing on the dying process. I don't know how you can really learn about the deaths of patients until you experience them. As a medical student you're involved with dying patients in your third and fourth years, but all of your didactic teaching is in your first two years. Then when you're caring for dying patients there isn't any place to learn or talk about it.

"In residency and fellowship there wasn't much discussion about death. I don't recall being taught anything. In fellowship one of the attendings was a bioethicist. We had lots of thoughtful discussions about death and withdrawing or withholding life support, but no personal focus on individual patients. As a first-year fellow I cared for a baby with meningitis for four months. I was very involved in her care. The parents decided to withdraw life support. We had a big team meeting to decide. The parents asked to wait until Monday when those of us most involved in her care would be there. Monday came and we stood around her bed as she was taken off the ventilator. She died with her parents holding her. I thought somebody might say something, but no one did. Later in the day I had another disaster and had to get right back into the work. When you're new it's all very intense. You're still young and can take it. Later you have to learn to distance yourself."

Over the years, she has witnessed and participated in many deaths yet never had the time to talk about it. "It all stays there. Periodically you lose it and cry. Something minor will set you off. Or there's one death that hits you especially hard and you have to grieve."

To teach young physicians how to cope with patients' deaths it would help "to know what other people went through, both older doctors and your contemporaries. It's a process. You find your own way and don't realize that you're on a journey. No one really tells you about their experiences." She and her colleagues "talk about the patients, but we seldom talk about our own responses. We deal with death more than most other specialties. People in our field are fairly well defended in their coping. Talking about how one feels comes across as being confrontational. We work serially and our colleagues in the trenches are the nurses. I talk with them more. Their role is different than ours. They're more involved physically and only have one or two patients at a time. They've cared for some of their patients for a long time and the deaths are quite emotional. Other patients are short-term and the nurses don't feel as much. Different nurses deal with patients' deaths in different ways. Some are more emotional and some are more technical."

IV

"I'm able to turn my emotions on and off. To be emotionally involved in a patient's death is painful but honest. What's more difficult is going back to work after something difficult has happened and just moving on. If you're honestly present, feelings tend to build up. I can turn my emotions on and off as I need to, but I have the self-awareness to recognize when I've been squashing my feelings down too long.

"I'm pretty good at psychological insights into my own and the families' reactions to things. I can be very honest with families. I try to be kind, but I don't beat around the bush. I can be emotionally present for them if they need that. I try to modulate my emotional involvement depending on the patients' and the families' needs. I see my role as trying to make patients' deaths as tolerable as possible for the family. There are some deaths that are worse than others. I try to orchestrate each death so that the family can be all right with it and not have any regrets. That's my goal.

"Doctors can use patients for their own emotional benefit. We have to remember that what we do is for the patient's well-being, not our own. I do get positive emotional feedback from my interactions with families. There can be a tendency to use that to meet your own needs. We have to be aware of that and keep our focus on the patient's and the family's needs, not our own.

"Sometimes I think I should be tougher and not allow my work to invade my personal life. I don't have many boundaries between the two. I don't compartmentalize well. I take stuff home with me. My husband is very supportive, but I think he wishes that I didn't bring it home so much.

"I find a lot of solace in the residents and the nurses. Nurses can't escape, while doctors can walk out of the room. They're forced to be present. When a patient is dying they usually only have that one patient. They take control of that family and that patient. There's a sense of shared experience. Failed code deaths involve a whole group of people. I have a sense of responsibility toward them to show that we ran a good code.

"My weaknesses are a result of fatigue and overwork. It takes energy to empathize! If you're overworked, busy, or tired, you can't do it. You keep pushing feelings aside until you go on vacation and then cry for two days about all the grief that you've absorbed. I feel responsible for everybody. Meeting the staff's and the family's needs is more important than my needs at the time. I have a sense of responsibility and a need to care for others. In doing that I'm fulfilling my own needs. I see some pretty horrible stuff. If it isn't dealt with it tends to hang around. Then when you have time to reflect, anything can bring the tears on—a song, a person. It takes a while to recover. It's like when you experience death the first time around. You're stunned, then numb and spacey for a while. The recovery from reliving one's grief is similar to grieving immediately after the death of a family member.

"It's a very solitary experience. There's not a lot anyone can say or do. The most they can do is to be there and acknowledge that it's been hard. The most disappointing times are when you've had a bad night, a sad death, or an awful week of deaths. No one acknowledges that. If you're up all night with a child and he dies at six-thirty in the morning, nobody on the next shift wants to hear about it. There's all this stuff you've experienced that no one wants to hear about. For friends who aren't in medicine it's hard. They're so horrified by what I do that they can't really hear about it. It's too awful for them. Friends and family are so overwhelmed by a horrible death that my grief seems trivial. They can't understand how I do it. My husband is as supportive as his personal level of happiness at the time will allow. Right now, he's down, emotionally tapped out. He's very supportive when I bring things up and it's obvious that I'm hurting, but he doesn't seek it out. I wish he did. I have a hard time feeling like a burden to others. I like to be self-sufficient. If I make him talk about it with me I feel like I'm being a burden. He was much more supportive when I was a fellow. Now he tends to personalize it to his own experience; 'what are we doing with our lives?' It pains him for me to talk about it. It brings up a painful reaction in him, about the sadness around us and about his feelings of mortality. I view it more like 'get on with it, it's your job.'

"My stepmother is the best at being supportive. She's a psychologist and a medicine junkie, a doctor want-to-be. She specializes in really disturbed people. She loves to hear my stories. If it's in the paper she wants to know all about it, both the medical and the emotional side. She also has psychological interpretations that are more intuitive than the reactions others have. It's nice to have someone who wants to hear about it. Most friends and family aren't able to hear it; it's too difficult for them. I need to tell the story. People who listen are very helpful. I have one colleague who's in the field and we talk a lot about our cases.

"The worst deaths are those where you feel that you made a mistake or didn't do your best. I'm not sure that I've made a mistake that directly contributed to a patient's death. I may not have chosen the best path of care and that contributed to the death. Or there are some cases where you need to do something that may kill the patient, like intubating them, even though you know that they'll die anyway. I try to be honest about my contribution to the situation and try to learn something from it that will help the next patient. What we're here for is to care for the patient and to provide the best care that we can. That takes precedence over our own emotional needs. My responsibility is to learn something rather than wallowing in guilt, which is ultimately selfish."

V

"Sometimes I think about my own mortality, especially after the sudden tragedies like car accidents and random violence, things that highlight that life is a crapshoot. People with chronic diseases and cancer illustrate the same thing. Those of us with no tragedies or medical problems are incredibly lucky. It makes you a little nervous if you're a person who goes through life thinking that you're protected, but we see that life doesn't spare anyone. We just had a family in which the father is a doctor and the mother a PhD. They had a child with cancer that got a bone marrow transplant and then died in the unit after two months. That death was hard for a lot of us. They were so like 'us,' a nice upper-middle-class professional family with two children. It hit really close to home. I don't have children and don't have the same visceral response that people with children have when a child the same age as their own child dies. But I know that something bad could happen to anyone I love.

"Often the older the child the harder the death or tragedy, like a boy with a serious football injury, a 'real person' with plans and a girlfriend. I have a very hard time dealing with adult patients dying. The patient could be one of my friends or siblings. An intensivist deals with so many children dying. You learn how to speak to parents. You can do it without a lot of thought. You have a way of approaching parents that becomes your style. When you have to shift to an adult's wife and children that style doesn't work. It doesn't fit your usual pattern. It's much harder for me to deal with an adult's death."

She thinks about the mortality of her family members "pretty often, daily or weekly. I think my father had better hang around for a long time! I worry about him, his health, his dying. It would be devastating for me. He'd abhor being sick and a burden. I always felt that he'd be the last one to die. If everyone else died and he was still there I could go on. If I lost him it would be losing everything. He's the one whose approval is the most important to me. My husband is older and has a bad family [health] history. It's too painful to think about losing him. It would be very painful to lose my father. Losing my husband would be . . . I don't know what I'd do. I tend to keep going and to suck it up. I'd probably do that, but I don't know how I'd be able to be part of the world.

"The other day it occurred to me that I'm turning forty this summer. I'm halfway through my life. It seems too short. The average life span isn't long enough to get tired of life. I want to keep going until I can't do it anymore."

Lee allows us to see another side of her independent strivings; she is very dependent for emotional support on her father and husband and does not know how she would go on without them. The PICU may function as a kind of secondary family for her, a place where there are both supportive people and people she can support and where the intense demands of patient care distract her from her inner life and provide a structure within which she can thrive.

VI

"In the P I C U the child is usually unaware that he's going to die and is sedated and comatose. In a 'good death' the family has come to terms with what's going to happen, can be present in the moment, and has had a chance to say good-bye and to do what they need to do so they don't have regrets. We're very able to make death comfortable. The hard part is helping the family to get to a good place and to not have regrets about how the death was handled."

A "bad death" is "sudden and unexpected. It's hard to make those good. They're things like a terrible accident or a chronic disease that suddenly becomes acute. In our setting the children aren't usually aware. They're brain-dead, have neurological damage, or are heavily sedated because of severe physical problems. Acute deaths are intubated and sedated. If they're going to die of a chronic illness they go to the floor [the medical ward]. I remember a time when I was a fellow. The patient, a teenage male, had a necrotizing pneumonia. We put him on E C M O, but the pneumonia ate away his lungs and there was nothing we could do. He was sedated, but awake and aware. His parents could talk to him and he could communicate with eye movements. I don't know if they told him he was going to die. It completely freaked people out when he did!

"I remember another patient, a fifteen-year-old on hematology-oncology. He'd failed chemotherapy and needed a bone marrow transplant even though the chances were slim. He came in with typhlitis, an inflammation of the bowel, necrotizing enterocolitis. His bowel was very inflamed and he was septic. After twelve to fifteen hours, it became clear that we'd need to intubate him. His chances of being cured of the cancer were small and his parents didn't want to put him through it. The parents spent an hour with him and talked about his going to heaven, playing golf with an uncle who had died, and about the people he'd meet. He asked to see his brother and sister. They went in for about five minutes. I was in another room. After they left the nurse came and told me that he'd just died. He suddenly flat-lined! It was a creepy experience. He knew he was going to die and the death was very peaceful.

"Children know a lot more about their own deaths than we think, and they understand more. Depending on their developmental stage they understand in different ways. Even if they're not told they're dying they understand more than we give them credit for." She has not had much experience talking with children about their deaths. "Sometimes I care for teens and young adults. I talk with them in the form of securing advance directives. Otherwise it's pretty uncommon. We don't deal with conscious children that often. I believe that children need to be informed and given more opportunities to discuss it. If it does come up we're pretty straightforward and honest with the children if they're old enough to understand. It's so infrequent that I'm not as polished at speaking with the children as I am with their parents. My abilities to help parents and families have gotten better. Sometimes parents don't want to tell their children that they're going to die. That's awkward. We talk with the parents about it long enough until they understand how important it is. It takes time and energy to do that.

"Parents want to know what their child's chances are, the statistics. Sometimes they ask about the dying process and sometimes they don't. If they don't I explain it to them. If the child has acute respiratory distress syndrome and respiratory failure then we'll have to give them medication so they'll be comfortable. If the parents want they can hold the patient. After we take out the breathing tube, the child may or may not try to breathe. We give them an idea of how long the patient will live.

"Most parents want to be sure that their child won't suffer. Occasionally a parent will say that they don't want the patient to breathe at all; they want it to be over. We explain that we don't do euthanasia but that we'll make the child comfortable. The respiratory drive is a very primitive force. Some parents want the monitors on and some want them off. Sometimes you discuss these details and sometimes you don't. I try to be present in the moment, empathic and honest. I try to keep the family focused." These experiences are not traumatic for Lee, "but they're exhausting! Every so often we get a crop of deaths in the same week. By the time you have these discussions with families they've gone through a lot already. When you have the death discussion you've already had a lot of talks with them."

VII

Lee's colleagues "have different degrees of self-awareness. Some become overinvolved with certain patients and uninvolved with others. Some don't deal well with death. When they know a person is going to die, they remove themselves. I feel that when we withdraw life support, I should be the one who does it. It's my responsibility. I cope with patients' deaths by being personally involved. If I go too long without being emotionally involved I start to not enjoy the job. It's a way of focusing to be part of the patient's death. After doing this for a long time it's pretty easy to become emotionally uninvolved. One of the older physicians is rather gruff and aggressive with people, but he can be great at dealing with sick children and their families. He's kind and involved. It's very different than his usual persona. He's emotionally available.

"I'm not sure that coping is the right word to describe how we deal with death. Coping implies that a death doesn't affect you. There's a critical balance between being too aggressive and not being aggressive enough, about not being afraid of what needs to be done. My tendency is to be somewhat overcautious. I'm very aware of that. I try to be clear if in deciding not to do something it's because that's the best answer or it's because I'm afraid to cause more harm. Others are more interventional and aggressive.

"There are different kinds of deaths. There's the failed code death. That doesn't happen very often in pediatrics. In those cases you have to be personally removed, a technician, and not allow your emotional response to get involved with the decisions you're making. There are a lot of planned deaths, children who have unfixable diseases or whose families have decided that the burden of continued treatment isn't worth it. Sometimes we elect not to resuscitate or to withdraw care with the understanding that the patient will then die. I try to assess how much my emotional involvement will be of benefit to the family as opposed to satisfying my own needs.

"The other physicians are well enough defended that it doesn't interfere with their functioning. You either develop your defenses or you drop out. Most of them are very compassionate with families. Those who've been in the field longer have better-defined coping strategies. Our primary responsibility is to deal with patient deaths in a way that's most beneficial for each individual family. We also have to act in a way that supports the nursing staff. We have to take care of the patients and the unit. Secondary to all of that is to integrate your own personal strategies. Some people are able to be more personally involved; others need to stand back from it at the end. You need to be able to function well but still remain empathic in order to stay in the profession. Coping effectively is a quality you bring with you.

"Intensive care attendings have different personality types. Those who are good at it pay attention to detail *and* stand back to see the big picture. They're able to be flexible. Adrenaline junkies don't do well in the field. It's not like an emergency room where you're 'saving lives.' It's about paying attention to detail, weighing the pros and cons, multitasking, and integrating a lot of diverse information. That personality type is attracted to intensive care.

"Younger physicians have less-developed coping strategies and less clearly thought-out concepts of death. It often comes up in the context of withdrawing life support. They don't communicate clearly with the families about what we're doing and its intent. They don't communicate clearly with the nursing staff. There was a recent incident in which the nurses brought up the different ways in which we withdraw life support. When we discussed this, our concepts were similar. I assume that the differences lie in how we communicate our decisions.

"One of my colleagues has a hard time dealing with patients' deaths. He gets very involved with some families, especially those with a higher standard of living and others who gravitate to him. When they get attached, he thrives on it. He takes the deaths of their children as a personal failure. If they die unexpectedly, he obsesses about it until the postmortem is back and he's exonerated from having caused the death. He wants to make it right for them. He thrives on them depending on him. There's not a lot of consistency in the way that he deals with death. If a patient is falling apart or is a failed code death he flogs them unmercifully until he's sure that the patient will die. I also know that we all sometimes misunderstand each other's intentions in these situations.

"Everyone will be responsible for some patient's death in the course of his or her career, making a mistake or a wrong decision, although it's pretty uncommon. We're also responsible for those patient deaths that we don't manage optimally, making errors of omission rather than commission. It's more critical to look carefully at those deaths rather than at the rare mistakes."

At the end of our interviews, Lee acknowledged that they had been "a bit tiring emotionally. It's kind of like going to therapy! I did it because it's important and to support my colleagues. It's an important project and we need to talk more about it. The format has the potential to be a lot more powerful than survey-like projects about life and death. In my current job situation I don't get a lot of emotional release. My mother's birthday and Mother's Day occurred in the last couple of weeks, work has been stressful, and I don't feel that I'm in a position to connect emotionally. It's more of an intellectual connection. I'll be on-call on the anniversary of my mother's death!"

She admitted that she had not let herself get too emotionally involved in the interviews. "I haven't gone home and cried! At this time in my life, with the way work is going and dealing with my mother's death, I don't have the energy to fall apart and then pick it up again. It's been very positive to articulate my views and not have them judged. You see my insights and intuitiveness as gifts.

Others sometimes don't. Some parts of our job are very hard to explain to people. It's hard to abstract out the essence of your experiences. Everyone in our field will relate to and understand the situation. I don't know how people without those experiences will see it. As lengthy as the interviews have been, they're not long enough. I'm not sure how accurate my abstractions of my experiences and memories are. I feel a responsibility to the field to portray them accurately."

8

"It's not about me, it's about the patient."

Over the course of many years as an attending physician on the hematology-oncology service, Dave has learned to subordinate his emotional needs to those of his patients and their families. While he believes it is important to recognize and acknowledge one's affective responses to the deaths of children and the pain of their parents, he recognizes that the tragedies he encounters in his work "aren't about us." He believes that physicians must meet their emotional needs outside of work and not allow themselves to become so overwhelmed by their feelings that they are unable to function in their jobs.

I

"During my senior year in medical school I did a PICU rotation. A couple of deaths there had a real impact. The horror of it got to me. I don't remember crying, just being stressed. One was a two- or three-year-old girl with 95 percent burns after a house fire. She was quite charred. I told the family that our main focus was on pain management. It was very difficult and traumatizing for the family. The other one was a two- or three-year-old boy whose mother had left him at church for a mother's day out program. He went down a slide, got his jacket caught, and was hung. He was brain dead. The parents were devastated and so was the priest at the church. Those were shocking experiences. You realize how quickly a life can be gone; two healthy people that in a flash are dead. It brought home how fleeting life can be. You know it, but it smacks you in the face. I see death so frequently that . . . it's a sick thing—but one of my motivations for having three children was to end up with at least two."

Early in his career, he notes, "I had a lot of balance in my life. I was newly married and had a rich life outside of the hospital. I was very enthusiastic about my work. I realized that I liked caring for really sick children. The work was very gratifying intellectually and emotionally." Yet the memories of those early deaths are still there. "Even when I have Alzheimer's, I'll remember those two children. They're powerful images, like 9/11. I still remember the ER bay and what it looked like. I'm not sure that there's still any emotion tied to those experiences anymore, just the memories.

"The first cancer death I had was a fifteen-year-old country girl. She had AML [acute myelogenous leukemia] and relapsed. I still remember her first and last name even though it was seventeen years ago. I'd been on call one night, had not slept, and was going home the next evening after thirty-six hours of work. I stopped by her room and said good night. She said, 'You look tired.' I said, 'I'm going to go home and just die.' She said, 'That's not very funny.' I said, 'You're right!'

"Each death is different. They're all sad, especially when you know the child or family well. You grieve a bit, not like what the families or the nurses go through, but you're sad, go to the funeral if you can, and shed a few tears. I'm much more affected by the deaths from drug toxicity than the relapses. Sometimes things go wrong. Those are much harder personally. You feel something close to guilt and you do some second-guessing.

"Communicating with the families and expressing my sympathy for them helps. The ability to do something helps. It's meaningful for families when doctors call them or come to the funeral. I get a lot of strength from my family and my church and from just vegging out. Often after a difficult death, I realize that I've spent a lot of time in front of the television.

"The worst times are when a child dies due to a side effect of the treatment. That's the most horrible situation. There have also been a couple of times when, despite trying, we haven't been able to get a patient's pain cared for and the process of dying was very painful; you have a sense of helplessness. It's tough when the child reminds me of one of my own children, either because they're the same age, share certain personality characteristics, or their parents remind me of my wife or me. A connection with my personal life makes it more difficult. One patient had the same birth date as my son. When I went to see him, it was like being hit in the face.

"All of us, if we have a series of deaths in rapid succession, get beaten down by them. It's numbing, like you're under a cloud. It takes your focus away. It decreases your ability to say just the right thing to families, to provide comfort care. We're going through that now. We've had eight or nine deaths during the nursing strike. It's hard on the families not to have the nurses here that they've bonded with. This week a great kid, Tommy, died. His parents were immigrants and very interesting. His father is in landscaping and his mother manages a store. Tommy had an illness from which he shouldn't have died, Burkitt's lymphoma. It has a 95 percent cure rate, but he was in the 5 percent that die. He was the only child of a really nice family. He was a basketball player being recruited to go to college. He won everyone's heart, and it was especially hard. You felt that it shouldn't have happened and that you'd let the family down. They were so sad and there was a lot of wailing. In their tradition the grieving process is very loud and that enhanced the sadness of it. His mother said to me, 'I had so much faith in you. This wasn't supposed to happen.' All I could say was, 'Sometimes we don't win.' That one really got to me. The children's deaths don't all hurt you equally. Some you've gotten closer to. He was one of those and I really felt the loss."

II

Dave grew up as the second of two children in a blue-collar family in northern Georgia. "My parents' families were poor. My mother was a high school graduate and my father quit school after the seventh grade. They both worked full-time in textile factories. They

wanted their children to have an education. My brother's an engi-
neer. Getting an education made us very different from them."

Dave's primary childhood caretaker was his paternal grandmother. "We were very close. My grandfather died when I was six
days old. I took his place in many ways. She was my babysitter until
I was twelve or thirteen years old and she played a big part in who
I am."

His family was Scotch-Irish and Southern Baptist, and religion
played a large role in his early life. "My parents were very involved
in the church. We were there three times a week. Culturally, the
church is a big part of life in the South. It was woven into everything
and was an overpowering presence. Conservative Southern Baptists
weren't mean then! I have fond memories of the church."

Death was discussed openly in his family. "I don't remember being
protected from it. My parents were from big families and there were
lots of relatives nearby. It was always important to show up for view-
ings and funerals. I went to a lot of them as a child." Death was something "that would happen sometimes. It was part of life and it was
sad. My father took his own father's death hard and got a shot of a
sedative from the family doctor. My mother cries easily and is emotional. Southern Baptists talked about the heaven and hell thing. It
seemed like the person who'd just died always went to heaven. There
were deathbed confessions. Death was always talked about a lot in
church. 'You could die tomorrow—what's going to happen to you
then?' After death people went to heaven or hell. The idea was that
people never really die, they move on to the next thing.

"We coped with death by being there for friends and family members. We invested time and emotion supporting one another. The
events weren't entirely sad. You saw family members that you didn't
see often. My parents' church provided food and meals for the
deceased's family. My mother was in charge of that effort for
twenty-five years! She had a telephone tree that she'd initiate. Everyone had preassigned dishes to bring to the family's house. They still
do it. It's a very Southern thing to do. Food is important in the
South."

His first experience of death was at the age of seven or eight, when his aunt almost died. "She was in her forties and had a stroke. She was in a coma for about a week. I remember it vividly. One night I talked with my parents and cried because I thought she'd die. I was very upset because I was close to her. She eventually made a near-full recovery and just died at age eighty-four!

"My mother's parents died when I was twelve or thirteen. It really affected me. It was very sad. They were quite poor. My grandfather was sick and probably had Alzheimer's. He was being worked up in the state hospital when my grandmother died. She was only sixty-two and was staying with us, and I could see that she was sick. She'd been diagnosed with congestive heart failure. She died unexpectedly in the hospital. There was a phone call in the middle of the night. I remember my mother running around crying and calling her siblings. I was mainly upset for my mother, upset to see her so distraught. I was very close to my parents. My grandfather's death about a year later had less of an effect. It was sad but also a relief. He wasn't able to care for himself and lived with us and with other family members. He wasn't very communicative. At the end he was hospitalized thirty miles away. Even though my parents both worked full time they went to see him every day.

"I dealt with their deaths by spending time with the family. In the South burials occur a few days after death. The time between the death and the funeral you spend all of your time with the family at home or in the funeral home. My mother was the oldest child. When her parents died the whole family came to us. There must have been forty or fifty people.

"The death that got to me the most was my father's mother when I was in my twenties. I think about her much more now than about my other grandparents. Her death was very sad because we were so close. I was the closest to her of all the grandchildren because I spent so much time with her as a child when she was my babysitter. I spent as much time with her as with my parents. She was ninety-three when she died. The last six years she was in a nursing home. She was a delightful person. She'd had a hard life, raising children through the Depression and running a small farm and a grocery store. One of her children became an alcoholic. She had a tough life, but she was a happy person.

"This past summer my aunt died and I went home for the funeral. I spent time with family members. I talked about her with my cousins. I get emotional easily. The death of my own parents will be very difficult. They're both in their seventies now. I haven't experienced the death of someone close to me in a long time. Their deaths will be pretty devastating and emotional."

III

Intellectually, Dave's first love was mathematics. "I wanted to be a math professor. I guess I got sidetracked into medicine. In the small town where I grew up several of my friends' fathers were doctors. I saw how hard they worked and I didn't want to do that to myself! Then during my sophomore year in college I realized that medicine was the area in which I could do the most good. I started taking pre-medical courses. I saw myself working as a primary care doctor in Appalachia or the inner city.

"From the beginning I found cancer to be a fascinating topic even though I hadn't had any personal experience with it in my family. In my clinical years I found the cancer patients the most compelling, because of their stories and their courage. As a third-year medical student I can remember putting pressure on the nose of a three-year-old patient with leukemia while we waited for the platelets to come. I had my best experiences with hospitalized patients and I liked the variety of inpatient and outpatient care that you get with oncology.

"What we learned in medical school about death was adequate, but not stellar. There was a required ethics course in our first year. It was very good and dealt with death as a topic. We also had an introductory psychiatry course that dealt with death. The psychiatrist who taught it showed lots of videotapes of dying people. He didn't believe in the Kübler-Ross stages. He thought that the last stage was withdrawal. I remember one tape of a dying woman. He was discussing with her the arrangements to be made for her children. She seemed disinterested. I think he was right. The last stage is disinterest.

"No amount of course work can prepare you for the death of a patient. You have to experience it. We didn't have any preparation in our third and fourth years. There weren't any debriefings. There still aren't. When we have a death we talk with the residents and medical students a little, but there's no structure to it. Structure would be helpful. You don't know how a death will affect you until it hits you in the face when you're tired, when it's unexpected, or when you might have done something differently. You have to be in the role to really experience it. It's a bizarre job! To experience death as often as we do and to go through all those experiences really affects you as a young physician. I don't remember being taught how to deal with it. There's no training about the caregiver's own experiences and how to cope. You just develop it over time. You start experiencing deaths in the third and fourth years of medical school as you care for people who die. How you deal with it is based on what you bring to the table. Nobody teaches you. It's based on your personal background and upbringing. It's not that you distance yourself, but there is one thing that helps me to deal with a death or with breaking bad news. It's realizing that it's not about me; it's about the patient. If I'm so devastated that I can't work I'm not helping people. If I weren't doing what I'm doing all the children would die. We can't win all the battles. Nobody taught me that. I worked it out for myself over twenty years in medicine.

"My background also helps me to deal with it. I grew up in a poor blue-collar family. I know how to communicate simply. That's hard for a lot of doctors. The current balance I have in my life also helps me, having children, a family, and outside interests.

"There should be something built into the clinical curriculum for medical students, times to sit and talk about the deaths of patients, about how you feel and about your role. They might be with a facilitator, an older physician with a group of four or five students at a point in their education when they've had some experience with patients' deaths. It would be an opportunity to learn how more experienced people deal with patients dying. When I was a fellow, we had a psychologist on our staff who met with the fellows once a month to give us the opportunity to talk about the stress of dealing with children with cancer. It was like a Quaker or Alcoholics Anonymous meeting, a supportive place to talk and express your feelings.

"I wish I'd had better training in how to deliver bad news to people. In my field, few deaths are unexpected and death is a relief in most cases. I have less trouble dealing with death than with giving the news that the cancer is back, with telling parents when I know what will happen. You know the odds aren't good and you're telling the parents that their child will die. That's more stressful than the death itself. It's very sad. We develop very close relationships with our patients and their families over time. With a relapse it affects you personally. You know them and you feel bad. You've grown close to them and you know that they'll be going through a painful time and experience."

"I really enjoy the work. I care for very sick patients. There's no one that I can't help. I get to know the patients' families. I see people at their best and their worst. Cancer's like a magnifying glass on peoples' lives. The fact that most children are cured helps. Seventy percent are cured! That helps you to deal with the other 30 percent. I have many more good days than bad.

"The only thing I don't like about my work is the hours—sixty to seventy hours per week. I'm happy to be in academics, where I get a mix of clinical and research responsibilities. If I were only doing clinical work it'd be harder. It's good to have a rich life outside of medicine. It helps me to cope with the stress.

"I feel that I'm making a difference. I'm also glad to be paid reasonably well compared to my parents. I have a lot of job satisfaction." However, the job can be very stressful. "There are many days on which my cortisol levels are pretty high! It's hard to deal with angry, needy families. The hours get to you, too. I always have the feeling that I should be writing papers and research protocols. I feel a responsibility to those things as well. There's not enough time to do all the things I wish I could do. Another thing I dislike about my job is that in academic medicine you're more respected as an internist than you are as a pediatrician. We're second-class citizens.

"I'd like to do what I'm doing now for another five to ten years and then spend more time doing administration and have a lighter clinical load. I don't want to be a full-time clinician in my fifties and sixties. The weeks on service are really grueling. It's harder now at forty-two than it was at thirty-five and it'll get even harder. I'd like to be in more of a visionary role, preferably in cancer rather than pediatrics, so I'm thinking more about women with breast cancer than about babies with diarrhea."

IV

Dave copes with the deaths of children "fairly well. I've had a lot of experience. I've been in oncology since 1988. Since 1990 I've focused primarily on brain tumors. We don't do as well in that field. Brain tumors only have a 55 percent survival rate. Acute lymphocytic leukemia is now approaching 90 percent [survival]. I don't like it that our [brain tumor] survival rates are lower [than for leukemia], but I think that I do a good job of helping the families through it. I'm a good listener. I hear the patients' and the parents' thoughts and fears. I'm kind and gentle. I feel that I have the strength to deal with the families. I remind myself that most of our patients don't die. People have different abilities to feel guilty. At this point I don't feel it. When a child dies I don't feel that I've failed. That helps me to get up in the morning and carry on. As a young physician, I can remember being in tears and feeling guilty.

"I'm entering a time when deaths hit me less than they used to. Sometimes I worry that I'm a little less empathic than I should be. I've dealt with death so much that it's become part of the work. I see older doctors with their grandchildren. They get soft again, the way they were in the beginning. That may be a motive for retirement! It gets too painful. It starts to get to them again.

"I'm reasonably good at helping kids to cope with their deaths.

A lot depends on the age of the child. I talk pretty forthrightly with teenagers. I also take my cues from the family. 'Do you want me to talk with your child about dying? Do you want to talk?' I help parents with what to say. With younger children I talk about it when they bring it up. They fear pain and being alone, the idea of not having their parents around. I emphasize that to the families and recommend that they spend a lot of time with them and that they give them permission to die, reassuring them that they, the parents, will be all right. It's common for children to worry about what'll happen to their parents. The child is the center of his or her own universe and it can be hard for a child to imagine how his parents will go on without him.

"My weaknesses appear mainly when a bunch of deaths come together. There's a limit to how caring you can be over and over again in a short period of time. The children toward the end get short-changed."

What he says to terminally ill children about their deaths "depends on their age. I may say nothing to a young child unless she brings it up. I talk about changing our goals and no longer fighting the tumor. At some point the tumor will take the child's life. We focus on her not having pain, keeping her as happy as possible, at home with the family or taking a Make A Wish trip (the "Make A Wish" Foundation, at www.wish.org, grants "the wishes of children with life-threatening medical conditions"). We focus less on death itself and more on life between now and then. We discuss symptoms of dying. I deal with brain tumors. I tell my patients that there will probably be headaches and vomiting. Most children with brain tumors go to sleep and go into a coma. I share that process with them. I tell them that they'll be getting sleepier and that eventually they won't wake up.

"Some children want to talk about it a lot and some don't. I have a conversation with the parents so that they can answer the child's questions rather than our answering them. Most children want to talk about it with their parents. Whether they talk to me depends on how close they are to me and how well they've known me in the past.

"They want to know what will happen to them. Will they go to heaven? What happens to their bodies? They're often concerned about being in a cold, dark place. What will it feel like? I tell them that it's just their body that's there and that they won't experience cold or dark. Those questions are tough to answer, especially if you know the child well and are close to him. The afterlife questions are particularly difficult because you're dealing with belief systems. Your and the family's beliefs may not be the same. It's not church and my role isn't that of a spiritual advisor.

"Parents ask if there's anything else to be done. Some hope for a miracle cure. They're very focused on the symptoms. They don't want to see their children suffer. They don't ask what will happen after death. Their questions make you very sad and they're tough to answer.

"It's hard to know when you've crossed the line between cure and comfort care. How do you know that you're there? Some families move too quickly. Others want to try things even when the child is on a ventilator. In most cases you've gone through all the things that are likely to work and the tumor is back. We also try new, experimental treatments. We'll go through one or two of those. Sometimes you hit a real home run with them, but once I've been through a number of things and the tumor or leukemia is still growing, I don't have trouble saying that I think we need to change our goals, or that we don't have anything else to try that makes sense. I'm not ready to do that quickly. I try everything that might work, plus one or two long shots. Once I've done that, I'm comfortable saying that it's time to shift into the comfort mode.

"In the beginning I talk with the families about how we'll care for them from start to finish, whatever the outcome. You give them the statistics of the chances for cure. I also talk vaguely about the odds the second time around. Usually I limit it to 'If things don't go well, we'll still care for you throughout the process.' Usually the families and the caregivers come to the conclusion that it's time for comfort care rather than cure at the same time.

"My colleagues provide a fair amount of support when one of my patients dies. Informally, everyone asks how you're doing after a death. We have a monthly support meeting primarily for the nurses. The meetings are important, but we don't just wait for them to happen. We talk at our rounds and at psychosocial rounds. Right now we're focusing on reintegration of the nurses after the strike. It would be helpful to have a formal debriefing, some kind of opportunity to sit down after a death and go through things, especially early on in training.

"My wife is very supportive. I'm an old staff guy now. Deaths are just part of our life. We don't talk as much about work as we used to. She's a good listener. So are my children. I haven't shielded them from what I do. They're generally aware when I have a patient die. They're more aware than most children that children can die, but their denial is still pretty strong. It must be developmental. My thirteen-year-old son had a classmate die this year. I was amazed at how well he coped with it. I heard about it on the late-night news. The next morning I talked with him and told him that a car had hit one of his classmates getting off the school bus. He said, 'I know, my friend called me last night.' He and his friends had talked about it a lot. He didn't want to go to the funeral. He coped with the death by raising the boy in his own estimation from someone he just knew to a good friend."

Friends and acquaintances provide very little support. "They come undone. If I talk about what I do, it stops conversation. They're blown away. It causes them pain, so I don't talk about it with them. I look primarily to my spouse and family for support."

V

"I'm comfortable with the fact that I'll die someday. Hopefully it'll be a long time from now. I find that my mortality is brought home more by the deaths of young parents. One parent in my children's school died of a melanoma, another of a car accident. The deaths of my patients make me more aware that my children could die. I don't think about it very often. Occasionally when my wife comes home late and there's no phone call and it's raining out, I get flashes of car wrecks. All that may change when my son starts driving!

"I've never had a 'near-death experience.' I did have an accident once that could have resulted in death. My wife, another couple, and I were hiking. It was the end of spring break, very rainy, and we were driving around the mountains in north Georgia. We came to a waterfall. It was only a mile hike in from the car. The waterfall is usually not very impressive, but that day it was. I wanted a picture, climbed out on a rock, took the picture and slipped. My friend tried to get me to take his hand, but I was afraid we'd both fall in. As soon as my feet hit the water I immediately went under. It was like being shot. I remember thinking very calmly that 'this must be what it's like to drown.' My next thought was, 'Drowning is a real possibility here.' Both thoughts were very calm. Then my head popped up. There was a huge log, half submerged. I grabbed it with both arms, but the current was so strong that I couldn't hold on. As I slid under the log back under water the log broke my watchband. My parents had given me the watch for high school graduation. I caught a branch in my hand. I thought, 'You've got to drop the watch!' I did, put my feet down, touched the bottom, and was all right. How calm I was in the water comes back to me and is comforting. I'm sure that if I'd stayed underwater longer I'd have panicked, but those thoughts of the calmness keep me calm about the process. So I don't worry about death that much. I hope it's of old age or that my parachute doesn't open!"

VI

A "good death" "is a death from progressive disease and not from a side effect. You see it coming. Preferably it's at home, we've done a good job with pain control, and the child is surrounded by his family. When you talk to people who're going to die they want to die at home. It's better to be surrounded by the people and things that have made up your life. A few months ago we had several families that refused to take their children home to die. Some of the staff, both nurses and doctors, went along with it. For the nurses in particular, caring for those dying children filled a need in their lives. That happens in the hospital sometimes. Caregivers overstep their bounds. It's condescending. We aren't giving families enough credit. Sometimes you lose sight of the greater good by satisfying your own need to care for people. My feeling was that we did those parents a disservice. I wanted them to be able to look back and say, 'Look what we did for our child.' A good death is at home. Even families that were initially resistant to it have been so glad they went home and had that time.

"A bad death is unexpected, from a side effect, and especially if it was something preventable that might have made a difference; like a child with a fever who's brought in too late. A lot depends on how accepting the family is of the death. That has a big influence on how bad a death is for the staff.

"Children have a developmentally appropriate understanding of death. Younger children, toddlers and babies, only understand that they're hurting. As they get older the main thing is not to be alone. With a teenager it's harder. They have a better sense of what they're losing and are going to miss out on." Dying children can be helped to cope with their deaths "by providing them with a situation in which their family can be there most of the time. It also helps to give them the opportunity to talk about it, especially with someone who's been trained as a listener. It's important that I help them with their pain. If a child is very sad, I'll start them on an antidepressant. I've done it a couple of times and never regretted it. If they only have a couple of months left, why should they be sad? The first child I did this with was an eighteen-year-old girl with a low-grade astrocytoma. In the hospice she was very sad and tearful, but after two weeks on the antidepressant she was almost giddy! Then there was a six-year-old with a brain-stem tumor. She was very sad, angry, and aggressive. Her behavior was disruptive to the family's life. They asked if we could put her on an antidepressant. She benefited from it enormously, and it affected the entire family's life."

His colleagues' abilities to cope with the deaths of children "vary from person to person. There are six of us now. Five out of the six of us do well, although we each do it differently. We're there for the families. We're appropriately sad. We're good about sending cards to the families and going to funerals. You do it for the families and for yourself. It's a meeting on a human level when the professional relationship is over. One of my colleagues gets quite squirrelly around patients' deaths. When patients relapse or die, he gets grumpy and difficult to work with. My sense is that he doesn't deal well internally with patients' deaths.

"My colleagues are able to deal with deaths in a way that doesn't interfere with their work and with their ability to meet their patients' needs. It's not about us; it's about the patients. That's the weird side of this job from a psychiatric perspective. In one room you're spreading joyful news and in the next one you're telling someone that the cancer is back. You just have to do it. What you feel personally isn't dealt with well at the time. A colleague once said to me, 'Oncologists cry more at movies than other people do.' Your feelings come out at odd moments. We get more release outside of work than on the job.

"Sometimes they try to keep fighting the cancer beyond reason. Part of it has to do with their discomfort in dealing with death when it's inevitable. When death comes, they deal with it well. Dealing with the anticipation of death is tough. Some hold out hope even when it's not realistic. It's kinder and better for most patients to actually deal directly with death. We should let them know what they're up against rather than being patronizing.

"I never sit in the room and listen to my fellow doctors giving bad news, so I don't have any direct knowledge about how they do it. We don't get any training in how to help children to cope with their deaths. I'm not sure that there's anything written about it. We try to be honest and not hide things, but we also try to be developmentally sensitive. It's different for a four-year-old than for a fourteen-year-old. We take our cue from the children about how much they want to talk about it. Parents often ask us what they should say. Sometimes we'll say that it's all right to stop fighting the tumor and let go.

"People who go into hematology-oncology get a lot of experience talking about death. Our group is forthright with both the children and the parents. It's also a very sensitive group. They're honest, caring, and gentle people.

"There are times when you're at a loss for words. There are also times when we get beaten down with a string of deaths close together. It's numbing. It decreases your ability to empathize with the child. The well is dry. You can only deal with so many things at one time. You have no chance to recharge your batteries.

"It's really important for caregivers to realize the impact they have on patients. We have such a position of power and can have a powerful effect on them. I saw a neurologist when I was in college. After I had an E E G he said, 'There are a couple of abnormalities, but I don't think we need to go looking for a brain tumor.' For the next couple of months every symptom made me think that I had a brain tumor! We can say things that are devastating for our patients. Doctors often have no clue what an impact they're having. We need more training in medical school about communication skills. I also think that it would help medical students to have focus groups with family members about how physicians helped or hindered their grief experiences."

9

"People don't know how long the pain from the death of a child lasts. It takes years."

A unique feature of Paul's background is that he, unlike the other physicians I interviewed, has lost a child of his own. That loss, a sudden, senseless tragedy, and the years of grieving that followed have brought him a unique understanding of what the death of a child is like for parents. When a child in his care dies, he knows from experience that the parents' journey is only just beginning and that it will be years before they have dealt with their loss sufficiently so that it is not a raw and ever-present wound. His instinctive gentleness, tempered by his own suffering, have made him a role model for younger staff in how to help families through the loss of their children and into the lengthy grieving process that will follow.

Paul recognizes that having a child diagnosed with cancer makes parents feel helpless and that many struggle to regain a sense of control by doing research on the Internet, searching for a magic bullet, and micromanaging the details of their child's care. He understands and empathizes with the parents' struggle, although in his heart he knows that there are times when bad things just happen and that there is not always a solution for every problem. "It's as if I have a secret. I know that there's no control, but no one else seems to realize it."

I

Paul was two or three weeks into his internship when he first experienced a child patient's death. "The child had Chédiak-Higashi syndrome, an immune deficiency in which the granules of the neutrophils [white blood cells that fight infection] don't release appropriately so they can't kill bacteria. He had a fever and died of a bacterial infection. The immunologist was angry with us. He felt that we hadn't jumped on the fever quickly enough. Because of that it wasn't a real positive experience. I felt bad. As a new intern you want to do the right thing, and it's the ultimate bad outcome if your patient dies. As I went along I put it into perspective by understanding what an appropriate evaluation of a sick child is and by putting that attending physician's personality into perspective. We residents had discussions among ourselves. 'Should we have done something different?' We also complained about the attending. I wasn't attached to the child because I didn't know him well. My pain was more from feeling that I hadn't done something right. As I became more comfortable with my abilities as a pediatrician I could focus on helping the children and the parents through this terrible event and worrying less about my medical skills.

"I allow myself to get sad with the parents. It's a sad time. It helps parents to know that others are sad about the death of their child. The person I trained with was stoic and private. Since my son's death I've realized that parents appreciate others' sadness for their child. I get tearful around families and give them hugs. It's been a developmental process to see how families grieve and to see how important it is for them.

"Some families have a problem letting go. They have a greater sense that they're in control. Some are like that up to a point, but then they switch to the palliative mode. Others can't bear the pain of death, and as long as you're going for cure you don't have to think about it; your focus is on the hope for a cure. For some families their religious faith helps them to deal with death. Those with strong beliefs in an afterlife are often willing to say, 'This isn't working. Death isn't the end.' But you can't really generalize and there are some very religious families that can't give up. The families that have the hardest time stopping are those with an illusion of control or those who just can't deal with the pain of their child dying.

"Despite my ability to let myself feel sad and empathetic, there's still some degree of separation. With some patients I lose that separation and it feels like a personal loss. I'm sadder than usual. There was one patient, a teenage African American boy that I'd cared for at another hospital, who came here when he relapsed. He had little social support, but he was a neat child. He got himself to his clinic visits. He was very personable and upbeat, a friendly guy who liked to crack jokes. He came here for a bone marrow transplant. It went well, but he got chronic graft-versus-host disease. I was trying to get him through it and he was depending on me. He asked, 'You're going to get me better, right?' I liked him and that made me feel more obligated to cure him. Then he developed a progressive neurological condition and ended up on a ventilator. The family wanted to withdraw life support before the medical team did. He was nineteen at the time, but he had no end-of-life documents so the family was making the decision for him. It wasn't clear to me that death was inevitable. I liked him, he was depending on me, and the family wanted to take him off the ventilator. That was the last death where I had significant, prolonged pain. I really wanted him to get better. I'd tried to cure him and thought that I'd be able to make him better. I had a sense that I'd let him down. I usually don't take it that personally."

Paul's comments illustrate the tightrope walked by even the most skilled and experienced physicians in their attempts to balance closeness with distance in their relationships and communications with dying children and their families. It is a balancing act that no one gets right all the time.

II

Paul was the oldest child in a family of four, two boys and two girls. His father was a family practitioner and his mother a homemaker who suffered from depression when he was in high school. "She wouldn't get out of bed for days at a time. She had ECT [electroconvulsive therapy] and antidepressants, but they didn't help much.

Six months before I left for college she 'woke up.' Then she developed epilepsy and had to take anticonvulsants. She died of a massive stroke when I was twenty.

"I didn't understand what was going on. She wanted to be a good mother, but she wasn't because she didn't interact with us much. We had to be very careful what we said. If we thanked her for something, she'd feel bad because she wasn't that way all the time. If we got her a birthday card that read 'You're a good mom' she'd get upset because she knew she wasn't. We went on about our business. My sisters ran the house, cooked meals, and did the laundry.

"Death wasn't talked about often. There wasn't much opportunity because not many of our relatives or close acquaintances died. Even after my mother died, we didn't discuss it very much. My father had patients that died, but he didn't discuss them at home."

Growing up, Paul was taught "all the religious stuff, an afterlife and going to heaven if you were good. My mother was the first person I knew well who died. There was a period of mourning and then we moved on. She'd been sick for a long time, and I hadn't had a close relationship with her for years because she was sick and in bed. I was sad and it was a shock because she seemed to be getting better. I was in Mississippi taking a year off from college and working on a farm. I came home, took three or four months off, and then went back to Mississippi."

Growing up, "I wasn't convinced there was an afterlife or that people went to heaven. By high school I was more of an agnostic; I didn't know. I'm not sure that I know now. I remember in high school being pretty clear that I didn't believe in heaven, but I didn't have a clear idea about what does happen. I thought that you should grieve and then move on. That's what my father modeled. He was remarried within one or two years after my mother died.

"In the small town in Oregon where I grew up the doctors took turns being the local coroner. One night a teenager was killed on a motorcycle. They called the coroner and it turned out that the boy who was killed was his son so they called my dad instead. That really shook my dad up. He came into my room, woke me up, and sat by my bed. He told me what had happened, but didn't say anything else. He looked upset.

"The boy who died in the motorcycle accident was sixteen and I knew him from school. I was a senior at the time and he was younger. There was another guy in high school that I'd known well in grade school. His father was killed in a logging accident. When I was a sophomore in high school, the president of the student body was killed in an auto accident. Someone had been drinking. Also the father of a good friend died of alcohol-related problems, liver failure. They were Roman Catholic and very religious. I was sad for the family and for my friend. I didn't know his father well. He used to drink a lot. I'd go over to visit and he'd be drunk, semi-joking and semi-belligerent.

"I don't remember those deaths affecting me much. They didn't cause me to think about my own mortality. That's kind of surprising. It was probably due to family modeling. My father was very wrapped up in his work. He wasn't that open with the family and he worked a lot. I remember being packed up for vacation and he'd have to go back to the hospital for a couple of hours. He didn't spend that much time with us. His set of priorities may have contributed to my mother's depression. She went to Berkeley, was a Phi Beta Kappa, and then ended up in the middle of Oregon with this guy who worked all the time.

"The expectation in our family was to get it together, do what you're supposed to do, and get on with things. I did a lot of sports from seventh grade through high school. There was some sport every season. My father hardly ever came to any of those events because he was busy. He didn't even come to my college graduation. There wasn't much discussion of feelings or much emotional support. We learned to deal with our feelings internally and to get on with what needed to be done. My mother was more emotional than my father was. She liked interacting with kids, and other children would come over and talk with her because she was open and friendly. Sometimes my friends would come over and talk to her when I wasn't even there."

III

"I tried to avoid medicine as a career. People asked me if I wanted to be a doctor like my father and I'd say, 'I don't know.' In college I wasn't sure what I wanted to do. I majored first in history and then in biology. I liked science and people, and so I gravitated toward medicine because I didn't have anything better to do. I didn't want to go to graduate school. Pediatrics was the first rotation I did and I liked it a lot. I liked children. I didn't find anything else that I liked as well. I realized that in family practice you have to know a lot about everything. I liked oncology because of the close relationships with families. I decided to do a fellowship during my third year of pediatric residency. I was looking for jobs in general pediatrics but wasn't finding anything I liked. One day I walked into the hematology-oncology office and the division head, a friend of mine, asked if I'd like to do a fellowship. I talked it over with him a few times and then did it. I liked caring for oncology patients, more because of the psychosocial part than the biology. You have an intense relationship with patients and families coupled with hardcore science. Others are more attracted by the science."

His feelings about his career choice "wax and wane. If I were in college again I wouldn't go to medical school. There are the time demands, it's very stressful, and you have to do more and more with less and less because of the reimbursement issues. I frequently think about doing something else. I'm working on a BA in geography part-time. I wouldn't miss the medical science, but I would miss the interactions with families. Things are changing and there's less prestige in being a physician. I don't have big ambitions such as being a division head or a chairman.

"My worldview gets in the way of my leaving medicine. I believe we have an obligation to care for each other. If I have medical skills but quit and become a cartographer, is that okay? I also like the lifestyle. I can afford to take vacations and live in a nice house, but then you work sixty to seventy hours a week.

"I'm also bothered by the stress. It comes from always having questions if I'm doing the right thing. I'm well trained, smart, and probably doing as well as anybody can. Then there's the platonic ideal of the perfect oncologist and trying to approach that. I'm more in the latter category, trying to get closer to perfection but never being close enough. I always feel that I could be doing better. If you make a wrong choice children die. If you don't take a fever seriously or make a wrong decision about dosing, children die. I've made decisions that I'd like to take back. I had a patient with A M L [Acute Myelogenous Leukemia]. She had a low-grade fever and her blood counts were low. I wanted to put her in the hospital, but she was disappointed because she'd just gotten out so I let her stay home. Later that night she got a high fever and was admitted; she ultimately died of an infection. Would it have made any difference if I'd admitted her earlier that day? Do you make them go to the Emergency Room or not? There are lots of decisions to make and I always want to do the right thing.

"There's also the stress of dealing with difficult emotional situations. I can deal with the sadness better than the anger. It seems like there are more angry parents these days. People have a sense that they have more control and can make everything work out. The parents get angry to the point that it interferes with the child's care, and the emotional stress of dealing with them can be wearing after a while.

"As director of the hemophilia program I have to deal with budgets and spreadsheets, but I don't have any training in it. I don't have training in supervision and managing personnel. It's frustrating to feel like you're never doing well in any part of your job. I don't publish much and don't do research. You never have the time to do any part of your job as well as you'd like. It's hard to choose to do less and it's frowned on to work half time.

"Some days I see myself resigning in a year or so and going into a different career. Some days I'd like to spend more time on the hematology side of my work. Most people aren't expert in hematosis and thrombosis and I like that science a lot. I think about becoming the regional expert in it. If I had to pick an ideal career I'd be in a pediatric hospice program, but we don't have one. The hospice programs care for children and adults, and I like to help patients and families through the dying process. It's important to do it well. I'm increasingly aware that death is a part of life, but our society doesn't deal well with it. Someone dies and people expect that you'll quickly move on. A lot of us, like me, had little experience with people dying while we were growing up. It's a part of the life cycle that's neglected and it's something you can help people with. People have this sense that we can control the situation, but I think we have a lot less control than people believe. As an oncologist I have to talk people into doing things. They come in with all of these articles off the Internet and are looking for a magic bullet. We often spend a lot of time debating about the therapy. It's not a team approach; it's more adversarial. You have to prove that you're doing the ultimate. In hospice work, you're able to focus on keeping the patient and the family as comfortable as possible. There's a sense in our society that if things don't go well it's someone's fault rather than that bad things happen. There's a sense of control when there really isn't. It's tiring to deal with those kinds of issues. The parents get into micromanaging, trying to seize control when they feel out of control.

"I can empathize well with families and get a lot of positive reinforcement from that. When I was on call as an intern, a child was dying of leukemia and I went into the room at night. The lights were off, the mother was with the child, and the child had labored breathing. The mother was very sad. She didn't want to talk so I hung out. I didn't know what to say so I said nothing and after a while I left. One or two years after he died she told me that it had been helpful that I'd just been there. I did it by accident."

Paul received no training in medical school about how to cope with the deaths of patients. "Medical school has it now, but there wasn't any then. My very first patient in my third year was a dying patient. The child was comatose, so I interacted with the family. There was no discussion—you were just thrown in there. Physicians are trained to make things better, but there are some things you can't fix. It's hard for physicians to acknowledge that. Just being in that position goes against the grain. I didn't have any training in residency either. I've never had any training about how to deal with death and dying, although I've had some exposure in the last five to ten years being on panels with medical residents about end-of-life issues.

"One panel I was on had a fourth-year medical student and an adult oncologist. The oncologist said, 'I never go to funerals because I don't want to intrude on the family.' I didn't use to go because I was trained not to. My mentor was very good, but there was a distance between him and his patients. I tried to do that for a while, but over the years I've realized that you have to reach out to families a little, to give them a pat or a hug to show them you're sad too and have tears. Going to the funeral shows that you miss the patient and care about the family. Families are surprised, but glad. Sometimes it's awkward. If there's a funeral you've failed, but it helps you to see that there are limits, that bad things happen. It would be good if students were taught early on that such things are okay. I wish that I'd been taught what the families are going through, what the care-givers are going through, and about managing the two in a way that primarily helps the family, but also helps the provider. Some people aren't cut out to be in a specialty where a lot of patients die. We had a family-practice resident, a great physician, but she was sad all the time because she couldn't separate her work from thoughts about her children. She'd ask, 'What if it was my child?' and would act very sad and tearful."

IV

"My wife and I talk about the patients' deaths a lot. We lost our son." A thief had been in their neighborhood fleeing from the police. He broke into their house and took their son hostage in the boy's bedroom. When the police arrived and asked if they might search the house, Paul and his wife were not even aware that the thief was there. Negotiations between the police and the thief began, but when they failed to make progress the police decided to have a sniper shoot the thief through a window. The sniper missed and the thief became enraged because of the trick. Fearful for the safety of Paul's son, the police broke into the room and shot the thief, but in the process also shot Paul's son. He died a few hours later.

"Since my son's death, I have a much broader and better perspective of what it's like for a parent. It provided a level of insight that I wouldn't choose to have, but that made me more empathic about how long grieving takes and about the stages you go through. It's not that you can't do a good job without that experience, but I do a better job since he died than I did before."

Despite his personal experience of a child's death and his empathy for the parents' loss, "I sometimes get burned-out about the whole process. Sometimes I don't feel as empathic as I'd like to be. The deaths of some children affect me more than others. Overall, I feel that I do well. By nature I'm willing to listen and to be patient and I'm less judgmental than some. I can let people do things in their own way and I don't feel that there's a right and a wrong way.

"I cope with children's deaths by talking to my wife and getting out of the hospital and hiking and walking. She listens. She knows the sadness of a child dying. She doesn't try to talk you out of being sad or offer suggestions. That doesn't help. I don't talk about it with friends. Sometimes it's hard to compartmentalize. Since the death of my own child I sometimes personalize deaths because I know what the families are going through."

V

"Over the years I've become more cognizant of the whole life cycle. I know that death happens. People can do it with dignity and grace with the assistance of others. I don't particularly fear death. It's part of the life cycle. Maybe that's part of getting older. I do think about it more than I used to.

"My son's death made me hyperaware of the uncertainty and capriciousness of life. Bad things happen out of nowhere. For years after my older son died I'd go to work every day and think, 'I hope my [younger] son doesn't die today.' I worried about it every day. When something unexpected happens to our patients, it reinforces that sense of the unpredictability of life. I try to be patient with people who think they have control, parents who are always on the Internet or are hypervigilant, watching to make sure you wash your hands or hook up a tube properly. It's hard to have a child with cancer. It's total loss of control. It's almost like I have a secret. I know there's no control, but everyone else thinks there is."

He thinks of his own mortality "more often than I used to, but not very often. When I think of mortality I think of how insignificant our lives are. Very few people make an impact beyond their own and their children's lives. Does what we do make any difference? Why do good things? Is it because you might end up in heaven? But if you don't believe in heaven why do them? I frequently think about how much doing good is enough. Can you say at some point, 'I want to take it easy and not work so hard?' Do you have a moral obligation to continue when you know more about something than most other people do?"

VI

Paul's definition of a "good death" is "pain-free, having the family close at hand, and having a sense of what's going on. I'm sure that at some level all children that die have some sense of what's happening. They're not getting better and they're more tired. It's important that the child has time to say good-bye. Sudden death is hard because there's no time for that, but I know that the families are just as sad whether they have time to say good-bye or not."

A "bad death" is "being in a lot of pain, being afraid and alone, and not having support from the family because they're in so much pain that they can't support the child. I'm struck by how often children hang on for the sake of their parents. If the parents say, 'It's all right, you don't have to hang on for us,' then shortly thereafter the child dies. I consider that supportive because the child doesn't need to worry about the parents.

"At some level children understand that they're dying. I'm not sure that they always understand the permanence of it. Parents try to protect their children and don't talk about it and the children don't talk about it to protect the parents. That often contributes to the child being more anxious.

"It would help if we had an environment in which it's all right to talk about death. We don't want to force them to talk about it, but we need to make it acceptable to discuss death so that we can tell them what's going to happen and can help them to deal with their fears. If you're willing to share your own fear and sadness it gives the children permission to do the same. If you're always cheerful and stoic it makes it like a taboo subject.

Terminally ill children "don't often ask direct questions about death. I've had a few ask, and what I usually say to them is 'We've tried everything we can and we can't cure the disease.' I tell them we'll take care of them and keep them out of pain. I tell them it's all right to ask questions and that it's all right to talk or not to talk.

"At some point we all deny what's happening by not using the words death or dying. It's very sad." Here he became tearful. "I appreciate the courage it takes to ask those questions. It's hard to do and I admire them for doing it."

Parents ask "what the end of life will be like and how much pain their children will be in. Many ask what the cause of death will be. We seldom get philosophical questions about mortality. I have the experience to answer their questions so I feel that I can help them. Part of it depends on how much of their sadness they share with me. I know what the parents are going through. I know how long it's going to take. If I bring up my son they try to take care of me! Two parents don't grieve in the same way. It takes years before you're back to normal. After a child dies no one wants to talk to the parents about their dead child because they think it'll make the parents sadder, but the parents want to talk about it. It validates the child's life and makes the parents feel better."

VII

Paul is not sure how well prepared his professional colleagues are to cope with the deaths of children. "We don't talk about it much and we don't debrief after the death of a child. There are very few opportunities to be collectively sad. The nurses are trying to do it, but the physicians don't. Sometimes you can tell a physician is really sad, but it's uncommon to have that verbally acknowledged. I don't think that we do a good job of supporting one another. Everybody in our group has been doing oncology for many years. They've developed their own coping mechanisms, whatever they are, but there's an expectation that you have to hold up your end of the workload. There's no time to take a breather and be sad. Sometimes I worry that I'm not sad enough! I'm too busy or too tired to be very sad. There's so much to do and so much stress that I sometimes worry that I'm becoming less empathic."

He sees his colleagues' ability to function on the job regardless of how they feel as a strength. "They have supportive families. A lot of us go to funerals. Is it positive or negative to have sad things happen around you and not fall apart? You compartmentalize. You can be empathic if you choose to, but you can also walk out and close the door."

A weakness of his colleagues is "not keeping in touch with families. I've learned through personal experience that grieving takes a long time. We could do more if we kept in touch with families longer. Also some of us don't acknowledge the futility of further treatment as soon as we might. As long as you're still fighting you don't have to deal with the sadness that the patient is going to die. Some are very good at it, while others go on too long. Sometimes we keep treating not because we want to but because the families want to. All of us probably sometimes end up treating longer than we'd like because of the family. As a fellow, I had a patient who was seventeen or eighteen. She was a girl and was engaged to a boy who was on a Mormon mission. We diagnosed an abdominal tumor and eventually we couldn't do anything more to cure it. The family refused to let us talk about her dying. Up until the day she died, they were planning her wedding."

10

"I love caring for young families and sick babies."

Diane's early experiences with the cultural traditions of medicine
suggested that physicians should react to their patients' deaths stoically and not get emotionally involved. Gradually, however, she
has come to realize that it can be helpful for both the physician
and the family when the medical and nursing staff show that a
baby's life and death has affected them as well. She is fortunate
to work with a close-knit group of mostly older women who have
grown up together professionally and are able to provide each other
with emotional support. She is grateful for this because the world
outside of medicine is not prepared to deal with the tragedies of
babies dying or being born with severe abnormalities that leave
them with little if any possibility for a quality life. Over the course
of her career she has seen her field evolve from the Baby Doe era,
when physicians attempted to save every baby regardless of its condition, to a more considered decision-making process that brings
in the child's parents' feelings about the baby's ultimate quality
of life.

I

Diane's first experience of the death of a child patient in her care
was "a twin in the NICU. I was a first-year resident. She got staph
aureus sepsis [a type of bacterial infection of the blood] and died
really fast. She just fell apart. The family was Spanish-speaking and
I didn't interact with them very much. Emotionally I remember little about the case. We spent a lot of time talking about it. We hadn't
treated her with the right antibiotic to cover staph. It was harder on

the family because of the other twin. They had to keep coming to the nursery and dealing with her after the death of the first child.

"The deaths I remember with the most emotion were those during my third year of residency. I felt I was really in charge then. They were my patients and I knew the families better. There were patients whose deaths could have been made a better experience for the child and for the family or whose deaths might have been prevented. However, my overwhelming memory is that the deaths were an unnecessary flail for everybody. We worked hard to save everyone even when it was clear to all of us that you couldn't save the child. I was in training during the Baby Doe era and that had a big influence. There was a lot of fear about letting children die. In the PICU and on hematology-oncology, the doctors didn't seem to be able to give up. Baby Doe was about children who were denied medical care because of their potential handicaps and whose deaths were subsequently reported to the state. One was the case of a baby with a meningomyelocele [in which the spinal cord and its membranes push out through a defect in the spine]. The family and the doctors decided not to do anything to treat the baby. A reporter wrote a book about it called *Playing God in the Nursery* [Lyon, 1985]. It was written about one of the nurseries I trained in. It seemed that there was a lot of fear among neonatologists there during my training. They seemed to be unable to overcome the Baby Doe legislation. Other nurseries that I trained in seemed lower key. There they talked with the parents about letting the babies go. It was quite a contrast and it was wonderful! The field went through a period during which the goal was to get patients to survive regardless of their condition. That was before long-term follow-up studies. This year I was discussing a case with a colleague. She was having trouble disconnecting life support. I asked her if she thought that continuing to treat the baby would lead to a successful outcome. She said, 'If we don't do something the baby will die!' That's how I remember people thinking during my residency and fellowship. The field has changed now."

After a baby dies Diane tries "to find people on the unit who really cared about the family and the child and just talk with them. The nurses and the attendings do all the talking with the family and we tend to leave the residents out of the process. I'm not sure if that's because we're trying to protect them. I remember one resident who was caring for a set of twins. They had lovely, educated parents. Both of the children were off the ventilator and one of them arrested on the resident's night on-call. He couldn't resuscitate the baby and the parents were there the whole time. When we debriefed, the resident got to be there, but that doesn't happen very often.

"I have no problem admitting that we can't do everything. The most difficult thing is when you wonder if you've missed something or could have done something differently and when you're really soul-searching about what you could have done. We have a nice bereavement protocol in the nursery. The nurses do it and that relieves the physicians of it. They offer to bathe and dress the child. They have clothing the volunteers have made, handmade, beautiful clothing. They have a whole ritual they go through even if the family doesn't participate. It helps everyone to get closure. They offer to keep the baby on the floor or go down to the morgue and get it."

In the last paragraph, Diane shifts unconsciously from painful recollections of cases where mistakes may have been made to a description of the NICU's bereavement protocol. Structuring mourning by fashioning a remembrance of a dead child is an important part of the coping process for professional caregivers. It is a way for them to sublimate or transform their feelings at the loss of a child into a more socially useful form by creating a comforting memory for the child's parents.

II

Diane's parents were orthodox Jews and her family's religious background "affected me a lot. My father was from a very religious family, but my mother was reformed. My father's mother was always on her about knowing things and so she became quite religious. My parents were very vocal about educating the world about Judaism. We went to services on Saturday and weren't allowed out on Friday night or Saturday. At every school function we had to stand up and talk about the associated Jewish holidays. I hated being forced to do that by my mother! I wasn't allowed to take the SATs on Saturday."

Her family discussed death "fairly openly. I didn't have to face it much. My mother's father died when I was thirteen. None of the children went to the funeral. My father's parents died when I was a resident and I did go to their funerals. Death was something to take in stride. They didn't have a strong belief in the afterlife so death wasn't something to strive for. I was told to visit my aging grandparents frequently while they were still alive."

As a young person, Diane believed that "the soul goes into some kind of afterlife. I never thought about heaven or hell. You were taught to lead your life so that you left a legacy. You had to try to be righteous, not because you'd be rewarded but because that's what you were meant to do. There's an Orthodox prayer that ends 'I have been young and now I am old and I have never seen a righteous man go hungry.'

"Six or seven years ago I talked with my mother about whether or not her mother should be allowed to die. My husband's father is an obstetrician-gynecologist and his mother is a nurse. His father has been a good model for me about to how to cope with death. His whole focus is on the person who is dying, making them comfortable and helping them to die with dignity. The hidden message is that if you helped the dying person you coped well."

Diane's father-in-law taught her that by transforming your grief into high-level care you provide comfort both for the dying person and for yourself. This was a coping strategy employed by the more experienced physicians and nurses, who had learned that by making a child's death as comfortable as possible and by helping the child's parents to get through the dying process intact they were better able to deal with their own grieving.

III

In college Diane planned to go into public health. "I got a job on the Bogalusa Heart Study. One day the head of the project asked me how I liked my job. I said that I hated it; it was boring. He invited me to work in his lab. I went to rounds with him once a week and got more exposure to clinical medicine. At the end of my time there he talked to me and advised me to go to medical school instead of getting a master's in public health. I talked it over with my boyfriend, now my husband, and his family. Everyone thought it would be a good idea.

"Initially I thought I'd be an adult nephrologist [kidney specialist], but I didn't enjoy the adult subspecialties. With adults half of them wanted to die and we wouldn't let them and half didn't want to die and we couldn't stop them. I didn't like chronic illness so I switched to pediatrics. In pediatrics the patients have someone who cares about them and they have a support network. That's not always the case with adult patients. I also liked acute care medicine. My choices were the PICU, which I found emotionally very difficult, the NICU, or the Emergency Room. The NICU gave me more opportunity to do physiological research and I really enjoyed working there. My first Saturday on call as a resident in the NICU I worked from six-thirty A.M. until nine-thirty in the evening and had fourteen admissions. All of us were totally busy and I was in a great mood. The attending said to me, 'You should do this!'

"This is definitely the right field for me. I'm less satisfied with academic medicine than I am with neonatology. In academics the emphasis is on clinical productivity. I spend three to four hours a day on junk that's related to billing. The academic part of my career has suffered as a result of that. I still love the teaching part. Research is hard to keep doing. It's so slow and you realize that you're not going to change the world.

"I love caring for young families and sick babies. We do a great job with them. I love the teaching and administering the unit, trying to improve the delivery of care." She least enjoys "the emphasis on productivity in terms of money. We're a huge profit center for the hospital and the pediatrics department, but that comes at a large cost."

In the future she plans "to stay where I am in an academic position with a major emphasis on clinical administration and the delivery of clinical care. Those are the things I really like about what I do, and I get positive feedback. Research will be a minor part of my work."

In medical school "they didn't teach us anything about coping with patients' deaths. During my fourth year, I was on internal medicine. It was a very busy night. There was a man in his sixties with metastatic carcinoma who was flipping out and there was a twenty-six-year-old Puerto Rican man who was dying of leukemia. His family was having a hard time and the residents were constantly being paged to them. I spent the entire night with the Puerto Rican family watching their son die. I helped his mother give him a bath and put on his clothes for the funeral. I felt somewhat intrusive, but I was assigned to be there. It was pretty sad. Around four A.M. I started crying hysterically and the charge nurse sent me home.

"During medical school we were taught to just buck up and handle it. You weren't supposed to cry. I did a NICU subinternship during my fourth year and when the babies died the residents cried. That was a real eye-opener. There were lots of discussions about how to deal with death. The resident was a British anesthetist. She got to be head of the PICU after a year of residency. She was very senior and comfortable talking about death. Even during residency it wasn't acceptable for the residents to cry when patients died. Many people believe that you have to be emotionally separated from the patients, but I think that seeing the physician cry helps the family to see that it's all right to cry, to see that even those caring for the child are sad. The nurses in the PICU didn't cry, but those in the NICU did.

"We need to teach doctors about talking to people about death, about giving bad news, about listening to people while they decide, and about helping them to make their decision without putting our own ethics on them. I didn't have any formal training during my fellowship, but we had an ethicist, a former Jesuit, and we did consults with him. I was able to seek out the help I needed and I feel comfortable with that part of my job. I wish I'd been taught more about how different religions view death and about how important it is for Catholics to get a priest to administer last rites. I didn't have a good feel for how to do that."

Dealing with patient deaths by "just bucking up and handling it" is, in my view, ultimately destructive for a physician's emotional life and for her relationships with patients. While it has a positive side in forcing the physician to function regardless of her feelings, it can lead to a certain callousness and off handedness in patient relationships, as reflected in Shem's book *The House of God*. Diane, whose religious tradition honored the dead and whose physician father-in-law provided a compassionate and humane role model, found such an approach to patient deaths very unappealing. She was glad to discover a clinical setting, the N I C U, in which it was acceptable and even encouraged to express one's sadness at the death of a child.

IV

It helps Diane's coping when she believes "that we couldn't have changed the outcome and when we're well-supported by other staff members. We once had a baby with a lethal congenital anomaly, but after ten days the baby still wasn't dead. The mother called us and brought the baby in. It was the most awful anomaly I've ever seen. It was monstrous! When the mother unwrapped the baby, the nurse and I started crying and yet the family had been dealing with it for days. One of my physician colleagues with training in ethics came and did a bunch of different sessions for the nurses and doctors. He's been wonderful in helping families and staff and does regular rounds on our unit. It's nice to have someone from the outside come in, look at your situation, and help you to formulate a plan. He meets first with the family to figure out what they want and need and then he meets with us to figure out what we can deliver.

"I never bring my work home even though it's hard to leave death at work. It's not a part of my job that's easy to talk about or to show people. It's easy to talk about our successes! In the old days I did. There were just the two of us then. Now when I come home the focus of our lives is the children. We don't have any downtime. We work in shifts! Sometimes I'll call home and prepare my husband if I've had a particularly terrible day."

The support provided by her colleagues is "very good. There's a network set up to provide it. I've been able to call on colleagues to help me when I need it. I remember three times when I worked in another hospital and needed support, but didn't get it. All three times I was unprepared for the child's death. One time a resident had injected subcutaneous heparin [a blood thinner] instead of lidocaine [a local anesthetic]. We didn't figure out what had happened until the baby bled to death. The other times were incidents in which the babies were asphyxiated. In both cases I thought they were getting better and I wasn't prepared for the deaths. We didn't have a good supportive network there.

"When you work too hard you're more susceptible to feeling over-whelmed. Here we separate day and night call and we can take the next day off and sleep. When you're tired you have no perspective and no downtime to think things through. Here I do. One opportunity is signing the baby out to another doctor at my level. That's really helpful. Sometimes I call the morning attending and ask her to come in early to help me out. Neonatologists are famous for not getting consults from other specialists. We're the primary care providers for our patients and we have more experience than the specialists do.

"We review every death. Maybe we're not always as honest as we should be, but usually we are. The only thing that we're really miss-ing is the follow-up with families. The death of a baby is different than the death of an older child. It's the death of your dreams rather than of an individual you already know. There are two types of deaths. In one something happened during the pregnancy and the parents knew in advance that things would be bad. In the other the parents expected a healthy baby, but things went bad in the end. It's also hard because what should have been a happy event turns into a real tragedy. It's hard for the families to get support and hard for their friends to know what to say."

V

The connection between her work and thoughts of her loved ones' and her own mortality "is something I've never really come to terms with, especially the death of my children." Through tears she continued, "That's one reason I couldn't deal well with the PICU. I couldn't bear to have normal children come in and die—like a child hit by a car or who developed leukemia. My own mortality doesn't worry me too much, but the thought of my children dying does worry me. There's an African curse—'May your children die before you die!' When I was pregnant the first time, it was a fundamental change. I really bonded to the baby. That's one thing about Judaism. You don't prepare for new babies. You have nothing in your house, no clothes or toys. Lots of Jews don't do that, but in our family we didn't prepare for a new baby until it was born.

"I think about my children dying when I read about other children's deaths, like when I read about children killed by a drunk driver. I don't think about it when I'm dealing with a dying baby." Thinking about her children dying "makes me sad. It makes me realize that I haven't prepared myself for that. I'm not ready to deal with it. Two of my children had children in their classes die. I don't remember that happening when I was growing up." She doesn't think about her own death very often, usually "every year when I renew my life insurance! I haven't updated my will for ten years."

Working with dying children "makes me want to live each day." Here again her eyes became moist. "And to end each day in a way that people would remember me positively."

VI

A "good death" is one in which "the family is there. The child is being held. We do that even if the family isn't there. We make them comfortable, although it's harder to know with babies if they're in pain."

A "bad death" is one in which "we've spent all the time at the end trying to save the baby without paying attention to the fact that the baby's dying. We haven't been able to help the family. The worst thing is when the family isn't there and we don't know if they've had a chance to deal with the baby's death on some level. We just had a set of twins. The mother refused to see the twin with anencephaly [no brain]. That's common with congenital anomalies. The mother didn't want to hold him or look at him. It's harder for the parents if they're not there when the child dies.

"One of the hardest deaths I ever went through was a girl with osteogenic sarcoma. She tried to commit suicide because she was scared and depressed. That was very hard for me. A lot of children with recurrent cancer give up hope before their parents or doctors do, so they're not given the opportunity to refuse further treatment. I can't think of anything worse than being a teenager with cancer. They lose all their hair and become Cushingoid. I'd have a hard time with pediatric oncology."

After a baby dies the child's parents often ask "if they could have another baby with the same problem. It's a way of asking if they were responsible. Sometimes a father will say, 'My wife smoked marijuana. Did that cause it?' Some are concerned about how to talk to their children about the death. Should they bring the children to the nursery? I tell them that if they feel comfortable they should bring them. If the children are younger I recommend they bring someone along who can take the children. If the children are older I advise that they let them be there as much as they want and that they answer their questions honestly. If the children need help we offer to get it for them.

"It's usually pretty easy to reassure the parents that they didn't cause the problem. One difficult thing is people's beliefs about God. I'm not comfortable mentioning God. One of my other colleagues sometimes says to parents that 'This is a decision God has made.'"

VII

"Neonatologists have all coped with babies' deaths so much that they've developed a good comfort level. Some of the subspecialists withdraw when we decide not to proceed with correctives. They write, 'The neonatologist will manage the rest of the care.' That's always seemed a little odd to me. We've worked so often on planned deaths that we make it easy for them to bow out.

"It's easy for us to talk about death with families. We feel comfortable bringing it up and explaining that a baby can have death with dignity. In antenatal consults most of us tell the parents that if we think things are hopeless we'll tell them. The nurses are also on the same level. You can talk about death without being stigmatized that you're giving up. We're good at supporting each other. We spend a lot of time talking with each other and determining the limits of care we can live with.

"We're not as good at following up with the families. In San Francisco we had a set protocol for follow-up. We haven't done that here. I'm not that comfortable about interfering and knowing when to leave the families alone. I don't go to the funerals. I want my space and time when I'm given bad news, and it takes me a while before I'm ready to discuss it with someone else. I'm happy to sit in the room when the baby dies, but I also offer to leave.

"It may be that I don't follow up because of my discomfort at invading their lives again. In San Francisco, the social worker, the doctor, and the nurse contacted the family after three months and offered to meet with them in person and discuss the death. I did the same thing in my first job. Then I had a horrible experience with one family. I met with them on the unit. They were falling apart and in desperate need of help. It made me gun-shy. I finally did get them help. Here, when I'm worried I'll involve a therapist to help them. I don't have the training and don't know what to do.

"The nurses are really good about recognizing and dealing with pain in the babies. They're comfortable giving low doses of morphine. It relieves the families if they're feeling that their baby is not in pain. The nurses also create a lot of memorabilia for the family. They save some hair and find things that belonged to the baby for the parents. They send the families cards and make follow-up phone calls to them. Most of the nurses are older and more mature and have a perspective similar to that of the older physicians—that death is just a part of life. You treat it that way. You try to make the best out of it that you can. There's not a culture of blame surrounding death because it's a team process and no one is left wondering if they did something wrong.

"There was a cardiology baby once. They were called in because it had a bad blood gas. The baby was waiting for a heart transplant and we were trying to get I V s in when the baby arrested. After the second round of trying to resuscitate the baby I suggested that we stop, but the cardiologist didn't want to. After the third round the father asked that we stop. We did. The cardiologist was furious. He didn't have the kind of I V line he liked. He filed an incident report. There's always something that you could do better, but if you do your best probably the outcome would be the same.

"We blame each other for lots of things! Infections, lines not staying in, or when things get missed. Like when the nurses are understaffed and forget to feed a baby. Often the nurses can't do the job because they're understaffed. Sometimes they have to take five babies. The strike nurses wouldn't take more than three. The nurses here are frequently understaffed. It must save the hospital a lot of money!

"Maybe we're too accepting. We give up more easily than other places do. We don't run codes for hours. Usually after twenty minutes we stop. I'm not sure if that's good or bad because best practice is still the lowest mortality. Death has become a part of my life. I deal with it on a regular basis. Our unit has more children die than any other unit in the hospital and yet it's still a fairly infrequent occurrence, about twenty-five or thirty a year."

She thought it would be helpful for young doctors and nurses "to have a program to debrief them after a child's death. It'd be nice to have fifteen minutes on the shift to give people a chance to talk. Frequently there's not enough time. The more people you hear talking about patients' deaths the easier it is for you to figure out your own style. Sometimes it's pretty uncomfortable! Often in the N I C U the resident is left out because they're not on that shift and we didn't check their schedule. Usually we debrief at the end of each shift. The nurses and doctors cry and express their feelings.

"The N I C U is a team of people who've worked together for a long time. All the staff was trained here and there isn't much turnover. The nurses and doctors have grown up together. They're comfortable expressing their feelings. I think that's because there are so many women. Also the nurses are very much included. The bereavement protocol provides closure for the nurses."

I mentioned that I had heard a number of physicians describe how difficult it is to take care of "PLUs" (people like us). "One of my colleagues is able to overcome that more than the rest of us. She wasn't raised in an upper-middle-class family. Sometimes we make it harder on PLUs based on how we think we'd respond. We once had a Cambodian family. That helped me to realize that there are many different approaches to what's right. They're more accepting of death and don't want extreme procedures done. The parents didn't want anything done for the baby. They kept asking, 'Can we go home now?'"

Consciously or unconsciously, Diane and I omitted one very important topic in our discussions about coping with death, the suicide of her N I C U colleague a few years before. In a close-knit, supportive community such as the N I C U her death undoubtedly had a devastating effect on those who were left behind. That neither of us thought to mention it suggests to me that it may still be a topic that is too painful to discuss.

11

"I know I'm not God, but I always try to save them."

Sarah, an attending physician from Israel, works on the hematology-oncology service and specializes in bone marrow transplants. Initially, she dealt with dying children's parents rather
bluntly, not softening her message with platitudes. Gradually,
however, she realized that she was being "overly direct" to keep
herself from crying. As she learned that it is appropriate for her
to express emotion in front of a dying child's parents, she became
more outwardly empathic in her approach. "I always had the
empathy in me. I was just afraid to use it." It was the death of her
father and her subsequent grieving that softened her defenses
and enabled her to enter and learn from the world of her emotions
and better understand the depths of pain that the parents of dying
children experience.

I

Sarah's first experience of a patient's death was with "a little girl
from the West Bank who had leukemia and died. I went to visit her
mother and took a friend with me. I'd gotten close to the girl
because her mother was really different. She came from a small vil-
lage and was the principal of a school. She knew English so we could
communicate. I got close to her and to the family. They intrigued
me. I needed to visit their home to have closure with the mother.
The child died at home and I was sad. I don't remember anything
more than that. Visiting the mother and seeing that she was okay
helped me.

"I was quite involved with the family of that first child. Every so often you get very attached. I remember one patient particularly. I was in South Carolina and the patient was an adult about my age. He was a very nice person and in another situation he could have been my friend. He was from New York City and his wife went home to be with the children. He got very sick in a short period of time and the decision had to be made about the ICU and intubation, but I couldn't reach his wife. I left messages with all the airlines because she was supposed to be on her way down. It was as if I'd stepped in and become his caretaker in addition to being his physician. I realized that it was wrong and it was very hard for me. He had to go to the ICU and later I had to send him for surgery. I lost the boundary there. I cared about him, not like a physician, but like a friend. I was more than sad when he got sick. I felt like I was losing a friend. I had this need to be with him and watch over him all the time. Everything was very emotional. It was almost like I took him on emotionally.

"When we talk about children's deaths I can remember when the patients were very sick, but I don't remember the deaths themselves. I know when they're going to die so I have my defenses up. The traumatic point for me is when they get sick and when I realize they're going to die. Then I focus on the family and turn my emotional energies to them. It's probably healing for me, too. It's harder to do that here in the hospital because the really sick patients go to the PICU where we're not part of the process. We've met with the PICU doctors to discuss it, to figure out ways that we can be part of the dying process and help the families. It helps to go the funeral. Sometimes I call the families or send a card. They often don't like to be called because it's a reminder of the death."

A patient's death "is a failure. I know that I'm not God, but I always try to save them. I don't promise that I'll cure them, but I hope so much that I can. I get attached to the children. They're so cute and have such beautiful souls. We had a girl who was dying a couple of days ago. She was so happy to be admitted to the floor. She was a nice child. It's hard to see them suffer. In that respect it helps to let them go."

175

II

Sarah grew up in Israel as the only girl among six children. Her father was a lawyer and her mother a homemaker. Her parents were both Jewish, her father from a Sephardic family in Syria that had immigrated to Israel when he was two years old and her mother from an Ashkenazi family that had lived in Israel for six generations. The differences between her parents' ethnic groups were "like those between the whites and the blacks in the United States. The Ashkenazi felt that they were the elite while the Sephardic were considered blue-collar. However, in Jerusalem the Sephardic were viewed differently because they'd been in Israel for a long time. They were like an aristocracy, a bit like 'old money' here, and my father was considered one of them. He did very well and was a leading person in the country. At one point he was nominated for President of Israel. My father's reputation and fortune soared in the 1950s and 1960s. When I was young we were just like every other family, but when my youngest brother grew up we were well off. My mother liked the Sephardic culture and so we children grew up being very proud of it.

"As my parents got older they talked about death, but when I was a child they didn't. After my father's death I asked my mother if she thought that there's a heaven. She said no, but did say that she thought she'd see him after she died." Sarah was taught that after death people "go up to the sky, up there. He or she is no longer here. It's a spiritual world, a big place, and everyone goes there, good and bad." As a child she struggled with this concept. "Did they all go to one place or did they just disappear?" She did not think much about death as a child, but "after I started working as an oncologist I really began to think about it a lot. Maybe it was in the back of my mind all along, but as a child I felt that you had to be tough, swallow your feelings, and go on."

Growing up she experienced the deaths of her maternal grandparents, a young cousin, and a friend. "My grandmother was sick, went to the hospital, and died. At the time it just seemed like the way life is. My mother's father lived with us and died in our home.

I was thirteen and remember that because of his death I couldn't go to a party. I was more upset about missing the party than about his death! My cousin died of leukemia when he was six and I was eleven. We visited him in the hospital. It was sad and I felt sorry for his family. One of my brothers was his age and they were friends. I thought about my brother and how difficult it was for him. I also had a friend who killed herself because of a boyfriend. I'd introduced them so that felt strange. Her death preoccupied me, but I'm not sure how it affected me. I thought about it, felt sad, and wondered if it were my fault. I don't think I felt guilty. He broke her heart. It was my responsibility to see that they fit better. I was fourteen or fifteen at the time."

The most traumatic deaths in her early years were those of her paternal aunt and uncle. "My father's father, who was in his nineties, had died a year earlier. We took part in the memorial service, seeing the family, and eating well. My father's brother and sister came to the funeral from another city. On the way back home, after a long day, their car crashed and they both died. He was in his thirties and she was in her fifties. It was the first time I'd seen my father cry. It surprised me," she said tearfully. "My father was like a rock and always handled everything. Of all his siblings, those two meant the most to him. His sister had raised him and his brother was a 'wonder child' with lots of promise. He was my father's protégé."

III

Sarah's interest in medicine developed gradually. "I was a secretary in the Israeli army and got bored. To improve things I applied for and was later accepted in an officer-training course. They put me in a job that was similar to that of a social worker and I was also a special officer for women's affairs. I oversaw the well-being of a lot of women in the service, but I liked the social work part better. During the attrition war of 1968 and 1969 many soldiers were wounded and killed. I had to go to their families and be supportive. I visited the wounded soldiers in the hospital, brought them goodies, and asked if they needed anything. I didn't know what I wanted to do so I took career tests. They said I could do anything! I thought back on my experience in the Army and decided to go into medicine to take care of people and to make them better. I also liked the energy of the hospital. My former husband, who'd just started medical school, encouraged me and told me that I'd like it."

She chose pediatrics because "I had children at home and needed to know what to do when they were ill. I did well on pediatrics. I started with neonatology. I liked the action and the high energy. I did it for a year and a half and after that it wasn't so exciting anymore so I tried gastroenterology. It was very brainy, but it didn't do much for me. Then I went into hematology-oncology. That was really exciting and combined both intellectual and personal challenges, but after a while the workup and management seemed too predictable and routine so I moved into bone marrow transplantation. There's so much that I can do in this field and it feels like I have more impact on patient outcomes. The patients are sicker, it's more exciting, and I can do so much more.

"I'm very satisfied with my career choice. I like the excitement. Things are changing and evolving all the time. I like the fact that we can cure or at least help so many patients. I like the interactions with the families. Over the years I've realized that we want the families to love us. They give us so much. I like being trusted and the trust is very deep. It goes along with the dependency they have on us. I like that, too. It's the relationships you build that keep me in the field. They treat you as much as you treat them. I learned this over the last few years as I began to open up more. They need that from me—to know that I'm human. It also helps with patients who aren't doing well and who are dying. You can discuss the death with the family more easily. I don't tell them everything about myself, but if they ask I tell them some things. Sometimes I regret it and think, 'They didn't need to know that.'"

She does not like "working in the corporate medical world. I don't deal well with the system. In my heart I'm a rebel! I'm also troubled by the death and dying. The long working hours were more of a struggle when my children were young. My ex-husband thought it was a big problem, but now it's not an issue."

In the future she sees herself "eventually returning to general pediatrics. At some point you want to slow down. The world of transplants is too demanding. It's always been my dream to be a country doctor, to serve the community, its needs, and those who aren't privileged."

"I don't think we were ever prepared in medical school for patients' deaths. At that time children weren't told they were dying and they weren't part of the decision-making process. In Israel there was a little bit more arrogance toward patients among physicians, more like it is in Europe. That may have changed by now. I found my own way. That's okay, but I wish I'd been taught that there's an issue there we have to deal with. We focused on cure, on health, on the positive. We never dealt with the negative. We focused on the 80 percent that survived, not on the 20 percent that didn't. Our focus was on healing rather than care. Medical schools should help us to deal with the dying part as well. That insight came to me when my father died. He was very important to me. After he died I got a book on Oriental beliefs about death. It said that death is a part of life, a part of the life cycle. That was like an illumination! Then I met a man whose mother was sick. I dated him while she was dying at home. There was something normal and natural about her and her husband's acceptance of her death. It was so unlike my father's death. My father was a very strong man and our family was patriarchal. I had five brothers and it was a man's world. There was all of this strength and power. Then all of a sudden my father crashed and died. He was dead in three months. I used to think that I'd go back to Israel and care for my parents, but this place became my home. He died while I was here. He wasn't supposed to do that! For many years he was my idol. Then I was on my own."

During training, "I didn't learn a lot from others. In residency I saw that deaths were hard on everybody. In fellowship I was taught how to talk with the patient and family about death and dying. It was good, but insufficient. Many of my teachers were in denial. They didn't want to deal with it. I remember one. When he had a patient that was dying he was always in a rotten mood. We learned not to talk to him. In my first job we had a psychologist on the team so we talked about it more, but I was never taught how I should cope emotionally with the death of a patient. I should have sat in more often when the attendings were talking to patients and families about dying. The nurses are much better prepared to cope with patients' deaths than we are. Maybe it has something to do with the reasons that we chose our fields."

IV

As for her ability to cope with the deaths of patients, "I'm improving. I'm better than I was. I've had a lot of experience. I'm very honest, sometimes to the point of shoving it in your face! Then it's a weakness, but sometimes it helps to tell patients the truth. Sometimes I say horrible things to people. It's much better with patients I've known over the years. I've gradually learned to soften what I tell them and to empathize. Empathy was always in me, but I didn't show it. My overdirectness was a defense mechanism so that I wouldn't start crying with patients and families. Over the last few years I've learned that it's okay to cry with them, but I have to be the strong person. Recently I had to tell a mother that there was nothing more we could do. I cried more than she did! Families often worry that when there are no more attempts at cure you won't care for them anymore. Increasingly I see my energies shifting from the patient to the family.

"My strengths lie in being with the family and trying to give them information and support. After the death I go to the funeral or service. I don't have to talk to them, just to be there and to be part of the process. Professionally I always go back to see if any mistakes were made. Usually I try to have a conference to see if we missed anything."

It makes it difficult to cope with the death of a child "if the parents are angry, accusative, and not trusting. That's the most difficult part. You can't fix the problem. It's a given and you just have to take what you have. I also don't like it when the child dies when I'm not around."

Her colleagues are very supportive. "After my first patient died everyone came and said they were sorry and hoped I was okay. I was surprised. Then I realized that they do it all the time. I haven't experienced that in other places."

She gets little support from her friends or family. "There's one person I can talk to, but usually I don't. It's too much for him. He says, 'I don't know how you do it.' Sometimes I'll say, 'I had a bad week, a child died.' He's afraid to ask about it! It would be nice if my friends were able to listen and to not be so scared."

V

"I thought about my own mortality when I cared for adults, but not when I care for children. It does make me think that we won't live forever. I haven't thought much about mortality over the last ten years. My children, on the other hand, were very concerned about it when they were younger. I didn't know how to deal with their worries.

"Many of my colleagues see a sick child and they reflect on their own children, especially in the beginning of their careers, but I always completely separated my children from the children I cared for. I didn't experience a connection. I thought a lot about death while I was mourning my parents. My father died nine years ago and my mother two years ago, but now I don't think about it a lot. It's interesting how I keep it out of my awareness."

When she thinks about dying "it's more in a practical way, like what I need to do and how my children will react. Then there's another level. Have I done what I wanted to do in my life? Over the last few years I've thought, 'Is this it?' I've so many years left. I'm happy with what I'm doing. What do I want to do? Is this what I want from my life? My concerns have more to do with aging, not dying."

VI

A "good death" is one in which "the child is with his family and, depending on his age, with his friends. I think it's better when the child dies at home. He should be surrounded by his family, his things, and ideally in his room with his toys. There should be a lot of touching and hugging." A "bad death" is "in the hospital, on a monitor, with the nurse running back and forth, the doctor going in and out, and the family not there."

She believes that dying children know they are dying. "They know they're going to another place. They all have this vision of heaven and angels. They feel it more than they understand it. They have to have the feeling that their family is with them all the time and supports them and gives them their warmth. They have to hear about death early on. They have to hear the word death.

"I'm open and tell them what's going to happen. I hope that I'm sensitive—I try to be. I support them and I talk to them directly about their illness. I'll say things like, 'We're not going to give you treatment anymore.' Sometimes I can't communicate with the patient. Some children won't talk with you. I wish I could learn ways to communicate with them. I'm thinking of my last two patients. They were very sick and they didn't want to talk. So I talked to the parents, but I'm not sure they delivered the message."

Terminally ill children do not ask her about death. "They may ask somebody else." The parents ask "how it's going to happen, when it will happen, will it be painful, how will the child feel, can you do anything? Can we bring our parents? Can we bring the dogs?" She's happy when parents ask her questions because it shows they're dealing with the fact that their child is going to die and allows her to help them with the dying process.

VII

She admires her colleagues' ability to "talk with the family about death before the child dies. They're able to express their sadness.

Some are able to sit with the family and cry with them, but also to understand that the family is suffering more than they are. The goal is to combine empathy with professionalism. Sometimes their empathy is too great. They can't step back and get too involved. I once had a patient who married his home health nurse!

"Some people can't say to the family that the child is going to die and keep on treating the child. Then there are those that detach themselves from the family when they realize that the child is going to die. They leave it to the nurses and social workers. I think that you have to make yourself available to the families. They often complain that when there's no treatment left they're neglected."

PART III

NURSES

T he role held by nurses in the care of dying children and their families has much in common with the work of physicians, but it is usually more personal and more intense emotionally. Nurses in intensive-care settings are always at the bedside and can seldom walk away to do other things, even such mundane tasks as having lunch. As a result, they are present during children's and families' most vulnerable and painful moments and must field the questions and deal with the feelings that families are often unwilling or unable to present to the doctors.

Most of the nurses I interviewed had chosen their professions for different reasons than the doctors had. Several recalled experiences of being cared for by a skilled and compassionate nurse and wanted to emulate in their careers that person's healing and supportive role. They were drawn to nursing less by an interest in science or prestige than by a desire to provide care to other human beings in a deeply personal and intimate manner. There were, of course, practical considerations as well. Nursing training is not as long as that required of physicians; it pays well, is in high demand, and offers more lifestyle flexibility in terms of variable shifts and hours. The profession is also not as consumed by the reimbursement and liability hassles that undermine the work-lives of physicians.

Many of the nurses spoke about the importance of their religious and spiritual beliefs in sustaining them in their work. Without such beliefs, the children's suffering and deaths would seem meaningless and overwhelming. Most thought it would be impossible to work for long with dying children if one did not have the hope that the children or their souls or spirits would be in a better place some-day. "You have to believe that after all their suffering the children have earned a free ticket to heaven."

Nurses in critical care see themselves as advocates for the child and her family. They usually know the patients and parents better than the physicians do because they spend much more time with them. They may be more likely than the physicians to call for the active treatment of a seemingly incurable disease to stop and for palliative care to begin. While there is seldom a sharp demarcation between curing and caring, the nurses may perceive it earlier than the physicians. This creates an important and potentially useful tension within the treatment team that causes all participants to reexamine what they are doing and to ask whether or not it is ultimately helpful for the child.

Having children of one's own deepens the identification of caregivers with their patients and with their patients' families. Transferring the profound feelings one has for one's own children onto the children one cares for can create an overwhelming and unbearable sense of pain and loss. Even the most experienced and psychologically well-defended nurses and physicians are vulnerable to moments when such identifications suddenly confront them "like a slap in the face." The physicians have more opportunities to distract and remove themselves from these situations and thus have more control over them. The nurses, however, cannot usually leave the room or retreat to another aspect of their work when their feelings about the patient or his family become too intense. At such times, the collegial support of other nurses can make all the difference. Physicians are more likely to be isolated in their roles, but nurses are surrounded by colleagues who understand what they are experiencing and can offer a hug, a break, or a listening ear if the nurse is able and willing to ask for help. One of them compared critical care nurses to young soldiers in combat. "Only the other soldiers know what you're experiencing." Friends and family, while sympathetic and caring, are often so shocked by the situations the nurses encounter that they are the ones who need support and comfort and are unable to recommend anything beyond the question "Why don't you quit your job?"

Collegial support is especially important for younger professionals in helping to normalize their reactions to traumatic situations. The shock and horror they experience early in their careers during an especially ugly death or resuscitation often provoke powerful emotional reactions not ordinarily experienced in daily life. Being able to talk with older, more experienced colleagues about how you feel can be very helpful, confirming that it is "normal" or "natural" to feel overwhelming sadness, guilt, or anger in such situations. Senior colleagues can also model ways to deal with these feelings without becoming immobilized or burnt out. It can be difficult for both young nurses and resident physicians to open their hearts to older colleagues because of concerns that they will appear weak or unprofessional. Moreover, the hierarchical and highly competitive environment of a teaching hospital appeared to me to make it especially difficult for attending physicians, as compared with the nursing staff, to ask for support.

It was my impression that the nurses, at least in this hospital and on these units, were more satisfied with their professional lives than were the physicians I interviewed. Much of this appeared to be due to the intense interpersonal involvement they had with the patients and their families. The physicians were pulled in many directions at once and seldom had the opportunity to get to know the patients and families they interacted with as well as the nurses did. Their focus was more often on the technical and administrative sides of health care, such as treatment planning, medical decision-making, fiscal management, and those banes of physician life, interacting with insurance companies, regulatory agencies, and lawyers. While the nurses were not spared these responsibilities, the nature of their work required intimate caregiving contact, and offered the satisfactions brought by these most basic of all human relationships. Physicians rarely felt that they had time to pursue that level of caregiving.

The nurses also appeared to have much more control over their work lives than did the physicians. They worked regular shifts, could often structure their shifts to allow them substantial blocks of time off, and were not ordinarily on call. Most were not involved in research or didactic teaching and so did not experience the nagging pressure of these additional, and usually unpaid, responsibilities that are expected of physicians working in academic settings.

Of all the narratives in this book those of the nurses seemed to me to convey the most passion for their work. Whether this is a reflection of the closeness of their involvement with patients, their perhaps greater willingness to expose their deepest feelings, or of the characteristics of people who are attracted to nursing rather than to medicine is not clear to me. However, their intensity and dedication are a testament to the fact that nursing and medicine, at their best, are ultimately labors of love that one undertakes to serve others, to cure disease, and to diminish pain and suffering.

12

"No one understands what we do and no one can empathize with what we're going through except us."

Katie is twenty-five years old and has only worked in the neonatal intensive care unit (N I C U) for three years. Her psychological defenses for dealing with patients' deaths and families' grieving are still evolving, and she is very much in touch with the trauma of the tragedies she encounters. As a result, her reactions to her work have a freshness and immediacy that is less evident in the more experienced nurses and physicians. Her youth and sensitivity help her to appreciate an almost transcendent quality to her work. She finds that the support she gets from other nurses is the key to helping her to understand and bear the emotions she feels when babies die.

I

Katie remembers clearly her first experience of a child patient's death. "She was born at twenty-six weeks. She was a twin and very sick at birth. I like to care for sick babies and that often puts me in the situation of having to face the baby's death. This baby was initially not expected to live, but despite that she did. She kept getting better each day, and the staff and her family started to have some hope. I was the first person to get to hold and bathe her. She had facial anomalies, but I was attracted to her because of her sad face. There was something about the way she looked at you and absolutely melted when she was held. She loved being held, but for a long time she was so sick that she couldn't be. I tried to give her extra attention because she'd gone without physical contact for so long. Multiples [twins, triplets] are always paired, so I also cared for her brother. After a few months she improved enough to go to the level two side of the nursery. She'd beaten the odds and we planned to send her home along with her brother after they learned to eat.

"Unfortunately, hospital-acquired infections occur even in our unit. She got a virus and it consumed her. The little reserve she had was quickly expended and ultimately she died. A part of me is very angry about that. I feel like she didn't have to die. She had conditions that could have caused her death later in life, but to have her die of an acquired infection was very frustrating. Her brother got sick too, but he had much greater reserves than she did and he lived. We tried her on different types of ventilators, but nothing worked and eventually her body systems started shutting down one by one. When the ventilators weren't able to keep her blood oxygenated the doctor called her mother to come in during the night. It was so painful to see her holding her dying baby. I'll never forget the horrific wailing sounds she made as she held her baby and bargained with God, pleading for her daughter's life.

"Eventually the parents decided to take her off the ventilator. We withdrew support and gave her morphine as a comfort measure during the dying process. I was unprepared for what happens to babies' bodies when they die. Things come out of their nose and mouth and any other areas that have been punctured, like IV lines. Their bodies become cold and stiff and their tongues protrude from their mouths as their face and body begin to discolor. The parents were horrified and I was in shock. Our attending was great. She said reassuringly to both the parents and to me, 'That's perfectly normal.' It really helped me to see the attending crying during the process. The baby's parents were screaming hysterically. Having the attending cry made the nurses think it was all right to be sad and it showed the parents that the doctors cared. As the baby gasped for each breath I listened periodically for a heart rate until her heart stopped beating and the doctor confirmed her death. All the while her brother slept quietly in his carrier, completely unaware of his sister's fate.

"After babies die, we nurses do the postmortem care. We dress them up to make them look alive. We have makeup and special clothes and blankets. We take pictures and make a memory kit for the parents. After she died and the parents stepped out of the room I realized that after working sixteen hours and being emotionally and physically drained I didn't have enough left in me to do the post-mortem care. Fortunately her other primary nurse from the day shift was called and came in to help. After we were done taking pictures, bathing her and doing footprints, handprints, and obtaining a lock of hair, we dressed her in a hospital-issued T-shirt, wrapped her in hospital blankets, and put her in a body bag. The feeling of putting a baby in a body bag, which is similar to a giant-size zip lock, is quite unnerving. At that point, as I tried to understand the overwhelming event I'd just experienced, I wondered if I could continue in this profession.

"According to protocol the nurse calls transportation and they come with a fishing-tackle box and take the baby to the morgue— but for dignity's sake we put her in the bottom drawer of a bassinette and took her down. That was the first time either of us had been to the morgue, which was also a strange experience. Then to pick up the baby you'd once held in your arms and who'd looked back at you so lovingly and place her on a cold steel shelf marked 'for babies only' was excruciating. We walked back to the unit solemnly, neither of us saying a word, and I began to feel the completeness of my exhaustion.

"I'd been on for twenty hours and had cried through the whole experience. I finally went home and slept. My husband found me crying in my sleep and said, 'You've got to quit!' I took a week off and went to her funeral. It helped me to do that and to talk to her family. They kept thanking us over and over again. It was hard to know how to behave. They invited the other primary nurse and me to go to the gravesite. During the service the parents said a lot of nice things about the nurses. They recognized that although we weren't biologically related to the baby we, too, had formed an attachment to her and had bonded with her. They appreciated that we'd experienced parts of her life, both good and bad, that no one else had. That helped. In some sense I think they were giving us permission to be sad and to grieve with them.

"Ironically, I was working an additional job at the time, giving pediatric advice over the phone. The first call I got the night after the baby's death was from her mother. She called about the other twin. She wanted to know how he'd acted in the hospital, if he was fussy a lot, and if he'd had problems with his stomach. It was therapeutic to talk with her and to appreciate that there was another baby who was doing well and who desperately needed that mother's care.

"After the baby's death I was an absolute wreck. I was so overwhelmed, but I knew I wanted to go back to work and that I didn't want to take my husband's advice and simply give up. She'd been my primary baby for the entire four months of her life and I would miss her dearly, but I simply had to move on. After a week off I decided that the best thing I could do was to go back to work. The first night I went to a delivery of triplets. Two of the babies died and I had to do the postmortem care along with a colleague. Surprised and shocked, I was again unnerved and wondered how I'd deal with this situation so soon after her death. With much relief I found that it was easier because I wasn't bonded to the two babies that had died.

"One night at my pediatric advice-line job I worked with another nurse who debriefed with me about the experience of the first baby's death. She validated my feelings. She said it was all right to feel the way I did. 'Nurses experience those feelings. To take a dead body to the morgue is very significant. You have a right to be emotional about it!' She shared her own experiences and that helped. I'd finally found someone who understood what I'd just been through and who reassured me that things would get better and that I could continue doing this work. The residents who were on the night the baby died were really nice as well. They told me I'd done a good job. They were upset, too, and to see them struggling with it was helpful. Subconsciously I thought, 'I'll never let that happen again. I'll never get that close to a baby.' For many months afterwards I simply didn't sign up for primary babies.

"Around the time she died our best friends had a baby. My husband said to me one night, 'Hold the baby, it'll help,' but it wasn't the same. It wasn't her. It confirmed again that he didn't understand. How could I expect him to? He had no idea what I see and do on a daily basis. Eventually he apologized for saying I should quit my job and said that he'd simply felt helpless seeing me crying and not knowing what else to do or say.

"Each case is different. I'm definitely more prepared for what happens now and better able to help parents and myself. It doesn't overwhelm me like it did the first time. It helps a lot to talk about it. That first death really prepared me. Since that time some of my other primary babies have died, but their deaths haven't been so dramatic. I haven't bonded with any of them like I did with that first one and I think I'm better at predicting when death is approaching so I can prepare myself.

"There was one baby who was abandoned by her mother at birth and transferred here. The baby was very sick from the onset of his stay, and it was quite evident that he was going to die. However, the state had custody and they wouldn't let us withdraw support without legal and ethical counsel. I desperately wanted to hold and comfort that dying baby who was so alone, but for legal reasons he had to die on the ventilator. He'd never been held and didn't even have a name. It really affected me that no one had ever appreciated that the baby had lived. I was sad that we couldn't do more to comfort him.

"There's another one I remember. He was still hooked up to the monitors as he was dying. His mother came in and touched him. His heart rate and oxygen saturation increased just by her presence and the sound of her voice. The attending said to her, 'He waited for you.' It was very touching and we all cried. He hadn't responded to our voices or touch, only to his mother. It was profound."

II

Katie grew up in a family of four and has a brother who is one year younger than she is. Her father works as a truck driver and her mother is a secretary at a middle school. She was raised in a very small, all-white town. The family was Baptist and "religion was always a part of our lives. We went to church every Sunday morning and evening."

Her parents were very open in talking about death, although she has had no experience of death among her family or close relatives. "Some distant relatives died, but there was no crying because they weren't that close."

As a child she adopted her parents' religious views. "They believed in an afterlife based on biblical teachings. According to Baptist theology there's a heaven and an afterlife. If you're a Christian you go to heaven. You're given a new body. You go through judgment and live forever with Jesus. A mansion is prepared for you. You'll know people in heaven, but you won't act as if you're still in a relationship with them. All children go to heaven. It has to do with accountability, when you come to terms with your mortality and with your relationship to Jesus Christ."

What she knew about coping with the deaths of others "I adapted from TV, where I observed people crying and moving on. I was oblivious to people's inner coping mechanisms." The only experience she had of death as a child was that of the wife of the principal in her mother's school. "I knew her remotely. I remember it happening and the principal having to be gone. I was in middle school then. I don't know how he coped. I didn't go to her funeral, but my parents went. She died of a brain cancer over the course of two years. I felt no connection so I didn't have to cope. At that stage of your life you think you're immortal and you're not concerned with death. I never thought it could happen to my parents or to someone in my family. It seemed very removed and I didn't personalize it at all."

III

"I always wanted to be a nurse and I fervently pursued it. I was always good at taking care of others." She was drawn to pediatrics because "I've always liked children and had a passion for them and their well-being. I worked at a day care and did a lot of babysitting. In nursing school I liked my adult rotations, but I had the opportunity to do a N I C U rotation and I fell in love with it! I had a directed practicum around it and volunteered there as well. When I graduated there weren't any jobs in the N I C U here so I worked in the adult I C U for six months and then transferred. I hated the adult I C U! The staff was very unwelcoming. The nurses there fit the saying 'nurses eat their young.' They threw you to the wolves. One of my first experiences with death was there and it didn't go well.

"I loved the babies. I always have and I knew the N I C U was my niche. The staff is much more receptive to and nurturing of new nurses. Many of them exemplify the grandmother-persona in their ability to care for and nurture those younger than they are. The nurses as well as the management in our department are very caring and take an interest in you as a person as well as your development professionally. I also liked the intensive-care part—the technology is fascinating, and I liked our ability to intervene and do things that are pretty miraculous. I was awed by the resiliency of the babies, the tiniest of patients. Many of them overcame giant obstacles and survived despite the odds. It was inspiring to see a baby fight for survival. People ask me, 'How can you work there? It must be so depressing.' Although it's difficult to convey to the lay world, working in the N I C U is very rewarding. Most of the babies go home and most do fine. We do have a tough population, not just preemies, but surgical patients as well. Survival is related to their gestational age, but 80 to 90 percent of the preemies go home. Of the others, the majority go home.

"I'm very satisfied with my career choice. I don't anticipate ever wanting to leave. Working in a tertiary care center and one that's a university is very important because we see so much here and we have the ability to do so much. Sometimes we try alternative procedures when other hospitals won't. Going to a community hospital wouldn't be comparable. I love what I do. I love coming to work. The interactions with the babies are very rewarding. The interactions with the parents can be rewarding at times. You can bond with them, some more than others. Most of the babies are there for an extended period of time, making it easier to get attached to them and their parents. The staff in the N I C U is a huge positive factor. I have many good friends there with whom I also participate in activities outside of work. It's a very caring environment. The doctors there seem to really value the nurses' opinions and judgment. We work pretty independently and have a lot of autonomy. I like the teaching aspect as well, and working with the residents. I really like working twelve-hour shifts and only having to work three days a week. You don't take any work home with you. Once your shift is over, it's over. It's not like having to go home and grade papers.

"The work can be draining at times. It involves giving a tremendous amount of yourself. The nurses take care of others and don't always make taking care of themselves a priority. I've had to really focus on that. It's hard not to get very involved. I grew up in a sheltered environment and the social circumstances of many of our patients' families initially really blew me away! There were drugs and crime and sad domestic situations. After a while it all becomes commonplace and eventually you're not bothered by what you hear. It's very hard to see so many of our children go to foster care. That's a real emotional drain. Working with dying children has also made me apprehensive about having children. Because I work in the N I C U and see only abnormalities I sometimes forget that the majority of births result in normal newborns. When I'm pregnant I'll probably expect the baby to be abnormal and will anticipate different disease processes.

"When you go home and talk to your husband and friends they can't comprehend it. They have no way of understanding your job and what you do minute by minute. They don't have enough knowledge to know why certain experiences are more significant than others. Yet I continue to try to unload on them, breaking down sentences and explaining as I go along, only to recognize that you can't debrief with them. They don't appreciate the idiosyncrasies of the job that make it so special and yet so difficult. That's why nurses have a lot of friends who are nurses! Nurses are the only ones who can truly appreciate what you're saying and have related experiences to compare and contrast and to simply understand."

Katie has had to learn to take care of herself. "Before I went into nursing I was very active. I worked out and went to movies. When I went into nursing I gave all that I had. I came home after a twelve-hour shift and I had nothing left. I didn't go to the gym. I didn't care for myself as well as I should have. Now I've made self-care more of a focus. I recognize that I have a tendency to say yes to everything and need to develop the art of learning to say no for the sake of self-preservation."

In the future she sees herself "continuing to work as a staff nurse in the N I C U. I never want to go into management. It's too removed from bedside nursing. That's what I like, taking care of babies. Also there's more of a time commitment in management. Looking ahead, I want to have children and don't want to work more hours. I did a practicum in management and there's no part of it that I like. That's not who I am."

She is "very dissatisfied" with her nursing school preparation for dealing with the deaths of patients. "Nursing school in general is too caught up in theories and is very impractical—and even more so about patients dying. I never was taught how to deal personally with the deaths of patients. There was a death and dying seminar but nothing about how we should deal with death ourselves. We were taught about the grieving process but more about what the family would be dealing with, not that you could have a relationship with a patient that died and be grieving yourself. Then when it happens it's huge! It's overwhelming, and the feelings you experience are very confusing. It would have been helpful if it had been addressed. It's acknowledged that death will happen, but that's it. They need to help you to see that those deaths are going to affect you personally and to let you know that it's all right. It's implied that we're meant to be stoic, unaffected, and have no reaction. If we do respond that way it affects the parents and makes them think we don't care. Besides, I can't pretend to be so detached.

"The only thing we were taught in orientation was the bereavement policy, which is very task oriented. It never addressed you and your feelings. It tells you how to make a bereavement kit and complete the care of the body after the baby has passed. I'm in the process of orienting people now. One new nurse asked what it would be like to go through the death of a baby. I replied, 'They just give you the policy and that's it. They don't prepare you emotionally.' Often the residents are falling apart as well! I not only have to deal with what I'm feeling, but what they're feeling too, and have to try to provide support for them."

She believes it would help new N I C U nurses "to hear how nurses who've done it for a long time have coped. It would help to know what their first experience of death was like and to know that it's normal to feel overwhelmed by it. They also have to learn that it's important for us to support one another. Do you go to the funeral or not? How involved should we be with families? We did have one charge nurse who, after a baby died, said that it would be good for those who hadn't seen a dead baby to take a look. Looking at and handling a dead baby for the first time is an eerie feeling and nothing can prepare you for it. Nothing about their appearance or the way they feel communicates life, and the image of the first dead baby you encounter stays with you throughout the rest of your life."

IV

"As a nurse I have it pretty together and have good control over myself. The other night a baby died. I didn't have the baby. I was orienting a trainee to level three care. We shared our pod with a male nurse and it was his baby that was dying. He usually has it together, but as the baby died he seemed very rattled. Even if you're not attached to a baby you feel some sort of connection or at least an uncomfortable feeling."

When a baby dies, the most difficult thing is "doing the postmortem care. We do it so we can dress them up and take pictures. It's difficult to know the baby is dead and that you have to dress it up to look alive. Handling a dead baby is different. They feel different. They get stiff and their mouths stay open. We have to prop them closed with Q-tips.

"There are times when we go too far. You think that a death could have been easier if only we'd let go sooner. Sometimes you wonder why we go on and pursue life so fanatically when the baby's body is clearly telling us that it's giving up. Why are we giving blood and making changes on the ventilator? It's not going to make a difference. Why are we wasting all this money, especially when the family is all right with the baby dying? Sometimes I think we're doing it for the doctors. I think they sometimes feel it's a failure when a baby dies. On the night shift, the residents want to keep the baby alive until the attending gets there or the day shift comes on.

"The hardest thing for me personally is the parents' reaction. I'm not good when people are crying. When others cry I feel the need to cry and I don't like it. It makes me uncomfortable. I'm not sure how to comfort them, how to give them space and yet to still be there, especially if I don't know them. Afterward, debriefing is helpful. I've found people to debrief with who are better than those I talked to in the past. Now I don't go home and cry for a week like I did with that first one."

She sees her ability to realize "that a patient's death has nothing to do with you personally" as a strength in her struggle to cope with the deaths of her patients. "A lot of the deaths we see are due to anomalies. It's easier to rationalize those deaths. 'It wasn't compatible with life.' Talking about patients' deaths with other nurses helps. Going to the funerals helps. It communicates to the family that you cared about their baby in a special way. I also like having pictures of the babies. I keep them in my hope chest and they help me to have closure. The more you can have closure, the better. In one instance, a baby I cared for was in a horrible social situation. After he died I thought, 'He's better off not being there.' It also helps if the death happens in a peaceful way and we're able to stop the medical interventions and let the parents hold and appreciate their baby and the life the baby has lived thus far. It's not a big trauma when it happens like that. I use my faith as a coping mechanism, too, my belief that all babies go to heaven.

"I'm not always able to find an outlet for my feelings. I try to talk to my husband, but he just doesn't get it. He wants to fix the problem, but I just want him to listen. I tend to get really attached to the babies and their families. Some of the veteran nurses don't get attached or if they do it's in a distant way. They're very methodical. 'That's the way it is.' I think they have a harder time being compassionate with the parents.

"Another weakness I have is that I don't like to ask for help. I'm a controlling person and I don't like to give up any of my assignment, even if doing so would mean that I could provide better care for the baby whose death may be imminent. I think it's better when the assignments are such that a dying baby is the nurse's only assignment.

"We have a lot of new people now who don't have much experience. They don't cope well with babies dying. I was helping one and when the baby died she fell apart. I was able to talk with her and help her. The other night my trainee asked if she could do the postmortem care. That's a good thing for the new people to do, to have that opportunity."

V

"I project the babies' deaths onto the mortality of my future children, especially with viral herpes infections. Herpes can be deadly for babies. It's a dramatic, horrible death. So I tell my husband, 'No one is going to kiss our babies!' I worry a lot about babies. I worried with all of my nieces and nephews before their births and was hypersensitive to all the things that could go wrong."

She seldom thinks about her family members dying. "We knew a police officer who committed suicide and that made me think of my husband. What would I do if that happened? I can't imagine what it would be like. Seeing the officer's wife made me think about it. Someone had to carry her into the funeral. She was weeping hysterically. It was two and a half hours long! They have a seven-year-old son. I thought about what it would be like for him."

She "hardly ever" thinks of her own death, "probably because I'm twenty-five. Sometimes I wonder how my husband would react and what he'd do. He wouldn't know how to pay the bills or where anything is. I project the feelings of the parents of a dead baby onto my husband, thinking that he would never be able to handle a situation like that."

VI

A "good death" is one in which "the family can be involved and it happens in a compassionate way as opposed to continuing a lot of supportive medical efforts that aren't going anywhere. Privacy is also important. Unfortunately on our unit there are four babies per pod and everyone in the pod hears everything. I don't think that other families need to share in that experience."

A "bad death" is "when we go too far, when we've gotten to the point where we can't stop. We call it 'flogging' the baby, keeping things going when there's no brain function. It's not fair to the baby to have to endure all that suffering. Babies definitely feel pain. They make faces and grimace. When we take them off the ventilator and they're dying we give them a generous dose of morphine. It suppresses their respiratory drive so the agonal breathing or gasping is kept minimal. That can be very disturbing for parents. They see the baby suffering and they wonder if they made the right decision to stop. It's nice when the babies die quietly. It's also good if the death is organized and not a resuscitation or a code, and if the parents have had time to come to terms with the baby's death instead of having to make a sudden decision.

"The chaplains are great. Their presence is very calming. They know what to say and what not to say. We try to anticipate the death enough so that the babies can be baptized or that a priest can be called."

When a baby is dying the parents' questions can be "pretty pointed. 'When is it going to happen?' 'Why?' We usually get the doctor to talk to them about it. They also break the news about a terminal diagnosis. Sometimes the parents think out loud, 'Why did this have to happen? Why did it have to happen to me?' There are some things that you can't share with the entire family, like if the baby is dying from a sexually transmitted disease.

"Sometimes it can be very uncomfortable. You don't know how much the parents want to know. Will they be hysterical? Will they have questions? Will you be able to answer them? The discomfort is about not knowing what to expect. Sometimes they just want honesty, to know that there's nothing we can do. Sometimes you feel relief with their questions. You're relieved that they understand."

VII

"Some of the other nurses are very distant emotionally. That's how they cope, but it's not necessarily the best way. At the staff level we support each other, especially on nights. 'Could I help you put the memory kit together?' 'Are you all right?' The charge nurses [administrative nurses responsible for the nursing care on each shift] don't always provide that kind of support. I think it's because they're so busy and don't have a close relationship with the families, but one has to wonder if it's become too commonplace for them and they've hardened themselves to the intimate feelings associated with the death of a patient.

"The boundary issue is a big one. People go from one extreme to the other. Some almost join the family and for years have a very close connection to them. Others take it too personally; 'it's my fault.' They overanalyze everything, wondering what they did to cause the death. Others remain cold and distant, like it's just a part of their job.

"After your first death you learn to deal with it. You're over the anxiety. I feel well prepared now. It's easier if it's a death you're expecting. With each new experience you get more insight into how to deal with patients' deaths and how to best help their families."

After reviewing the draft of our interviews Katie wrote down some additional thoughts.

"Babies, despite their tiny bodies, make a huge impact with their lives, both on their parents and on the nurses who take care of them. Everything about them breathes life and their will to fight and persist is always evident. As a nurse and a caretaker of babies, for me it's a pleasure to get to experience their lives with them and to provide them with the best possible medical care during their lives, no matter how long or short they may be.

"Recently I took care of a baby who from the beginning was fighting against all the odds. As a micro-preemie of twenty-six weeks, his life got off to a rocky start and eventually he developed an overwhelming infection that ultimately caused his death. I took care of him after I completed the interviews. It was interesting to reflect upon my feelings during his life and especially when it became evident that he wasn't going to live. I felt like I was more effective with his parents and more comfortable dealing with them, and that I was more aware of my own emotions and coping mechanisms. I reached out more effectively to the nurses who were offering support and was careful about what I said around my husband, although keeping him informed.

"I became very attached to the baby as I saw him rally against the odds and give us glimmers of hope that he was still fighting. However with a massive infection and edema his physical heart simply could not endure, although the being inside of him was with us. He was clearly responsive to voice and touch and I encouraged and supported intimate moments between him and his parents.

"I cared for him day in and day out for the three short weeks of his life and in the last four days I cared for him almost 75 percent of each twenty-four-hour shift to ensure that he got consistency. The last night I cared for him before his parents made the decision to withdraw support, I spoke with his mother at length, listening as she poured out her heart because she was concerned that she, who had given him life, would now be taking it away. Knowing that they were planning to take him off support sometime the following day I hardly slept a moment, and at one P.M., only four hours after arriving home and with little sleep, I sensed that the end of his life was near and decided to go into work early to be there for the family, for him, and for my own grieving process. His parents had never held him until the day he passed away and I reflected on how sad it must be to hold your baby for the very first time knowing that it would also be the last time, and how you would want to hold on to your baby forever.

"After his death I was glad to see that our medical director chose to have a debriefing about his life and death. I found the debriefing very enlightening, comforting, and reassuring. I wished that I could have shared more during the debriefing about what a special baby he was, about what I had shared with him and his family, and about the special hours his family spent with him after he died. However, I knew that if I uttered a word my composure would crumble and so I chose to be brief in my remarks.

"The words of the person who ran the debriefing were very touching and reassuring. No one understands what we do and no one can empathize with what we are going through except us. She emphasized how important it is to support each other and to continue the work we are doing for the betterment of our babies and their families."

13

"I've seen way too many dead babies."

Allison has worked as a nurse in hematology-oncology for twelve years. Her close involvement with the deaths of more than one hundred and fifty children has left her with "a black spot inside that grows and grows." Although she loves her work, she feels that she is at a crossroads in her career and must find a way to reenergize herself to continue. The recent birth of her own child after years of trying to conceive has contributed to the intensity of her feelings; she now personalizes each loss in the imagined loss of her own child. The illnesses and deaths she sees every day at work have sensitized her to be overprotective of her child, checking him at night to be sure he is still alive or worrying that he will die from a bee-sting. She has begun to wonder if she should see a therapist because of the irrational intensity of her fears.

I

Allison's first experience of a patient in her care dying was "a thirteen-year-old girl with cystic fibrosis. I was working nights. She never had anyone with her in the hospital and so we became good friends. She'd become psychotic from a combination of hypoxia and her family's inability to discuss dying. Every time she closed her eyes she saw people dying and babies bleeding. She ended up in the P I C U on heavy sedation and died of a heart attack. I still have the ice-cream scoop she left behind.

"Her death was hard. I felt really close to her. It was more than a professional relationship. I felt bad about the way she died. There was so much dysfunction in her family and they weren't there for her. I feel better about a death when it goes well.

"I talked a lot about her with my coworkers. I didn't go to the funeral because I was working. I had a dream about her a week after her death and it made me feel a lot better. In the dream I was working and couldn't find her and I was frantic. At the end of the day I opened a big conference room door. The room was all decked out like for a party. She was there with a hat on having a great time. I said, 'There you are!' She replied, 'I was having a good time and didn't want to take my meds.' At the time I thought that she'd given me the dream from the other side to tell me that she was okay.

"I still think about her a lot, usually in the context of not getting too involved with patients. If I got that involved with every patient that died I'd be a basket case! I need to feel that any nurse would be fine to care for my patients, not just me. If I get in the position of thinking that only I can do it then I know I'm too close.

"Since then, for the most part, I've been less emotionally involved. After that patient, I got a new job caring for adults in a hospice. During the two years I worked there I got very comfortable caring for dying patients. So when I went back to working with children I was more comfortable caring for the dying. I've not gotten that close since then, although I've gotten pretty close to some.

"I used to work at an outpatient oncology clinic. They'd close the office on the days of funerals and we'd have a cake to remember the patient. That really helped. I got a birthday book and started writing down the days they died. We put up pictures of them at the office. That was nice. Here we don't have that kind of small, close-knit group, but I've kept the birthday book and we try to talk with one another about the children who've died. Four times a year we have a 'Celebration of Life,' an open house at which we light a candle for each child. There's a memory book with one page for each child with his or her picture on it. People write what they remember about them."

The most difficult aspect of a child's death is "the lack of bereavement care for families. We should have someone trained in grief work who follows up with families. Most families don't need it, but some need it a lot. They come with no support network and so we become it. Then the child dies and we say 'good-bye.' Since we don't have a trained follow-up person we have a voluntary system for the nurses to do aftercare, but I don't feel comfortable with it. It blurs my boundaries. I don't have time for it at work and I know nothing about bereavement counseling. We had a patient's mother who killed herself on the child's birthday after her death. She was mentally ill and jumped off a freeway overpass."

It helps "to do something to remember them in the future, like writing in my book. When I do that I'm done. A year ago a friend and colleague commented that I seemed to be getting cynical about the outcomes of our patients so I counted the number of children in my book. There were one hundred and fifty! When I was a nursing student one of my mentors had a poster that read 'Expect A Miracle.' I bought a stamp with that saying on it, but I gave it away a couple of years ago. However, now that I've had a baby my feelings have changed. I'd do anything and put him through anything for the smallest percentage that he'd be cured."

II

Allison's father was a sales manager and her mother stayed at home with the children. After the children left home, her mother got a degree in counseling. "She was always interested in how people feel. She was very into PET [Parent Effectiveness Training] and taught workshops when I was little. She would deliver 'I feel' messages like 'When you do that I feel . . .'"

Her parents were American-born Caucasians who had "eclectic" religious beliefs, although both were raised as Christians. "My family celebrated Christmas and Easter, but otherwise we didn't attend church. I grew up in a Jewish community and attended Hebrew school during the fourth through the sixth grades. It didn't work out because I wasn't Jewish. Then I attended the Presbyterian Church in middle school and was pretty involved. I went to a Roman Catholic high school. Not surprisingly, I'm now a Unitarian!

"My mother's mother was a medium who communicated with the dead. I'm not sure my mother bought into it but some of it rubbed off. She believed in the 'white light' and put it around us in the car. It protects you from evil. We'd do a little prayer, 'Please spirits, protect us.' She had a belief in the spirit world and a karmic belief in reincarnation. I still do the white light with my baby at night. My own views of reincarnation are unclear. There are more people now than there used to be so how can there be enough souls to reincarnate? On the other hand I've met children with an 'old soul' quality.

"My grandmother had dementia and died four years ago. She got into a great nursing home and the family believed that her spirit guides were watching over her. I hope she's watching over us. She belonged to metaphysical groups in the twenties and thirties and after her death we found books and books of notes. My mother called them her 'spook groups.'

"When I was little I didn't know anyone who died. There was a neighbor who did, but we kids didn't attend the funeral. In high school my best friend's brother was killed, hit by a car while riding a bike. It was devastating. He was a great person and I felt that maybe he was too good to continue. It made me feel a lot more vulnerable. His family was overcome with grief and the community was devastated. There was a huge funeral.

"My family didn't talk much about death. You went to the spirit world, 'the other side' as my mother called it. There are nice things there, whatever you like. You get to see other people who've died, people you missed." As a young person Allison did not think much about what happens to people after they die. "Most of the people I work with had a lot of experience with death when they were younger, but I didn't. I believed that after death it was a pleasurable experience for the person who'd died and that everyone else was sad."

Her family modeled coping with death by "expressing your emotions honestly. Whatever you felt you should express. If you expressed your feelings you'd get over it." When her friend's brother died "it was very hard. I liked him a lot and was quite sad. I realized that I could lose my brother to whom I'm very close." She coped with the death by "being supportive of my friend, whom I love. Her brother was the only boy in a Cuban family, the star. It was a really big loss. For years afterward his room remained untouched. It was kind of spooky. I put most of my energy into trying to help her. I tried to get on with life. Her whole family spoke Spanish so I couldn't be as helpful as I wanted. Talking about it now I realize that I don't cope with my emotions about most of my patients who die. I don't cry. I just trudge on and get on to the next patient."

III

"In high school I had no idea of health care as a career. After two years of college in San Diego I lived on my own for two years in San Francisco, including a summer at Yosemite. I had two experiences with health care, one with a great nurse, one with a horrible nurse. The horrible one was in Yosemite, where I was hospitalized for an infection. She didn't bring me any food or a phone. I remember crying and crying and no one did anything. She didn't even tell my parents. The good one was a nurse practitioner I saw in San Francisco. I saw her for routine things and she was nice and helpful. I was working three jobs to pay the rent and decided I needed a better job and that to get one I needed to go back to school. I read a list of things that nurses do and I thought it looked good. I had a dream and when I woke up I knew I was going to Humboldt State. I just knew that was what I needed to do. I called and got an application even though I didn't know if they had a nursing school. It was the turning point in my life. Humboldt State was perfect! I'd never been there, but when I drove into town I felt like I'd come home.

"My first job was in a general pediatrics unit that was half hematology, half oncology. I liked it because of the oncology patients. You got to know the patients and the families well and it was intensive. Now I have a hard time coping with parents who are upset because their child has a cleft palate!

"I'm very satisfied with nursing and pretty satisfied with hematology-oncology. I'm not very satisfied with my present unit. I love being a nurse. It's hands-on, helping people to get through things like coping with bad procedures and teaching them about their bodies. I like the hours, seven A.M. to seven P.M., variable days, and two days on one week, three days the next. Without taking any days off I could have eight days off in a row! I also like the pay.

"Sometimes it's very hard from a demand perspective, running around with too much to do, but that's also one of the things I like about it. Today I woke up at three A.M. and couldn't get back to sleep because I was thinking about work. I was rehashing all that had happened and worrying about a patient's care. I have huge responsibilities at work. I don't like that. I sometimes feel like I have more knowledge than the residents or fellows. I sometimes feel like I need to say, 'Are you sure?' I feel that the patients need to be closely monitored by someone who really knows what they're doing. The attendings are so busy that the parents end up keeping track of what's happening to their children. In the last one to two years we've had lots of turnover and have new nurses working that aren't as competent as the ones we used to have. After the strike we had a lot of traveling nurses [nurses recruited by the hospital from other parts of the country to cover for the nurses on strike].

"My dream job would be to work in an adult short-stay unit with basically healthy adults. I'm getting burned-out with parents. It took me eight years to have a child. I had a hard time with pregnancy and have a hard time with parents who don't appreciate their children. I've less sympathy with parents who have entitlement issues—like free food and working the system. They're not working, have too many children, and their children are running wild on the floor. It's as if they're thinking, 'Now that I have a child with cancer I should get what I want.' I want a less-demanding job with less emotional baggage."

In nursing school "we weren't taught anything about dealing with patients' deaths. It would have been good to discuss it in some way, perhaps a 'taking care of yourself' course. The hospital culture isn't set up for self-care. It's built to work, work, and work. If I work thirteen hours straight I'm lucky to have a half-hour off for lunch!

"I wish that our managers were more empathic about how we feel when our patients die. I wish we'd been taught more about grieving and boundaries. It would be good if there were a way to get one-to-one support. I worked in a hospice for awhile. They encouraged self-care and it was the best job I've ever had. We had discussions about what to do to get over it when a person dies. You'd write them a letter or put a rose petal in a vase each time you thought of them. Here we do have Celebration of Life parties to recognize who the child was and to express your thoughts about the person, even negative ones. They're just with the staff nurses so you can be honest."

IV

She is "well prepared physically" to deal with the deaths of patients but "not as well prepared emotionally" as she'd like to be. "It's good that I have a feeling they're all right after they die. I have a belief in an afterlife. It would be harder if I didn't. I also don't get too involved with patients. When I do it's really hard and I don't ever get over their deaths. It's like a purgatory place. I'm going through it now with a three-year-old patient who died a year ago. I was very close to her. Her mother wasn't there much and I became almost like her parent. I can't get over it that she's dead. I think about her every day I'm at work. I wish she weren't dead. I miss her. I have another patient now that I'm close to. He's doing fine, but the other day I had this flash—'What if he dies?' It's my maternal side, when I become more than a nurse for the patient. That little girl lacked a real parent. I was setting limits on when she went to bed and making her food. She would hug me, touch my hair, and tell me that she loved me."

Her weakness is in dealing with dying patients. "I don't really deal with it. I may not let others openly deal with their feelings. My feelings get stuffed in. They're down there. Having a baby has made it hard. I don't want him to die! I hold him and think, 'I won't let you die!' Then I think, 'Why am I thinking that?' I've seen way too many dead babies. I go into his room at night to check if he's dead. It must come from my repressed feelings."

"I have fabulous coworkers. That's what keeps me coming to work. After you've been doing this for a while you can't talk with normal people anymore. Their work world seems so trivial to me. All they say is, 'I don't know how you can go to work every day.' My spouse is pretty good. I don't usually talk about work at home, but when something happens and I need his support he's really good about listening. He's been with me my whole career. Aside from him, my only support is from nursing friends. My mother's especially inept at listening about my job. She doesn't want to hear about it and she's a therapist! I think she doesn't want to know about sick children."

V

"I expect to die at any minute! I expect everyone I know to die at any minute. You never know what's going to happen. It's really hard for my baby and me. I should see a therapist. He's ten months old. One day we were outside, it was a beautiful day, and a bee was flying around. I thought, 'He'll get stung, have an anaphylactic reaction, and die!' I was panicked. 'I don't have any intubation equipment!' I often get that anxious, panicky feeling. I cherish him so much. He can't be replaced. We tried so long, eight years, before we got him."

Thoughts of her own and her child's mortality have "made me a more honest person in my relationships with others. I try to live my life like each day is my last. My husband knows I love him. When a coworker died last year it really affected me. [She died unexpectedly on a camping trip.] I was the last person to talk with her. The conversation wasn't as nice as I wish it'd been. She was calling in sick and I was busy. The rumor is that she died of an arrhythmia. I have atrial tachycardia. After she died it freaked me out, and I saw

a cardiologist about it. It could have been fixed with a catheteriza-
tion, but I figured I'd die during the procedure."

VI

"Part of a 'good death' is the preparation for it. The family has
accepted that the child is going to die. The child, if he's old enough,
has been able to talk about his death. It's important that the child
dies where he wants to die and that his pain is under control." She
mentioned the three-year-old girl she had been so close to who had
died. "She said, 'I'm going to die. I'll see Jordan [a former patient]
there.' In her play, her Barbie doll would go to heaven. We'd send
Barbie through the pneumatic tube system. We'd ask her where she
wanted to send her. She'd say 'to the lab,' because she always had
to have her blood drawn. One day she wanted to send her to heaven.
Later she asked where Barbie was. I said, 'She won't be coming back.
She's in heaven.'

"More children want to die in the hospital than I'd have imagined.
About half want to be at home and half want to be in the hospital.
Some parents don't want their child to die at home because then
they'll always be reminded of the death there."

A "bad death" is when "the symptoms aren't managed well and
there's a lot of pain or nausea. The parents aren't comfortable with
what's happening. Instead of accepting the death there's a breakdown in communication between the family and their caregivers."

Dying children understand more "than we give them credit for. I
think they know they're going to die long before anyone talks to them
about it. It's important to increase the parents' comfort with the
child's death. If they're comfortable that makes the child feel comfortable. If the parents freak out the child freaks out. Dying children want to be sure their parents are going to be all right.

"We nurses feel that we don't get to do enough to prepare dying
children for their deaths. The parents and the doctors don't want
you to talk about it. Most of our doctors want to keep treating the
children, hoping for a cure, when most of the nursing staff knows

they're going to die. It's harder for the doctors to say 'There's nothing more we can do and your child is going to die.'

"We try to help the parents to talk with their children. We teach them how to talk about death with them. It's very helpful when family members are open to talking but only about 10 percent are. There's a whole dynamic of the parents and the doctors pressing for a cure and not wanting to talk about death until the patient is actually dying and it's too late. Even when a child is in a hospice many parents aren't able to talk about the child's death."

She considers it a weakness when she doesn't "bring up death unless someone else has. I'm afraid the parents won't want to talk about it, that they're still hoping the patient will be cured. If the patient is a 'no code' I feel very comfortable talking about the child's death. If the child is a 'full code' it's harder." [A "full code" means "if the child stops breathing we'll intubate him and send him to the intensive care unit." Conversely, a "no code" means that if the child stops breathing he will not be intubated and will be allowed to die.]

"I believe it's up to the doctors to talk with the family about whether a child is a code or a no code. A lot of times it's the physician that's not ready. We have a patient with chronic leukemia who should have died many times over the past four years. He also has bad asthma. We've finally been able to have that child made a no code. We know he's going to die, but it has taken four years for everyone to get to the point that he's declared a no code."

When she talks with terminally ill children about their deaths "I ask them what they think it'll be like and let them talk about it. I take their lead. They usually have a clear idea about it. Older children like to talk about what will happen to other people in their lives, to do a will, and to plan their funeral. I don't have those conversations as much as I should. Some ask what will happen to them physically. 'Will it hurt? Will I stop breathing?' Depending on their age and what they're like we're usually pretty honest.

"Parents also want to know what the child's death will be like. They're afraid the child will have a lot of symptoms, especially if the child is at home, and they won't have us to help them. They want to know the stages of dying and what to do about them." She described the stages of death as "first the child doesn't want to eat or drink much, they stop peeing as much, and there are changes in their breathing and an increase in their pain and nausea. Then they develop air hunger, go into a coma, and two days after that they're dead."

She is pleased when the parents of terminally ill children ask her questions about the child's impending death. "It opens a door that's scary to open because you don't want to offend them. I know they're getting themselves prepared and the patient will have a good death. Some parents believe in a miracle until the child's last breath."

VII

Her nursing colleagues "help the families through the process and support each other, but they also overstep their boundaries, get too involved with the families, and don't take care of themselves. That leads to burnout, and you can't do the job anymore. That's probably the reason so many people have left." She defines "too close" as "spending time with families when you're not working, giving them your home number in case they need support, and spending your personal time here in the hospital with them. It takes away the family's ability to form their own support network.

"We all anticipate that there will be a time in the future when we can't do this work anymore. All of this grief builds up. It's hard to be as intimately involved with people as we are and then never to see them again. There's a little black space that gets bigger and bigger until you stop doing this job. If it gets to the point that my grief interferes with my ability to relate to patients in the way I want to then I can't work here anymore. For me, it's almost the same with the children who are doing well as with those that die. You have this intense relationship for a year and then they disappear and you don't know how they're doing.

"I've been doing this work for twelve years and I'm at a crossroads. Do I want to keep doing it? I need to be reenergized to keep going. In our job we have an overwhelming responsibility to cure these children or keep them alive. On top of that is the grief you feel about the children you've lost. There's not much discussion about it. There never seems to be an appropriate time to stop the cheerleading. It's too scary to talk about it in a group. You don't want everyone to know how you're feeling. It's better to talk one-to-one."

14

"Being faced daily with the fact that life is temporary and unpredictable seriously affects the way I live."

Kirsten wants to be in control of her emotions and is more likely to write down what she feels than to talk about it with someone else. The feelings aroused in her by the deaths of children can be overwhelming, especially now that she has children of her own and can put herself in the shoes of the parents whose children are dying. Early in her career she felt she was too closely identified with dying children and their parents and had difficulty dealing with her feelings about them. With experience, she has pulled back and now wonders if she has gone too far. She continues to think about where to set the emotional boundary between herself and her patients and their families. It is important to let families know that you care, but becoming so emotionally involved that you are no longer objective and helpful is too close. Her strong religious faith supports her in her work because she believes that dying children will be reunited with their families and will never be alone. She wonders how people without a strong religious faith can work in her field.

I

Kirsten's first experience of coping with the death of a child patient was with "a little girl about two years old who had leukemia. I didn't have children at the time. Coping before and after I had children was very different. She was in the hospital a long time and I cared for her, but she died at home. Her family lived far away, and I didn't attend the funeral. She was the first child I was connected to that died. It was hard and I was sad. The day I found out about her death I was at work, and I learned that I could be sad and still have the composure to do my job. It was easier that she died at home and I didn't have to attend the funeral. I remember being really sad for a while."

She dealt with that first child's death by "talking with my husband and continuing to work. I don't like to be out of control. If I have to be sad it won't be in front of my coworkers and family. With my husband it's okay because I don't have to put on appearances. That first experience taught me that I could cope with a child's death. Before it happens you don't know how you'll feel or how it will affect you. I thought I handled it all right. It wasn't devastating. I had a feeling of relief that I'd be able to cope with that aspect of the job.

"I have a firm belief in a just God. People come to earth to learn things they couldn't learn in any other way. Everything happens for a reason, but some events test my belief. My strongest emotional reactions are around those events when something out of the ordinary happens. We had a little boy in the hospital who was inadvertently given an overdose of medicine and arrested. He went to the PICU, had some neurological sequelae, and later died of his original disease. It didn't happen on my watch, I wasn't there, but he was my patient. I knew how the nurse that made the mistake felt and I knew how the family felt. Here we are, care providers trying to do our best and the families trust us. I was really angry about it. I wondered 'What was God thinking?' Some things you can understand, but there was no understanding that. Experiences like that trigger emotional reactions. A little girl was cured of her cancer and then died of croup in her mother's car. I felt sadness and anger. Why would she beat cancer and then die out of the blue? Another child I cared for had been cured of his leukemia after three hard years of treatment and then was killed on an ATV. Those kinds of deaths are the hardest. They make less sense to me. Other types of illnesses and deaths I can make sense of. It's the issues of unexpectedness and unfairness that make them difficult. They seem to be the cruelest and they provoke anger and sadness. I'm angry at the situation and the crueler it is the angrier I am. Maybe I'm a little angry at God or at the understanding I don't have.

"Other deaths that bother me are the ones when the children die of the treatment and not the disease. We use dangerous drugs and have to be aggressive. 'Do no harm' is our underlying principle, but we couldn't help as many children if we weren't aggressive. Yet it still bothers me.

"I remember a four-year-old with leukemia, a very bright, cheerful child with a terrible social situation. His parents dropped him off like the laundry. The nurses parented him. He went on to finish his therapy. I saw him again when he was eleven or twelve and he'd become a sexual offender. It made me so upset. I grieved for the life he should have had. He was in our system for three or four years and we didn't know to do anything about it. I had a grief reaction for someone that didn't die. I also had a lot of anger. I was angry with everybody that had failed him. Someone was hurting him all those years and we didn't know or didn't stop it soon enough. Now he was preying on younger children."

She copes with her feelings of sadness and anger "by dealing with them and trying to move on. After a certain period of time they seem to be gone, but at times you find they're stored up somewhere. I've been to funerals where it's hard to maintain composure. I think it's because of the cumulative grief. There was a Christmas tree festival back home where people would donate a tree to auction for charity. The families of children that had died often donated a memorial tree with pictures, a theme of something the child adored and the child's story. The first couple of years I went to it and read the children's stories. Eventually it got to be very sad and I couldn't go with other people. I learned to go alone and read all the stories at my own pace. It was very sad but also therapeutic."

Coming back to work after she had children, "I'd sit in when the doctors told parents that their children had cancer and couldn't help thinking of myself in their shoes. I'd need to cry after that. I got choked up and I had to work on that. In some circumstances, it's fine to cry but not when the parents are being told the diagnosis. There's a fine line between being sad and crying with someone and being so sad that you can't talk. That's not all right with me. Also there's my own personal control issue. I'm not comfortable being sad around other people. A little bit sad is fine, but sobbing isn't. I don't know too many professional people that are very emotional around others. The line of self-control is a little different for everybody. If I'm really sad I don't want to be around anyone.

"After I had children I distanced myself more. If you're too empathic it's like you're crying for your own child. Moving here also made things different. The philosophy where I trained was that children should die at home if it was feasible. Most parents seemed to agree. I never saw a child actively die. I didn't visit the body afterward. The children I was closest to died at home and I generally sent the families a note afterward. Here the milieu is different. More children die in the hospital. I seem to have an avoidance behavior that I've really had to fight. It's difficult to visit a dying child in a hospital room, and I have some anxiety surrounding those visits that I don't understand yet. I do visit when I know my presence is important for the family, but it's too hard on me emotionally.

"In our field we can be helpful whether a child lives or dies. We can make the road easier, but it's still very hard. We need to continue educating ourselves about how to make death easier for the family. I don't feel sad so much for the child as for the family. They have a long, devastating road ahead of them. It's different for every family."

The most difficult aspect of a child's death is "the unknown for my family. We all die. I don't know if my children will die when they're young or old. I worry about it a lot." Through her tears she continued, "I worry about it all the time. Accidents are more likely than illness. I think that being faced daily with the fact that life is temporary and unpredictable seriously affects the way I live. I generally don't sweat the small stuff and I know to be grateful each day for life's smallest blessings. I'm also very invested in security and freedom. Most of the big decisions in my life are a reflection of that."

II

Kirsten grew up as a member of the Church of Latter Day Saints. Her Mormon background was "the core of who you are, how you live, and how your family is. It was central, especially if you lived in Utah. I'm not as devout as my parents are, but I still practice. The town where I grew up was pretty diverse. I didn't feel different from the children who weren't Mormons, but I think they felt different from us. Mormon social life frequently revolves around church activities, but mine didn't."

Death was discussed "pretty openly, but I didn't have much experience with it. The closest death was that of a cousin when I was about ten years old. He was on a church mission in Florida and was hit by a car while riding a bike. It was a pretty big event in my life, the first time I was confronted by the fact that things aren't permanent. If that could happen to him and his family, then nothing was permanent for me either. I had a lot of fears about what could happen to my family, but I didn't worry much about myself."

She coped with his death "by thinking about it a lot and writing in my journal. I liked to write in there. It was very helpful. I was a pretty introverted child and was more likely to write things down than to tell other people.

"Overall I've been pretty lucky. Many people have to deal with a lot of tragedy growing up, but I didn't. There was a family up the street whose parents died in a plane crash when I was twelve or thirteen. I babysat for their children. The children were three and five and I remember them wailing at the funeral. I felt sorry for them, for the unknown of how their lives would play out and what would happen to them." Those deaths, however, were less significant for her than the death of her cousin. "I don't remember writing about them specifically. My mom went to the funeral with me. It wasn't devastating.

"My parents were honest about death and allowed us to talk about it and to tell them how we felt. They'd say that they were sad and talk about their memories of the person but wouldn't cry in front of us. I was taught that although separation is hard you live again after death. If you follow your religion you'll be with the person again. After death the spirit separates from the body, the body is buried, and the spirit goes back to God. There are degrees of heaven, and depending on what kind of life you live here on earth you achieve one of those degrees. Cremation was discouraged because the body and the spirit come together again. There's a Heaven and a Hell. They didn't talk much about how you got into Hell. All the people we knew were good people."

III

She chose nursing "because in two years you could get an associate's degree and make pretty good money. My dad wanted me to do it and my mom was a nurse, so I figured 'Why not?' Then I could make enough money to finish school in the field of my choice. The funny thing is that I ended up really loving it. You can do anything with a nursing degree. I worked at a children's hospital on the medical-surgical unit for two years. The care was integrated and I got training in hematology-oncology. My relationship with the patients there was more long-term. I saw the children for a year or more. I liked getting to know them and their families and having them get to know me. You felt like you were taking good care of someone. Then I transferred to the hematology-oncology clinic for seven years and moved up the ranks. I did a BS in the meantime and went to nurse practitioner school."

She is very satisfied with her choice of profession. "Emotionally it's very positive. You learn from people in crisis, about how to rise up. It's pretty amazing what people can do when they're hit with hard times and what the people surrounding them do, their communities, schools, and families."

She had to think awhile to come up with negatives about her field. "The information overload, the intensity, the pressure, my inability to keep up, and feeling inadequate. Also anxiety at having little peoples' lives in your hands."

In the future she sees herself "continuing on, developing an expertise in certain areas or projects such as program development. I have three young children so I don't see myself trying to rise up the administrative ladder. I want to have a balance in my life. I have a tendency to get compulsive, with tunnel vision. I'm competitive and too intense in some areas and I have to be careful."

She does not remember receiving any training in nursing school about how to deal with the deaths of patients. "I don't recall any discussion of death. No one that I cared for died. We did talk about how to care for yourself as a nurse so that you could better care for your patients. They taught us to care for ourselves holistically. If you're in a good place, balanced and emotionally healthy, then you're in a better place to help others. We were taught to be aware of our spiritual, emotional, physical, psychological, and social lives. If you could address those things in yourself you'd be better able to see problems in others and help them. We were taught in lectures and in discussion groups. Holistic care went throughout the curriculum."

On reflection she is not sure whether you can really teach a person how to cope with the deaths of patients. "You can give people a few tools and places to start. It's very personal and everyone does it differently. You can't really deal with it until it hits you head-on.

"I learned the most through others' modeling. Objectivity is the biggest thing. If you lose it you're not able to be helpful. That place may be different for everyone. You have to make sure that you remain helpful, not dealing with your own issues before those of the patient. You can overdo it, too, building a wall, being too far back, indifferent, and disconnected."

IV

"I'm very prepared to deal with patients' deaths in terms of maintaining my emotional health. However, at times I get anxious, utilize avoidance behavior, and distance myself emotionally. Balance is the key. You can't survive in this job if every death feels like a close friend or family member. It also takes a lot of courage to walk into a crisis situation and feel like you have the knowledge and ability to help someone. My personality is introverted and I'm not able to strike up a conversation easily. In a tough situation I'm prone to just being quiet.

"My family keeps me centered. They care. There was one child I was close to that died and the social worker called me at home. The child was a fraternal twin like my daughters. I was holding one of them, rocking her. I was able to just cry and rock my baby." Tearfully, she continued, "When terrible things happen in the hospital the place you want to be is at home with your children."

It makes it harder to cope "when the situation is too close to home. My colleagues can be very helpful with that. They know that different people are affected differently. It's absolutely fine to say, 'I can't do this now.' I used to have to hold the children down for bone marrow tests. If they reminded me of my own children my colleagues would let me out of doing it. The ultimate thing is the relationship you have with your colleagues. The closer you feel the more you can help each other."

Her husband "listens but doesn't say much. He doesn't know what to say. He hears but doesn't respond much. He doesn't tell me how to feel or how to act. He doesn't try to direct my feelings or thoughts. He listens to be supportive of me, but what I'm telling him isn't important to him. It's a duty. He cares about me but doesn't want to really get into it and have a philosophical discussion."

V

"I'm not afraid of death. I'm more afraid of someone close to me dying. The grief of living without someone you love is something to be afraid of. Life is temporary. Life after death is important to me. I think that you do live again and can be together again." She thinks of the mortality of her family members "very often, daily. Sometimes I think about it in an anxious, fearful way. It's motivating in a way and very grounding, a daily reminder of your priorities and the things you should be grateful for. And sometimes the fear is subdued and it's okay to just take life as it comes. The unpredictability of life motivates me to be as secure as possible. I have three beautiful girls. Even though I have a fabulous, loyal, providing husband I went back to graduate school mainly for the security and independence.

"No one knows how long they'll live or if they'll be able to raise their children. Hopefully that affects the decisions you make, teaches you to make the most of every day, and to spend time with your children now rather than later. If you died today would everything you'd done in the last month seem important or a waste of time?"

VI

A "good death" is "one that's planned. You have the time to work through the issues. If you anticipate the death you can plan for it. Some people, even with time, don't go through the steps. They can't come to acceptance. Others can. They seem to have a better experience around their child's death than those that are stuck do. The child's involvement is important. Often there are certain things they want to do or say or organize before they die or before they begin actively dying and feeling bad. There are issues around their personal belongings, stories or messages they want to write, and important mementoes for certain people. They like to have input about where they are. Most want to be at home. Different centers do it differently. Where I used to work they often utilized home health from the beginning of treatment, so there was already a relationship and an easy transition to end-of-life home care. Here more care is completed in the clinic so sometimes the transition is a barrier. Some families are uncomfortable having their child at home or want the child to be in the hospital because of pain-control issues.

"Having a frank discussion about death with the family is very important. Even little children want to know if they'll be alone and what they'll experience. That's especially true when the parents are separated. The children worry a lot about them and how they'll cope after their death."

A "bad death" is one in which "the family isn't ready or at peace.

They're not in a place where they could cope or accept or start working through the process. They're too involved with their anger at the medical team, at another family member, or at God, or they're in denial. Fear is another obstacle—fear of their inability to cope. Can they live without their loved one?"

Children "know more than we do about when death is coming. They know, even very young children." Hospice care would help terminally ill children to cope with their deaths. "It's not well received here compared to where I was. Hospices here have no role until the very end. It's hard to form new relationships at the end of life. It's better if the hospice or home health-care is integrated into the child's treatment early on. As a caregiver you can't bring up death until you've talked with the family. You have to find out what their beliefs are so that you don't contradict what they're telling the child. It's very hard and time-consuming.

"People with the expertise to help children cope with their deaths come from different disciplines. Where I was, the social workers were heavily involved. Here it's the nurses. We haven't been formally trained to do it. Having a relationship with the child and the family from the beginning is the key, and putting forth the extra effort as the goal changes from cure to coping with death."

If a terminally ill child asks her about death, she would "talk to the parents first, because I don't want to contradict their beliefs. If the child wants to know what I think about death I tell him. I say 'You'll never be alone and you'll always be with someone that loves you.' Otherwise, I'd probably be more of a listener and answer their questions. Parents often talk about what their children say to them and what their wishes are. The things children most commonly say to me about death are matter-of-fact statements like 'I'll see Jesus' or 'I'll go to heaven.'

"Most parents want to know when and how their child will die. Some want to know what will happen. Others don't. Some want to know how they'll know their child is dead. My idea of a good death is when the parents are able to hold the child. Some mothers have said they're afraid of not being there at the moment the child dies.

They sleep with them and don't want to leave them alone. 'How will I know when it's close, when I can't even leave them for a minute?' They often want our input about when it's time. They sometimes feel conflicted between releasing the child from his pain and wanting to have the child with them as long as they can. They want to do the right thing, but they're not sure what's right." The parents' questions "affect you more later, when you have time to think about them. While things are going on you know they need your help and you need to keep it together. Later on you feel sad and think about what it might feel like to have your heart breaking like theirs are."

VII

"People who've been in this specialty a while learn a lot and become pretty polished. When you first start it's tough. It's very hard to get the mix of empathy and objectivity right. I've been in the place of being too close and now I've backed up to where I'm not close enough." Some of her colleagues "cross the line and become too enmeshed in the families' lives, almost a surrogate family member. The families love it and would probably prefer it. When someone does that it makes it tougher on the rest of us. Families feel that should be the standard of care. There's probably not one definition of crossing the line. It's a matter of interpretation."

Some of her colleagues cope well with the deaths of patients and others do not. To cope well means having "an innate sense of what the family is and what they need. They're on such a roller coaster and their needs change. Some staff know that and some don't. The ones who don't do it well are very concrete and factual. They tell you that you should feel this or that. You need to be sensitive to what the person is actually feeling, not what you think they should be feeling. The good ones are sensitive to where the parents are. It's not something you can teach. You shouldn't be too distant or too close. There has to be a balance. Some of it you have and some of it you learn from experience. The families teach you as you go."

Her colleagues' biggest weakness is "avoidance. Nobody knows what to say all the time. We all say things we shouldn't say. I believe people are avoidant because of their discomfort. Do you want to delve into something when you're not comfortable with it? What if you get involved and don't know what to do or say? If you get involved and don't have a good relationship with the family, that can be negative, too. It's difficult to go somewhere when you're not prepared or aren't welcome."

15

"There's nothing right about a dead baby."

Caroline, a forty-year-old nurse in the P I C U, is a deeply spiritual person who is secure in her belief in God and an afterlife. As much as her beliefs comfort her, however, the pain of some children's deaths can be overwhelming emotionally, especially if that patient has touched her heart. The focus of her caregiving efforts is on keeping dying children safe and comfortable, answering their questions, and doing what she can to help their parents through this darkest time in their lives. In giving others excellent and gentle care, she replicates her own experience of being cared for as a frightened young woman with appendicitis who was away from home for the first time and without the support of family and friends. She wishes that her colleagues were more supportive and comfortable in talking about their feelings when children die. She would also like her husband and friends to be able to listen to the stories she needs to tell, but she usually finds they cannot bear to hear them. No one wants to hear about dying and abused children.

I

Caroline first experienced the death of a child patient when she was working as a home I V therapy nurse. "The baby had a chromosomal anomaly and not much of a life. He was just living at home. I didn't expect to feel any great sadness, but that was the first time it struck me that there's nothing right about a dead baby. Despite the child's handicaps his family had loved and cherished him.

"That experience taught me that a child's death will never be like the death of an adult. It will always be heart-wrenching. You can prepare yourself, but there will always be something about a child's death that touches your heart. We just had a baby born with a huge congenital anomaly, intraventricular hemorrhaging, and kidney and liver failure. It was a very little baby and everything was wrong. It coded five times in twenty-four hours and I knew things wouldn't end well. After all those codes the child would have had no quality of life and I didn't expect to feel any sorrow when he died. He was on the hi-fi [high frequency oscillator] and couldn't be held. We made the decision to take him off and put him in his mother's arms. She'd never held him and this was her only chance to hold him alive. I saw her later and she looked very young. She was asleep in the chair holding the dying baby. That was too sad.

"After a death like that, if I'm working with a person who feels like I do I might talk about it a bit. That night there was such a person. We talked and started to get teary so I stopped and wrote down numbers for a while. After a death in the PICU there are always a lot of things to write down. It's something I can do without concentrating hard and I can let my mind go where it needs to go, to acknowledge how sad it is, to repeat my mantra of helping people through their darkest hour, or to say a prayer to help the family. I realize that I'll not be able to do this job for years."

The cumulative sadness of all the deaths she has witnessed "changes the things that rile me up. When the mothers in my children's elementary school get all worked up over the theme of the class party they look preposterous to me. The sadness also changes me politically. The last few nights I've been caring for a horribly abused child. She had lacerations on her spleen, liver, and kidneys. I thought to myself, 'This baby can't pull herself up by her bootstraps. We as a society have a responsibility to her. As a society we'll be judged by how we care for her.' I also wouldn't be hesitant to write down something in her chart that might get me called into court. If someone was able to beat that child so savagely . . . there was so much blood in her belly that we didn't know if she'd be able to breathe. She may survive this beating but not the next.

"Over the years I've raised the bar on what gets to me and what makes me sad, but there are still some things that make me sad when I don't expect they will. There will be a small detail that gets to me. Generally, however, when I'm caring for children with chronic illnesses that have no quality of life I often feel they deserve to rest. The other day we had a child that had been in a car accident. He wasn't brain-dead, but he was in a permanent vegetative state. The family made the decision to withdraw life support and I felt that was the right decision. That death didn't take me a few days to shake out of my head."

Professionally, the most difficult aspect of a child's death is "if it was something we could have caught earlier. I always ask myself if there was something different we could have done. I try to learn something and to make changes so I can be more cautious. Once when I worked in the E R we had a baby with R S V [respiratory syncytial virus]. She looked all right, more like she hadn't eaten for awhile. We got an X-ray, and then just after I'd placed the pulse oximeter on her finger she coded on a mucous plug. We were able to resuscitate her, but as a result I became more aggressive treating babies in the E R. I used suction more aggressively and I put them all on cardiac monitors.

"Personally, the hardest deaths are those that are unexpected. Or the children are too similar to my own children. One of my children had mycoplasma pneumonia. He did fine, but shortly afterward we had a child in the P I C U with the same condition. It went to his brain and he had a demyelinating encephalitis. Those 'there but for the grace of God go I' experiences, the things that could happen to anybody, really get to me."

II

Caroline grew up in a family of four and has a brother who is two years older than she. Her father was an immigration lawyer and her mother helped him run his practice. The family was Roman Catholic. "We shared my father's German heritage in that we never missed a day of school and never gave in to illness. My mother, as an Irish

Catholic, was an expert on guilt—and she had a temper. My father was very kind, a quiet, unemotional man. He never raised his voice and never said no. He'd say, 'As you wish. You know where my wallet is.' I had so much guilt in me that I never took advantage of him. The only time he'd say no was when he was concerned my safety might be in question."

Her family was "pretty open about death. My mother came from a big family. They'd have a wake with the body in the living room overnight. My father was the middle of seven children. His mother died when he was seven and his aunt came to live with him. She did it out of duty, not out of love, and it was like the love was gone from his life. He was a World War II veteran and had been there at D-Day. He rarely spoke of it and when he did he'd get all choked up.

"My parents believed in heaven. After Vatican II, my father stopped going to church and wasn't outwardly religious. My mother believed in purgatory and heaven. She talked a lot about purgatory and said that was where she was going. She was pretty feisty and a bit of a martyr and thought she'd have to earn going to heaven.

"The first significant death I experienced was that of my maternal grandmother. I was the ninth of ten grandchildren and there was a big age range. The older ones did sixties things like living with people and doing drugs, things that horrified my grandmother, while I was president of the church youth group. I was her favorite grandchild and got her wedding ring and nursing school pin. Two days after she moved out to California to be near us she dropped dead. It was a huge moment in my life and very hard on my mother.

"The night she died I went outside, looked up at the sky, and had this feeling like I was hearing God's voice, and it said, 'It's all right. She's here with me.' I still feel my grandmother's presence and from that moment I've never doubted the existence of God. It was a very strengthening moment before a hard time.

"Right after her death my mother went away on a planned trip. When she came back she said to my brother and me, 'I hate you. I don't give a shit about you! I want you the hell out of my life!' She'd probably had a nervous breakdown. I went and stayed with another family for a couple of days. When I went home she continued to function as our mother, but she stopped saying every day that she loved us. I was fifteen at the time and I remember calling a friend six weeks after my mother had come home and saying to her, 'My mother said she loved me!' That meant the episode was over and things were back to normal. She never spoke to me that way again.

"My mother was a woman who functioned on the edge of panic most of her life and she just went over the edge. At the time I felt rejected by her. After my grandmother died she said, 'I don't have a family anymore.' That hurt my feelings. I told my dad and he said, 'She needs to knock that off. We're her family now.'

In addition to the death of her grandmother, Caroline experienced the deaths of her father's father and two of his brothers. "My father's father died when I was six or seven. He went back to the funeral with my brother and wasn't especially emotional. However when his younger brother died I remember saying to him, 'Daddy, why do you look so sad?' He said, 'It's not every day that you lose your brother.' When I was fifteen his older brother died and I flew back with him. It was an open casket funeral and I remember my uncle's young children standing by his body the whole day. I remember thinking, 'That's not for me! Why is everyone emphasizing death and not the hereafter?'"

III

"Being a nurse was something I wanted from junior high school. Sometimes I look back and think, 'I was a very good student. Should I have done more than this?' When I was a freshman in college I got appendicitis just before Thanksgiving. I was away from home and it was the end of the fall quarter so my friends were gone, too. I went to the emergency room at four A.M. and had sixteen hours of tests before having surgery at midnight. I was a very innocent young woman and it was my first gynecologic exam and barium enema. That was a lot for an eighteen-year-old girl to handle by herself. The doctors walked in and out and ordered things, but it was the nurses who helped me through it. I volunteered at the university hospital all four years of college to be sure that nursing was what I wanted to do.

"My first job in nursing was doing home I V therapy for both adults and children. Then I was a hospice nurse for four years. Those experiences helped me to read a family's culture and figure out how I should fit in. For example the Vietnamese don't want people to die in the house, and Hispanic families have a number of religious needs at the end of life. I also found that I preferred working with children. When I moved here I worked on the pediatric ward, but when there weren't enough child patients we cared for adults. There were always too many adult patients and I didn't like it. I also oriented to the N I C U and worked there for a year. I liked it a lot, but the work was too predictable and routine. Care was performed almost by the clock and the patients were generally more stable than in the P I C U. Then I oriented to the emergency room and I loved that! I gradually shifted over to the E R. It helped that I spoke Spanish. I decided to move to the P I C U for several reasons. First, I was tired of people swearing at me. Second, a drunk driver killed our paramedic. She was brought to our E R. None of us recognized her until after we'd cared for her. That must be some basic protective mechanism we have. She had four young children. It's very hard to watch a parent with children die. That was the worst night of my career. I also had to draw blood on the drunk driver and after that I kept getting subpoenaed. After her death I spoke at her funeral. The third reason was that after the nurses' strike the hospital retaliated by demoting all the charge nurses. My third night back they were going to put an agency nurse in charge instead of me because they thought I'd retaliate. I'd had a lot of contact with the P I C U and after that I asked them how they were doing after the strike. They said they were doing fine because their administration didn't retaliate. I sent an email and asked if there were any positions and they wrote right back and said 'Yes!'"

Caroline is satisfied with her profession "for now. I don't know many people that can work two days per week and make the money and benefits I do and also make a difference. The ER was staffed with people like me that have a dark sense of humor. The PICU isn't funny. I was on a PICU retreat a year and a half ago and our facilitator said, 'Wow, this isn't a touchy, feely group!' It was weeks and weeks after I started working there before people said hello. I worked last Christmas and it was a very sad night. After the death of a baby, one of the nurses I really like said to me, 'Merry Fucking Christmas!' That was her way to distance herself. There's no happy reason to be in the PICU."

The best part of working there is that "you help people through the darkest hours of their lives. One family said to me, 'When you come I know I can go to eat and go to sleep.' I tell the children I won't surprise them and that there won't be any needles they don't expect. Parents compliment me on my gentle manner with their children. My ability to speak Spanish makes a big difference with Spanish-speaking families who often have had no explanation of the child's illness. The PICU is also very challenging intellectually. I'm learning more about the heart than I ever knew before. There's a high level of expectation about what you'll know, and if you're chosen to learn about the heart that's a big compliment."

The worst part of her work is "watching children suffer and die. There's a sound parents make when they've just received the news that the child will die or that its brain is gone. It's a cry from the depth of their souls. It takes me three days to get it out of my mind. We're all one day from being one of those families. If one of my children gets a headache he gets an MRI, an MRA, and an EEG!"

In the future she hopes to become involved in management. "The job I've been waiting for just appeared, but I don't want to work full-time yet. I'm really enjoying the cardiac training and the idea of being part of a pediatric heart-transplant team is exciting. There are a lot of opportunities in my future right where I am. When my youngest son goes to college I'd like to work full-time in management." Her interest in eventually switching from clinical care to administration is related to "learning that I get terrific satisfaction

out of getting people to work together and achieve rather than feeling disempowered and griping. I'm good on my feet at politics and
can be in difficult situations without offending people."

She does not remember receiving any training in nursing school
about how to cope with the deaths of patients. "You meet a lot of
people who say, 'I can't take care of children, it's too sad.' At the
beginning of nursing school everyone wanted to be a pediatric nurse,
but at the end I was the only one. In nursing school they did talk
about debriefing after patients' deaths. You're also encouraged not
to get too personally involved with a patient. I don't recall being told
specifically how to take care of yourself. I do remember a very
unpleasant adult death. A woman was in a crowded, three-patient
room with just curtains between the beds. It had probably been a
two-patient room. She died during the night and lay there dead for
hours with people on the other side of the curtains. I'm sure they
peeked in. She died of breast cancer and had trouble breathing and
when she died she was in a position of struggling for air. I was really
upset by the lack of respect shown for the dead woman and her family and for the other patients and their families. Then we took her
down to the morgue on a patient elevator! It all seemed so wrong
to me, but I don't remember my nursing professor asking, 'Do you
need to talk about it?'

"There was a cover on the *American Journal of Nursing* that said,
'Do we eat our young?' Nurses still aren't as good to each other as
we should be and could be. There's a lack of empowerment in nursing. I remember a situation in my last job in which one of the nurses
had a baby and brought it in with her on the night shift to give to a
day-shift nurse who was going to take it home and care for it while
the mother worked. The next morning the day-shift nurse brought
the baby back to its mother. One of the managers saw it and said,
'I hope that baby hasn't been here in the hospital all night!' The
baby's mother was offended that the manager would think and say
that, but instead of saying anything to her she wrote a letter and had
someone else read it aloud at staff meeting while she sat there and

cried. I thought, 'Why can't she read it herself?' Nurses are too apt to take things very personally and then not confront situations directly. There's a nurse on our unit who is quitting because she believes she always gets the lowest-acuity patients, but she's never said anything about it and has never volunteered to care for someone she wanted to care for.

"There's also a culture among the nurses in the PICU that they know what they're doing and everyone else is an idiot. They refer to the NICU as 'the nursery.' That's offensive! It just shows that it's not good for nurses to stay in one job too long. It's helped me to move around so that I don't think other people doing different jobs are idiots."

IV

"I've seen a lot of children die and I'm a person of faith and that helps me. Every human being is spiritual, and you need to support that spiritual side. If parents say, 'I don't know what's going to happen after she dies' I'll say, 'I like how peaceful she looks. I like it that she isn't gasping for air.' Once when I was working in the ER a woman came in who had a spontaneous miscarriage and passed a fetus. Two of the nurses asked me to come and see the baby. They wanted a person of faith to see it because it seemed too cold to just put it in a jar and send it to the lab. They needed someone who'd think it was the loss of a life.

"It helps to know that a child is at peace and that they'll all go to a better place. If I see a family with faith I hope they'll find peace and will be better able to support one another. I ask God to work through me. That takes the pressure off when you're helping someone through her darkest hour. I used to think that I had to say something brilliant, but now I realize that it's being there, being present that helps.

"I remember a teacher in nursing school saying that every nurse carries five patients in her heart. There are children that really touch you. I once had a patient that couldn't stand me. I like that because you know the child has a brain and is reacting appropriately. He'd never even looked at me until one night when I was putting in a central line and he reached out, put his hand on my face, and looked in my eyes. I've never forgotten him. There's a patient with Down syndrome that I'm caring for now. His family has eight other children and they love him. If he were to die it would be very hard for me. I often think about him when I go home. He does whatever he can to vex me. He works and works until he gets the pulse oximeter off his toe. Or he keeps moving his arm so that it takes half an hour to get his blood pressure. Then he looks you in the eye. I love that baby! I often think, 'You've got to get off of that ventilator soon so your parents can hold you and so I can hold you, too!'"

After a hard death it takes "a few days to get it out of my head. I find myself telling my children, 'I can't handle you guys fighting in the car and then having to go off and watch a baby die.' One day I came out of the hospital and saw their three beautiful faces at the door waiting for me and I cried and hugged them all. That shook them up and so I try not to do it anymore. Then a two-year-old drowned in my neighborhood and I remember thinking, 'I can't have this at work and in my neighborhood, too!' People who let their children ride ATVs really upset me. Those things flip over and kill children! And then there are the people that speed through suburbs. What's so important that you'd risk the life of a child?

"Time helps me to cope with children's deaths. I work two days a week and have four days off before I have to go back. I get to return to a normal life more often than the others do. After four days off there may be a whole new group of patients on the unit. It also helps to be a person of faith and to have an intact family that keeps me busy. I have friends at work that I can talk with, especially friends from the E R who still come over.

"I'm very protective of my patients. I especially don't like the way we do organ donations here. [For example, if] the child has been shaken [so violently that it] is brain-dead but still has to have intensive treatment until the organ donation team can find a recipient.

They sit at the front desk only fifteen feet away from the patient's room calling all around the country through the night. The family and the nurses can hear their spiel twenty-five times; 'Do you want these corneas or this heart and lung?' There's all this shoptalk going on with the family listening. Plus you're hearing the story of how the child died over and over again.

Her coping efforts are made more difficult "if things hit home, if a child is killed by a drunken driver, or if the child wasn't wearing a seatbelt. I hurt for those children. If they survive how will they feel that their parents didn't take a basic safety measure like fastening their seatbelt to protect them?

"I'm trying to decide if coping is something you can be taught. I'm sure there are studies showing that people who participate in debriefings stay in nursing longer. Nurses need help to learn that you're going to have all these feelings about your patients and your work and that it's all right to talk about them. The experiences you have as a nurse change you. You need to know about that and be prepared to think about it. I was brought up in a right-wing Republican family and then watched all these young men die alone with AIDS because their families had rejected them.

"Last Christmas night when the baby I told you about died there were two new graduate nurses working. The death hit them very hard and they had to go off together and cry. I don't know what would prepare you for the death of a baby. You can find a lot of peace in an adult's death if it goes their way, if they're comfortable, and the family is at peace. With a child's death, even if all those things are true I always say in my head, 'There's nothing right about a dead baby.'

She and her colleagues "talk to each other briefly [after a child dies]. No one has ever called me at home to ask how I'm doing. Our unit is the most dog-loving place I've ever worked! Staff members will bring their dogs into the PICU to show to others and there are lots of pictures of dogs in the break room. People frequently ask how my dog is; they ask that more often than they ask about my children! The PICU also has the best food in the hospital because the staff is always bringing things in."

I wondered out loud with Caroline if the PICU staff are more comfortable showing their feelings indirectly through pets and food than by talking about them. "We don't seem to want to bring up our feelings at work. People who've been PICU nurses for twenty years aren't the most touchy, feely people. They have feelings, but they don't show them at work. The first time I saw a PICU nurse let go for a minute in front of everyone was after the death of a child that had fallen down some steep stairs. People fought hard to keep him alive because they thought the brain would be okay, but he died anyway secondary to pulmonary contusions and heart failure. He was coded at least six times, and there were four twelve-hour shifts in which the intensivists were in the room most of the time coding the child. It was very grueling on everyone. The parents said, 'Why are you trying so hard?' After the child died, one of the nurses hugged his primary nurse and cried. I told her that he'd gotten the best of the best.

"It would be nice if, after a patient died that you'd cared for a lot, someone would check in with you and say, 'That was a hard one.' Right now we have three open-heart surgery children that aren't doing well and they've been with us a long time. One has been there for ninety days and, as one of our attendings is fond of saying, 'These children are like sharks. They have to keep moving or they die.' The patient is in foster care as well, and we often think 'We're the ones that love him most.'"

Her husband and friends provide some support, "but I feel that I'm getting more than they really want to give me. They want to support me, but they don't want to talk about dead children and especially abused children. They say things like, 'I can't stand it; it's too awful; I admire you, but I don't want to hear about it; I could never do your job.' Even among people in medicine you hear comments like, 'That's the reason I left pediatrics, dead children.'

"I tell my husband and friends that I know it's hard for them to hear about what I do, but I need to talk about it. My husband works in the semiconductor industry and I'm not interested in that, but

I'm prepared to listen. Of course, talking about microchips doesn't make you squeamish or sad."

V

The deaths of children "reinforce that I have to be there for my own children. I say to my husband, 'We'll do whatever we need to do, but we have to raise these boys. My biggest fear is that I won't be around for them. For me, watching the parents as a young child dies is as hard as watching a child die. We once had a patient in the PICU who was a young mother. I'm not sure how she ended up with us, but it broke all our hearts that her children would be without a parent. That's a big thing that drives nurses, being there when someone needs them. I don't have the right to skydive!

"When my children are sick I'm more likely to deny it at first, but I'm thinking the worst. We wouldn't keep our children alive in a brain-dead, vegetative state like some parents do, but I also have to acknowledge that unless you've walked in those parents' shoes you shouldn't judge them.

"I don't think about my children dying. In the PICU if someone ever starts to say, 'That could have been my . . .' we stop them. We just don't say that at work. I don't allow myself to say or think 'What if this were my child?' My husband's father had a ruptured aorta so I'm more likely to think about him dying suddenly. He runs in races and I tell him that if he has chest pain he has to stop. He has no right to die on us!"

VI

A "good death" is "pain free. If the child has expressed a wish about who should be there when he dies, we make that happen. If it's a baby, we always try to let the child die in his mother's arms. We dim the lights, put music on, and have memory boxes to collect handprints and locks of hair. We also have Polaroid cameras to take pictures of the child. We try hard to meet the spiritual needs of the child and his family and to provide holistic support. All of these things help us, too. They are things we can do when a child dies." A "bad death" is one "that takes us by surprise, like an unexpected code. We feel better if we saw the code coming and were prepared.

"I believe children that are old enough seem to understand they're dying. We had a boy with a heart defect that would have been fixed in infancy here, but he was born in Mexico. He spent ninety to one hundred days in our unit and died because his pulmonary hypertension was so severe that we couldn't ever wean him off nitrous oxide. As he was dying he told his family and the staff, 'I'm going to be with the angels tomorrow.' The next day he said, 'I'm going to be with the angels today' and later that day he died. I've had children say they won't have a second bone-marrow transplant or they won't go on a ventilator. One of my patients was a boy with an aneurysm. He told his parents that he had a headache and they took him to their primary care provider, who told them there wasn't anything wrong. That night he walked into his parents' bedroom and said, 'Daddy, I'm going to die' and his aneurysm blew."

To help children cope with their deaths "it's very important in the PICU that the same people take care of the same children. That helps to create a relationship in which the children don't have to be brave. I took care of a boy who was going to have life-threatening surgery the next day. I asked him how he was doing and he said, 'Awful! I'm afraid.' When I asked what I could do to help he said, 'Make the operation go away.'"

Caroline believes she is good at helping terminally ill children cope with their deaths. "I'm very accepting of cultural diversity and speak Spanish fluently. Last night I took care of a boy who had either encephalitis or multiple brain tumors. The neurosurgeon had told the family that and left. I was able to talk to them about it and go over the possibilities. I told them it could be a difficult night for them because we didn't have any answers yet, but I assured them we'd keep him comfortable. I'm also very flexible and I try to provide the children with opportunities when they can be free to speak. I put their comfort and safety ahead of everything else. I'm not afraid to be their advocate. Once in a while if a family dislikes me I have trouble shaking that off. I had one family that thought we were part of a conspiracy to give up on their child and that I was being deceitful. I guess it bothered me because I'm the child of alcoholics, don't want anything to be my fault, don't want people mad at me, and want to please."

If a child asks her if he is going to die, she replies "'You know you're very sick now. Is there anything I can do for you?' Some will ask if they're going to die tonight and I'll say, 'I don't know, but I think it's possible' or 'I think you're very, very, very sick.'"

Children often ask about "the timing of their death or if they'll be in pain. School-aged children's biggest fear is that they'll be left alone and then die. When children have had head injuries and are confused, I always tell them where their parents are." When children ask questions about their deaths "it touches my heart, but I feel privileged that they've trusted me enough to ask questions like that."

The parents of terminally ill children are "more likely to vent than to ask questions. They ask if their child will die and about the dying process, what will happen. They ask if they'll be able to hold their child and, if it's a sudden death, if everything possible has been done. If I think I've helped the family and provided a safe space for them to share their feelings, then I feel good.

"In the P I C U we have a routine after a child dies. We make molds of children's hands, take clips of their hair, and help the families to bathe and hold the child one last time. When a child is nearing death you see a 'memory box' sitting on the counter and you know we're ready to go. Having a routine like that is helpful.

"During my first P I C U death I functioned as an interpreter with a Spanish-speaking family. The mother had given the child a Tylenol caplet, it ended up in his airway, he coded, his brain swelled up, and he died. The doctor who ran the code said some gentle things to the family and I told them that 'we can't maintain the blood pressure; there's no blood going to his brain;' and finally, 'We're going to stop now because he's gone.' The whole team was so grateful that I'd been there to interpret. They'd desperately wanted to provide the family with the same level of information as they would for an English-speaking family. A lot of nurses will come in to be with a dying patient that they have a particular bond with. If the life support is going to be turned off, the families want to be with someone they know."

VII

Her colleagues "don't take any better care of themselves than I do and some are worse. The older nurses have a pretty tough shell and the younger ones say that they 'won't do this job forever.' Their strengths are that they have terrific clinical knowledge. They're a very smart group of people and aren't taken by surprise. They recognize when a child is in multi-system failure and there's not much we can do. When that happens we have case conferences with the families, tell them we won't be able to overcome the child's problems, and ask them what they'd like to do. This helps us to assure that the families aren't blindsided. Even during a code the families can be part of the decision-making process. During a code one of our attendings will ask, 'Is there anyone in this room who has any suggestions before we stop? Is everyone okay to stop now?' He then says to the parents that the heart is no longer beating, that we can't get oxygen to the brain, and that there's nothing more we can do. The way we do end-of-life care in the PICU is very good."

Her PICU colleagues "very much want to help the children through it and to help them talk about it. We make up beautiful beds for the dying children. A women's group at the university makes a lovely quilt for each child. We take very loving care of them. With babies we use stuffed animals instead of restraints to keep the babies' hands away from their IV lines and ventilator tubes."

Some of her colleagues "can be inflexible. A lot of children with cystic fibrosis are in the hospital frequently and they always say they like the night shift better. They try to sleep all day so they can be up talking with the nurses at night. Some of my colleagues on the day shift say to them, 'You have to sleep at night.' When they say that I think, 'He'll be dead in three weeks, what does it matter?'"

16

*"You can't open your heart to everyone
and be grieving all the time."*

Karen's self-image from an early age centered on being a caregiver.
Now twenty-seven and a nurse on the hematology-oncology unit,
she believes that she has found her true vocation, helping children
and their families cope with terrifying illnesses and sometimes
the child's death. Her tenderness and affection for her patients
make her vulnerable to the deep pain of their loss. Even though
she has learned to maintain a greater emotional distance, there
are still times when she chooses to cross the boundary between
professional and personal involvement for the sake of a lonely or
a particularly appealing child. When those children die, her pain
is especially acute. She wonders if she will be able to continue
working in this intellectually and emotionally challenging field
after she has children of her own, anticipating that her identification with the suffering of her patients and their families may
become overwhelming.

I

Karen's first experience of a child patient's death occurred two
months after she had begun working on the hematology-oncology
unit. "I had a mixture of emotions. I was afraid because I didn't fully
understand the dying process but also curious because I needed to
learn more. I felt sorry for the family because they weren't there when
the child died. I also admired the way the staff dealt with his death.
At the time I felt more like an observer watching colleagues.

"I felt it was unfair that his life had been cut short and began to
doubt my spiritual beliefs in God and heaven. I also questioned the

way we treat cancer because his quality of life was relatively poor. He died around Christmas. I went home sobbing and didn't recognize or understand the emotions I was having. I had lots of dreams about death and losing people. I felt out of control. I didn't know the people at work well and couldn't talk with them. I was left to work it out on my own.

"After his death I slept a lot, cried, and read books and watched movies about death. I also talked with my mother-in-law, who's a nurse. I connected with her, but I was intimidated because I was brand-new. Was my reaction normal? Why didn't the other nurses seem as upset as I was? Was I taking it too hard? Later I made a close friend on the floor and learned that other people have similar emotions. The other nurses were just in different stages of their development.

"That patient's parents had been there with him all the time. Then one day just after they stepped out of the room he died. I see and hear of this frequently. Parents fall asleep and their children die. Children and even infants try to protect their parents. Perhaps they don't want them to witness the moment of their death.

"The more I experience the more I can give to the family. Initially it felt like I was continually taking and learning and later you're giving back. The families teach you so much. I've learned to listen more to what they and the child need. As time passes and I learn more, I feel that this is where I should be with my life."

After the death of that first child, "I was afraid of becoming a burnt-out nurse, disconnected from the children and families I cared for. You develop a special relationship with children and when they die it's extremely hard, but I've learned to process my grief and don't let it affect everything I do. However, my work and these families are such a big part of my life. I talk with my husband a lot. We've learned together what I need. Some days I need space. You learn how to use your resources and protect yourself. I believe you learn how to do that because you can't be grieving all the time. A little girl died last week. She and I talked and cried together, but I'm at peace with it and not feeling intense grief. Now I know more about what each diagnosis means, and more-experienced colleagues have taught me about preparatory grieving. I get attached but with the awareness that it may end. I've also learned how to savor each moment and rejoice in the good times.

"I remember one girl with whom I'd made a conscious decision to cross the line and get more involved. It hurt a lot. She had a limited support system and I wanted her to have someone by her side who cared deeply for her to help her in the final days of her life."

Professionally, the most difficult parts of coping with children's deaths are "the ethical questions about what we're doing, about the way children die, and about how long to continue treatment. I think that a child will die and yet we keep treating her. Then when the child dies, I ask myself 'Why did we choose to do all those treatments when three months ago we were pretty sure she'd die?' However, it's that one child who unexpectedly does well and proves you wrong that keeps you going. Sometimes we work so hard to cure and it's difficult to change focus or it happens too late. It must be hard for the doctors to look at the family and say, 'We don't have anything else to offer you.' Yet for us as nurses it's hard to do things we don't always fully support. Some of the pressure comes from the families, too, who want us to keep trying even when there's only a slim chance for cure. Some days I think, 'This is it. I'm done. I won't be a part of this kind of work anymore.' But I don't do that because of the families and the people I work with. Sometimes I also need to step back and think, 'How could we not give this chance to these children?'"

Personally, the hardest thing is "realizing what the child won't experience. It's a lost life. There was a little girl who talked about being a bride and so we had a Barbie wedding. We all remember it. She took her little ring and put it on Ken's finger and we all teared up. When she died she was only three years old.

"I believe everything happens for a reason. Every outcome is meant to teach us something. I came to this belief through my own spirituality, my personal and professional experiences, and what I've learned from others who've helped me to see beyond the moment.

When I came to believe everything has a purpose my work got easier and I could accept things. It's comforting to believe that because it takes some of the responsibility and strain off you. Now I don't question myself as much. It helps me to be able to continue to do this work."

II

Karen's father, an airline pilot prior to his retirement, grew up in Oregon and was raised a Baptist. "It was a horrible experience and made him anti-church. He referred to his uncle who raised him as 'a Sunday saint and weekday sinner.' He was physically and verbally abusive. When my parents first married, my father attended church, but later he stopped as his views of organized religion changed. My mother took us to church while he was working, but when he retired we stopped going. He came to view nature as his church, a place where he found solace and peace. When I was growing up, my parents had conflicts about church attendance. My mother, who was a Presbyterian, wanted to take us regularly, but my father voiced concerns. He used to talk about his frustration with self-proclaimed religious people like his uncle who felt they could do whatever they liked and then ask for forgiveness and go to heaven.

"Growing up, my life revolved around animals. That's where I learned about death. My sister had a tendency to be mean to animals. She once threw a gerbil in the air and hit it with a rock. I was always the caregiver and nurturer who tried to make things better and protected the animals as much as I could. If the animals died I'd try to make it the best possible death, much like I do now at work. I'd be in charge of the funeral, would make a little box, and would say a prayer. I talked a lot about our animals that had passed away. I didn't feel as free to talk about peoples' deaths because it was too painful for our family.

"My belief was that after a person dies her body is here on earth, separate from the spirit, and the spirit goes on to heaven. The body and the spirit are two different things. Then a couple of years ago my dog died. I was going to have her cremated, but I told my mother that I couldn't burn her. My mother said, 'It's just her body,' but I couldn't see her body and spirit as two separate things. When I go to a cemetery I believe the person's spirit is there and can hear you. I don't believe in hell. Everybody has some goodness in them.

"I used to think a lot about my grandmother, who died when my mother was twenty-five or twenty-six, about who she was and why she had to die. I knew some stories about her, which helped me to feel connected. She used to throw tea parties for the little girls in the neighborhood. She was a piano player and a good cook. There were lots of pictures of her and I was told I looked like her. Since I was little I've thought I'd get breast cancer and die young like she did. I felt at peace with the thought because it meant I'd be with her and my mother.

"Thinking back, I believe my thoughts about dying young had something to do with my grandmother, perhaps with finding a way to meet her. I felt cheated that I'd never known her and I wanted to so badly. I was always curious about her, but when my mother was diagnosed with breast cancer seven years ago I felt I had to get to know about my grandmother because by knowing her better I'd know more about my mother. There were so many parallels between my grandmother's, my mother's, and my life and I felt I needed to get to know my mother on a deeper level and also the woman who raised her. I pictured myself raising my children without my mother around and I wanted to be able to tell them about her as a person."

III

"Initially I thought I'd be a physician. I went to a special program in high school for people who wanted to be doctors. However, none of the doctors that came to talk with us said they'd go into medicine again because it wasn't about caring for patients but about steering clear of lawsuits and working with insurance companies. We had friends who were nurses and after talking to one of them I decided to go into nursing because I was most interested in patient care.

"In nursing school I did a rotation on adult hematology-oncology. I found it difficult to work with adults who were dying and trying to figure out what to do with their children and getting their affairs in order. With my mother battling cancer it was too similar to my personal life. It was different with children. One of the first children I worked with was actually excited and looking forward to going to heaven. I liked working with people at that stage of life and their families because it was a truly intimate experience.

"I love what I do and feel I'm doing work that has meaning. The children and their families teach me how to do my work. I feel really fortunate to be allowed into someone's life when he or she is experiencing illness and sometimes death. The child and family's lives are turned upside down and they are forced to examine themselves and create a new norm for their family. I feel privileged to work with the child and the family through that process.

"This is my first job. I love the people I work with. I've heard people say that nurses who work in specialty areas tend to be close because we can relate to what the others experience. Outside of work it's difficult to find anyone that truly understands. I appreciate the intimacy of our working relationships. We see one another at very vulnerable times. It's the emotional and psychosocial side that drew me to the field.

"The most positive part of my work is the relationship with the children and their families and what I learn from them. I admire the strength I see in children and their parents. It's also exciting to work in a field that's continually improving and looking for better treatments. The work is both emotionally and intellectually challenging. It's stressful, too, but it's a good stress. During the nurses' strike I felt really guilty about what I was doing to the patients and their families because we left them in their time of need. When I came back to work I was fearful about what the families would say about how the strike had affected them.

"The most negative part is that my family has difficulty relating to what I experience. That makes it hard to feel supported at times. When I first started, if I mentioned something they thought was upsetting they'd say 'Why not get out of the field?' I'd tell them 'Because I love it.' A colleague once told me that it's like war. You can only talk with your fellow soldiers because only they can understand what you're going through. That's why you're so close to your colleagues. They understand what you experience."

"I don't feel I had any preparation in nursing school about how to cope with the deaths of patients. I didn't know what happened to the body after death. We had a class on aging and death, but it was more about death from natural causes. We learned about Kübler-Ross and the stages of dying, but I wish we'd done case studies about what the patients are actually feeling physically as they die. We had the theory but no real practice. It was hard to be new and still learning what happens to the body during the dying process when the families were looking to me for reassurance. 'Why are his hands so cold?' I remember the nurses on adult hematology-oncology talking about a patient during rounds and saying, 'I'm sure he'll be dead in eight hours.' How did they know that? What do you do to help people that are dying? There should be a whole course on death.

"I had an experience during a nursing school rotation that really disturbed me. A nurse treated the body of a patient I'd worked with very roughly. The patient was only thirty-two and was recently married. No one had told me she might die and her death really surprised me. My clinical instructor and I talked about the unexpected part of it. I also talked with her about my emotional reactions. The patient died while her family was away. Her husband wanted to be in the room while we bathed her, but the nurse told him it'd better if he weren't there. Then she just ripped the pillow out from under her head and yanked out the Foley catheter. The patient was beautiful. She wore a bandanna that was always perfectly placed. The nurse tried to fix it, but she didn't put it on the way the patient would have worn it. I felt that the patient's spirit was still in the room and that the nurse was violating her body. I was so upset with her and promised myself I'd never act like that.

"One of the greatest things about nursing is being a patient advocate. For the most part I know the patient well and know many of their needs. One of the things I like about hematology-oncology is working closely with families. You learn about their conflicts, complex needs, desires, wishes, and personalities. The doctors have much more limited contact with the patients. When I started the job I wasn't prepared to be a patient advocate. How do you help a child prepare emotionally for death? I wish I'd been taught how to care for the family's holistic needs. What I know I learned at work from the more experienced nurses.

"I'm fairly satisfied with my on-the-job training, but everybody has a unique style in approaching the impending death of a child. There's sometimes conflict between the staff about when to tell a family that 'enough is enough.' It's hard to lose a patient when you've worked so hard to keep him alive. I feel empathy for the doctors' position because the families look to them to save their child. Caring for dying patients and determining what is best for them and for their families is a continuous learning process and very individualized.

"We try to find resources for the family to support them during the dying process and after the child dies. We have a Palliative Care Team that does a lot of that work. After a child dies some of us keep in touch. Others believe we need to let them go back to their primary support systems. Nobody tells you what the boundaries should be for nurses dealing with dying children and their families. You have to learn for yourself. I wish I knew more about the psychological aspects of working with families. We have one or two child life therapists and one social worker, but they're pulled in multiple directions. Many of the families' needs end up being addressed by the nurse and yet we've not been trained in how to work with them. It's also hard to make the transition between rooms. In one room the child and family are happy because they've received good news, while in the next room they've just been diagnosed and are shell-shocked, and in the one after that the patient is dying. We're always on an emotional roller coaster and it can be hard to meet the families' needs. It's easier when I'm close to the family. One of the things

I've learned is to let them vent. You support them as they work through the process. I can't imagine what it would be like to have a child die. I like it when the families express what they're going through. It's much easier for me to help them when they talk about how they're feeling than when they're closed off."

IV

Karen says she is helped to cope with the deaths of children "by my family, my nieces and my nephews. Whenever I've had a hard time I go to their house, play with them, and read them stories. Children always help you focus on what's really important in life, living in the moment and for the moment. My belief that everyone has a purpose and that once you've reached that purpose you're not needed here helps me, too. And my colleagues are a great source of support."

V

The deaths of child patients "make the thought of dying easier. They give me strength and peace about death. It's a normal part of living. You don't have to be old to die. I don't want to die, but I realize that it can bring peace to you and to others in your life. My mother is a cancer survivor and the children's deaths make me worry about her. I realize that cancer kills people and takes them out of our lives. It could take her as quickly as it does my child patients. She had her annual checkup recently. I get knots in my stomach just thinking about the possibility of her death. We don't cure everybody."

She seldom thinks of her family members' mortality. "Something has to happen that reminds me of it. My brother, who's a pilot, was recently in a really bad accident. He was riding in a bus on the way home from the airport and a truck hit the bus. When I saw him I hugged him and said, 'I'm so glad you're still alive!'" Thinking of losing one of her family members "makes me cry and feel at a loss. I can't imagine them not being in my life, not being able to hug them or talk to them, not being able to call or experience fun times with them. If they were to die I'd want it to be peaceful and painless."

Thoughts of her death occur "pretty frequently. Death is such a part of my life. I checked my e-mail this morning and learned that one of our patients died last night. I recently went to the funeral of a man who had committed suicide. He was the minister that married my husband and me. They'd moved away from here about a year ago. His suicide was a huge wakeup call for everyone. We thought everything was fine. What could we have done? What did we miss? If we were more aware of our own mortality it might change our daily lives. If I did it would help me to guide my life better and to think about the kind of impact I'd like to have on people. I hope I have a lot of life left!"

Frequent experiences with death "make me want to have a deeper relationship with people. I want every conversation to have meaning. I want to know everyone better. There's so much we don't know about one another. It probably irritates my family! They want to have a normal conversation and there I am sitting at dinner asking, 'I wonder what heaven is like?' Our lives get so busy and they're so short. They'd be better if we were more open with one another. A lot of the conversations I have with patients and parents are about deeper things. We just had a patient die, an eighteen-year-old. When we told her she would die she said, 'But I want to make a difference with my life!' We told her that she had."

VI

A "good death" is having "as little pain as possible and not being scared. I've seen children excited to be going to heaven! We need to help them to be open to that idea. Their deaths should be peaceful and their family and friends should be around them. I like the energy when everything about a child's death feels right. They need to be prepared to die and to know they're going to die. It's important for us to use the word 'die' or 'pass away' if they know that means to die.

"It makes me sad when people die unexpectedly. It's important for children and their parents to recognize what they think will happen after the child dies. It's difficult when they're in turmoil. If the parents aren't at peace with their child's death then the child gets the sense that it's not all right to die. You see children clinging to life and lingering until the parents accept the idea that they're going to die. Then when the child sees that her parents will be all right she dies."

A "bad death" is one in which "the child is in awful pain and the family is fighting and angry. Or the child doesn't understand what death is or sees it as a failure. It's also bad when the child is so sick before dying that he can't say goodbye. I once took care of a little boy. The moment he died he vomited up a lot of feces. I remember feeling horrible that this had happened to him and his family. It was dark and his mother was frightened. His sister, who was seven or eight, woke up just as he died and the room smelled horrible. She was so scared and it took a while before she could figure out what had happened. It's important for the parents and siblings to be prepared for what may happen to the child's body. If the family is at peace you can tell them what is happening and it's not scary for them.

"The experience I had around the death of the last child I cared for was nice. I didn't know the family well, but I connected with them and was able to guide them through the dying process. After he died, we made handprints with him and his family. They shared memories, tears, and laughter. The mother said, 'I'm so glad we could do this and that he wasn't hurting.'"

How much terminally ill children understand about their deaths is "based on how well the family and staff can talk about it. The family is very important in preparing the child for death. If the family is not ready to discuss death I can't do much to help the child prepare. I have to respect where the family is. Some children understand fully. They help with their funeral plans and tell you what they want. Others are taken by surprise. If the family is prepared the child will usually be prepared."

Terminally ill children could be helped to cope "if society were more open to talking about death as a normal thing. We're so unprepared for grief and how powerful it can be. From the initial diagnosis of cancer we as a staff should acknowledge to the child and his family that death is a possibility. We do give the statistics—saying, for example, that 'there's a 60 percent chance of cure,' but I sometimes think we wait too long before saying we won't be able to cure the disease.

"Every time I help a child through the dying process I hope that I get better at it. It's an experience-based skill. I used to think I had to have the right answer to every question, but now I see how important silence and one's physical presence can be. I think I'll continue to get better as I get more mature emotionally and spiritually. I hope I bring a lot of comfort and peace to the families. I'm a strong advocate for the child and the family around the child's death. I try to make the death the least intrusive possible. I try to help the children talk through their fears. I'm getting better at those conversations and talking with children about what they think will happen after they die. I hope it helps the families to know what their children are feeling. In my experience most children aren't scared of dying. Many don't realize that death is permanent. I'm getting better at listening to what the family needs rather than to what I think they need. We're not taught to listen!"

She finds it difficult "when a family needs me to say something and I don't feel I have the right words. If I knew more I could be a better advocate for the child and help the family to cope more effectively, assessing what they need and intervening according to their needs. Sometimes it's tricky to balance the child's needs against the family's needs. Sometimes we're forced to move too quickly from a curative to a palliative mode and the child isn't adequately prepared.

"I get impatient with the process of learning. I want to be good at my work now! I've done it for five years, but I'm only twenty-seven. There's so much to learn. I wonder if it will be different after I have children. The worst thing that has happened to me is having my dog die, and that was really hard!

"When children ask me about death I talk about heaven and ask them what they think will happen when they die. Do they believe in heaven? What do they think heaven will be like? Will they see people they know? I try to create a sense of anticipation so they don't think they're going to a scary place. Every child on our unit usually knows another child that has died so we talk about their friends that are in heaven. Most children are comfortable talking about their thoughts of death and I try to normalize that part of their lives. I recently had a conversation with a seventeen- or eighteen-year-old and helped him to talk about his fears of dying so young. He said, 'Some of us die sooner rather than later.' There was a big pause and I thought, 'He knows that he's going to die.' I said, 'Some people die when they're two and others when they're one hundred. We don't know why. There are no answers.' He was very open about it and we had a nice, quiet conversation. We both knew we were talking about him.

"Dying children often ask what happens to your body after you die. A few have asked if their parents will be all right. A teenage girl asked me, 'Why is my body doing this to me?' I couldn't answer that question. It's very hard to say that you don't know. Why was it she and not someone else? I wished I could give her a comforting answer, but I didn't know one. One five-year-old girl wanted to know if animals would be in heaven and what she could take with her. She was in so much pain and she kept asking her mother why she couldn't go to heaven now."

Children's questions about death "sometimes make me smile and laugh and realize how wonderful, innocent, and accepting children are. And sometimes they make me really, really sad that things aren't fair. Children who are older and realize the permanence of death make me really sad. They're thinking about all the things they won't be able to do.

"Parents of dying children ask about the physical aspects of dying. What will they see? How long will she live? What signs are we looking for? Most parents have never seen anyone die. My heart goes out to them because their first experience is their own child dying. There are also parents that feel guilty. 'Have we done all we can? Should we really stop treatment?' Some have spiritual questions, especially if they don't have well-defined beliefs. If they don't believe in heaven they may ask what will happen to their child after death. The child's death brings up a lot of questions for parents about their own beliefs. Parents that have a strong set of beliefs are really fortunate. If they don't it becomes an all-consuming problem for them and many times they'll want to speak with the chaplain.

"I don't belong to a specific religion so I have trouble answering their spiritual questions. I haven't yet seen a family that has said, 'This is it, when you're dead you're dead.' They need the comfort of believing there's something for their child beyond death. The same is true for the staff. I think it's one of the defining points between those who stay and those who leave. When a staff member struggles with her beliefs and can't come to a conclusion that gives her hope for the children, it's hard for her to stay in the field because all the children's suffering seems to be for nothing. After seeing all that the children go through one has to think that they'll experience a peaceful afterlife of some kind.

"The parents' questions are hard for me. I'm not a parent so I don't really understand the depth of their suffering and their responsibility at having to make big decisions for their children. My heart breaks for them. In many ways it seems more difficult for them than for the child because they survive and have to live with the decisions they've made. How do we guide them through the process and provide them with comfort? There's a physician on our unit that I've always looked up to as a mentor. I've learned a lot from him about what to say to parents. He's a man of few words. He's taught me how meaningful your presence alone can be.

"I don't think I'll be able to continue to do this work when I have children of my own. It gets harder and harder to care for children who are the ages of my nieces and nephews."

VII

"Staff that have faith in a higher being or power seem to cope better than those that don't. So do those who have worked here longer.

It also helps to have boundaries with the patients' families. Those who develop relationships with the families outside of work have a hard time when the child dies.

"My colleagues are very compassionate with one another. If one staff member is having a hard time we try to support her. The nurses' support group has increased peoples' awareness of how the children's deaths affect us all. Humor helps, too. When we asked one dying boy if he thought he'd meet God he said, 'He checks you in!'

"Their weakness is that they're sometimes not able to talk about how a child's death has affected them. If we did we could be more supportive of one another. I think people are guarded because of a fear of what others will think of them, but when they talk about it you can see this feeling of relief come over them. It seems there's always some degree of guilt and a sense of failure that we didn't succeed. You think back on the child's course of treatment and all the decisions that were made. Should we have done things differently? Sometimes the families look at you with the same question.

"Staff seem to work on the unit either for a couple of years or less, or for a long time. The people who stay seem to learn to cope with death and find strength and enjoyment in the children. Those who don't, experience the work as so draining that they can't go on. There are also people who stay for the wrong reasons. The job is hard on them and their boundaries aren't good, but they have a sense that if they leave they've failed."

CONCLUSIONS

Early Experiences with Child Patients' Deaths

One of the nurses summed it up best: "There's nothing right about a dead baby." The emotional pain and the sense of unfairness that surround the deaths of children can penetrate the psychological defenses of even the most experienced nurses and physicians, and empathy with the parents' loss, especially if you are a parent yourself, can feel overwhelming. Few people believed that they could work with dying children and their families without eventually paying an emotional price. "It is a black hole that just keeps getting bigger." That price might include becoming so consumed with work that nothing else—family, friends, or health—seemed to matter, burning out and leaving the field for less stressful employment, or withdrawing emotionally to such an extent that one had nothing left to give. Most, with the exception of those in the NICU, could not envision doing what they are doing now for the rest of their lives. They sensed that the long hours, physical strain, and accumulated emotional burden of caring for dying children and grieving parents would sooner or later push them into less taxing lines of work. Because of its emotional and physical challenges, dealing routinely with dying children in acute-care settings (apart from the NICU) seems to be the kind of work best suited to younger rather than older nurses and physicians.

Those most vulnerable to the pain of children's deaths were, not surprisingly, those new to the field—residents and young nurses. Their first and their most traumatic deaths often impacted them with the force of a sledgehammer and affected them so powerfully that for days they might feel very sad, cry frequently, and have difficulty sleeping, concentrating, and working. At such times their spouses or families might implore them to leave jobs that caused them so much distress. Yet they persisted and gradually developed the emotional calluses that are necessary to survive intact in such demanding fields. Learning how to cope with the deaths of children is a process, a journey that you make without realizing you are on one. It is a largely unconscious journey whose progress you observe only after the passage of years when you reflect back on where you were and where you are today.

All of those I interviewed, from the most to the least experienced, had a clear and often still troubling memory of the first death of a child under their care. Some of the deaths were memorable because of their horrible circumstances. A beautiful Japanese girl with leukemia bled out while the intern watched helplessly. A little girl was burned over 95 percent of her body in a house fire. A boy was accidentally hung while playing on a slide at a church daycare program. A child recovering from a serious illness aspirated a hot dog in the hospital and went on to die as the resident struggled to get her senior colleagues to make more of an effort to save her. Other deaths were remembered because of mistakes that were made, such as using the wrong antibiotic or not jumping on a fever quickly enough. The key factors that seemed to set these early deaths apart from subsequent ones were that they occurred when the nurses and physicians were new to their work and at a time when they had just begun to bear real responsibility for their patients. In professions whose goal is to make sick children well, the death of your patient, especially at the beginning of your career, is "the ultimate bad outcome" and a direct challenge to your sense of professional competence. For many it brings into question whether they have chosen the right line of work and if they will be able to continue to endure the pain of children's deaths and parents' suffering.

Subsequent deaths were generally less traumatic because the physicians and nurses had learned to defend themselves from the pain. Many found that distancing themselves emotionally from the children and their families made the deaths more tolerable and less like the loss of a loved one. Over time, however, most recognized that being too distant was not helpful for their patients or themselves, and they continued to struggle to find a balance between withdrawal and overidentification. Some learned to channel their energy and emotions into learning something from each death rather than beating themselves up for real or imagined errors. Others sought to reframe their approach to dying children and their families by devoting themselves to keeping the child pain-free and helping the family get through the dying process intact when further aggressive treatments offered little hope of cure.

Regardless of how well defended or experienced they were, none of my medical or nursing colleagues was able to maintain a professional and personal distance all of the time. Now and then a particular child or family would find a way around their defenses and they would become so attached to the child or its parents that the child's death felt almost like the death of a family member. This attachment might develop because a child reminded them of their own children or the parents reminded them of themselves or their spouses. An abandoned child, or one seldom visited by its parents, might provoke responses that were more like those of a mother than a professional caregiver. Or a child might have some especially endearing quality, such as unusual insight or a sense of humor, that made getting him or her better so important that death was experienced as a personal failure.

Deaths that were the result of treatment errors could also break through their defenses even after they had worked in the field for twenty or thirty years. Nurses and physicians in intensive care and hematology-oncology units employ treatments that have the potential to do great harm as well as good, and mistakes happen. Even though they know this intellectually and recognize that it is better to learn from their mistakes than to depart on a guilt trip, few seemed able to escape deep pangs of conscience and sleepless nights if they felt responsible for hurting a patient. The medical maxim *Primum non nocere* (first do no harm) is deeply ingrained in physicians and nurses and remains a guiding principle throughout their careers.

It is probably reinforced in those who care for children by the special and intuitive protective response that the young elicit from most adults.

From my point of view, the capacity to experience a certain degree of guilt after making an error is important in our professions, and its complete absence would be very troubling. We need to endure some suffering for our mistakes to keep us alert not to make them again. As long as that suffering is not persistent and disabling it is a necessary and sufficient requirement for our work.

Family Background, Personal Experiences, and Coping with Death

Reflecting on my colleagues' personal and family backgrounds has convinced me that, although training, experience, and the observed behavior of professional mentors and colleagues all contribute to your ability to cope with children's deaths, your most important teachers are your parents and family members. As one of my physician colleagues put it, "No one can teach you how to deal with a child's death. It's mostly about what you bring to the table." If a beloved parent dealt with death by ignoring it and repressing his or her feelings, then chances are that you will adopt a similar coping style. If your role in your family was to keep it together and remain calm during crises then you will probably behave that way on the job. If you learned that it was all right, and even a sign of strength to express your feelings and to talk about them with those around you then you will believe that is the "right" way to cope with patients' deaths. The cultural traditions of medicine have been more supportive of the former approaches of repressing, or at least suppressing, your feelings in the face of death and adopting a degree of professional distance from the suffering of patients and their families. Openly expressing feelings to colleagues and especially to patients and their families was discouraged and might be viewed as weakness or the loss of objectivity and professionalism. While these traditions are changing as more women and older people with broader life experiences enter medicine, they still prevail in the more "macho" procedural specialties like intensive care, where doing often predominates over developing therapeutic relationships with patients. Most of the intensivists I interviewed had learned early in their lives, long before they entered medicine, to compartmentalize or repress their feelings and to ignore or put aside their emotions.

Nurses were often drawn to their field by the experience of having received kindly and compassionate care at the hands of other nurses. Nursing appealed to them primarily for emotional rather than intellectual reasons, although the money they could earn also attracted some to the field. Even those who were academically gifted discovered that personal caregiving was more important to them than science or perceived prestige. The physicians, on the other hand, most often went into medicine because they were interested in science, had been excellent students, and felt an attraction to medicine because they could combine science with involvement in the more immediate and practical problems of treating diseases and helping others. It is also one of those fields to which very bright and ambitious students are drawn; it pays well and has a certain cachet among families and friends. The physicians I interviewed did not usually cite personal experiences of being cared for and a desire to emulate that caregiving in their choice of careers. Some did have physician role-models as young people, but those role models were as likely to make them not want to enter medicine as to inspire them because of the long hours involved. More often than among the nurses, medicine appeared to be a default career choice for bright, ambitious people who found that the world of science did not motivate them sufficiently to pursue a PhD. Interestingly, their decision to enter medicine rather than basic science was often tinged with a certain amount of guilt, as if they had "sold out" or taken the lesser path; "real scientists get a PhD."

Many of the nurses mentioned their religious beliefs as the bulwark of their work with dying children. Some wondered if it would be possible to remain in their field for long if one did not believe in an afterlife as an explanation and reward for the dying children's suffering. The physicians did not seem to have such secure beliefs about what, if anything, comes next, and most were, if not disbelievers, certainly agnostics who worried that once you are dead there is nothing more. They appeared to derive their comfort from helping dying children and, especially the child's parents through the dying process. They were able to give children medications to reduce their pain and to make them more comfortable. They were able to help parents to the realization that their child was going to die, to assist them in understanding that palliative care and not cure was now the goal, and to indicate ways in which the child's dying could be made easier and less painful. They were also able to educate parents about the dying process, to prepare them for what they would see, what they might expect, and how they would know that death was near. Some parents were unable or unwilling to accept this help, and the deaths of their children were often the most disquieting, disorganized, and distressing for all involved.

No patient's death affects you as powerfully as the death of someone you love. The stunning, sometimes overwhelming, impact of losing a parent, a sibling, or a child was experienced as orders of magnitude greater than dealing with the loss of a child patient, no matter how close you had become to the patient or his or her family. The deaths of loved ones often seemed to open up realms of feeling, especially in more stoic and rigidly defended people, that revealed to them for the first time the power of emotions for both good and ill. Several of the physicians only learned to truly empathize with others' losses after the death of a loved one. It is not that they were incapable of sympathy or empathy before but that the depths of their pain in loss led to a deepening and enriching of the empathy they could offer to others. Such a gift is, of course, double-edged. It opens the way to closer, more meaningful human contacts, but it can also make you vulnerable to overidentification with the patient and family and possibly compromise the objectivity that is so important in making decisions and recommendations about health care.

One of the striking aspects of the physicians' and nurses' stories was the positive and negative impact of individuals on their learning and decision-making processes. A high school teacher and coach suggested to a young man that to emulate him would lead to a miserable and impoverished life and that his student should find a more lucrative pursuit, such as being a doctor. A young woman witnessed what she judged to be incompetent psychiatric care of her brother and decided to become a competent physician who could help families to understand what was happening to their loved ones. A nurse was moved by the care she had received at a frightening and lonely time in her life and made it her goal to provide the same compassionate and loving care to others. A young physician watched the gentle, humane manner in which a more experienced physician treated the families of dying children and decided to be like him. The persons who marked the turning points in their lives were not prominent or famous people and might just as well have exercised a negative as a positive influence. Their words and actions were profound experiences and landmarks in the lives of the people I interviewed, and teach us what an enormous impact any one of us can have on those around us. Our real human legacy, if we are concerned with such things, may rest not so much on the reputations, publications, or monuments we leave behind but on those small, individual actions that others observe and incorporate into their own lives as beacons to follow or warning signs to avoid.

Medical and Nursing Education and Training as Preparation for Coping with Patients' Deaths

The quality and quantity of teaching and training nurses and physicians received in school and on the job oriented toward coping with the deaths of patients varied from poor and none to excellent and considerable. However, all acknowledged that coping with the deaths of children is not something that can be formally taught. "It can't be spoon-fed. You have to work it out on your own." It is a set of skills based on the coping strategies you learned while growing up that are later modified by life events, professional mentors, and experiencing what does and does not work for you in your coping process—and for some by psychotherapy. A few did think that learning about "self-care" in medical or nursing school and hearing from physicians and nurses experienced in the care of dying patients about how patient deaths affected them might have been helpful in preparing them for what was to come. "Then you'd know that the powerful feelings affecting you after a patient dies are normal." Others thought that working during medical or nursing school with dying patients such as those in a hospice and receiving concurrent instruction on how to deal with your feelings would have been good preparation for the time when you actually bore the responsibility for patient care. It must be acknowledged, however, that there were significant interpersonal differences in the ways in which individual nurses and physicians learned to cope with children's deaths. There is probably no single approach that is uniformly successful. Each student must be assessed individually and taught in a manner that works best for her or him.

There was agreement that it would be very helpful if hospitals provided confidential opportunities for nurses and physicians, especially for those early in their careers, to talk about their reactions to the deaths of their child patients away from managers and bosses. My experience suggests that hospitals are, unfortunately, reluctant to do so. This reluctance appears to me to have several determinants. The obstacle most frequently cited is cost. It is expensive to let nurses and physicians go away from their work and to hire others to cover for them while they process their feelings about a child's death or a parent's reaction to that death. It costs money to employ a professional skilled in listening who can organize and direct confidential encounters, and there is no immediate or obvious financial benefit to doing so. There are legal concerns about discussing errors and possible malpractice with others who might later become witnesses for the plaintiff. I also believe that there is, among some hospital and nursing managers, a certain institutional suspiciousness and desire to control what is discussed on the job, especially in an environment such as ours, where conflicts between nurses and management had led to a nurses' strike and vestigial ill feelings. It sometimes seemed to me that there was a perception among managers that you could best avoid problems by pretending they were not there or by dealing with them in an "instructional" rather than an "emotional" manner. Unfortunately, these approaches appeared to me to drive the process underground and reinforced a feeling among medical and nursing caregivers that talking about their feelings could be harmful to their careers. The real danger, however, is that unprocessed feelings about patients' deaths may lead to irrational, sometimes self-destructive behaviors like alcohol and medication abuse and to staff burnout and the loss of well-trained, highly valuable caregivers. I believe that money—and, more importantly, careers and lives—could be saved if hospitals established opportunities at work for caregivers to talk about their reactions to their very stressful and demanding jobs and to learn from their colleagues in a safe and confidential setting.

Coping with the Deaths of Children

Coping with the deaths of children is a highly personal process, but one that can be helped or hindered by a number of factors. All of the physicians and nurses found that focusing their energies on keeping the dying child as comfortable and pain-free as possible and on assisting the family through the dying process helped them with their own coping. Unfortunately, some families could make the dying process and the staff members' efforts to assist them and their child very difficult. The key issues seemed to be whether the family could gradually come to understand and acknowledge that the child was going to die and whether they could shift their efforts from working and hoping for a cure to making the child's death as comfortable as possible. Not all families were able to make the transition from striving for cure to palliative care, and the deaths of children from these families were frequently the most painful and least satisfactory. In addition, family members might be limited by their intellectual capacity to understand what was going on and why their child was not going to make it. They might be unable to let the child go because of their own emotional needs: "How can I live without him?" They might have cultural or religious traditions that interfered or prohibited them from "giving up." Or they might be alcoholic or severely mentally ill and unable to come to grips with the fact that their child was dying. In the words of one of the attending physicians, "If the family is dysfunctional the child's death will be dysfunctional."

The family's unwillingness or inability to acknowledge that their child was dying and to switch from a therapeutic to a palliative mode could be exacerbated if there were differences among the members of the treatment team about when "enough is enough." The nurses' most frequent criticism of the physicians was that some of them would never give up and would "treat, treat, treat" until it was too late to prepare the child and his family for death. Sometimes they felt that the physician was doing this more to meet his or her own needs than those of the patient. There is seldom a bright line between cure and care, and reasonable people will differ on when it is crossed. The most grotesque and unnerving deaths were those during which neither the treatment team nor the family could agree about when it was time to stop pushing for a cure. Those deaths became a "flail" for all, with extreme treatments, procedures, and resuscitations for the children, and a sense of anger, frustration, and despair among the family and the caregivers.

Personal support systems at and outside of work were very important. Many found that civilians (people outside of medicine and nursing) were of little help in their coping process. Descriptions of the emotions stirred up by interactions with desperately ill and dying children and their families were often so upsetting for nonmedical family and friends that it was not worthwhile trying to discuss them. "They get so upset that I end up supporting them!" Spouses varied in their ability to provide support. Those who were also physicians or nurses could understand what you were talking about, but they were often struggling with their own coping and had little energy to listen. Some spouses found it too upsetting to see their spouse unhappy or to hear about distressing topics such as death or abuse and would shut down prematurely. A very few were able to listen empathetically, to tolerate the pain of what they were hearing without falling apart themselves, and to keep from talking excessively or merely offering platitudes to help themselves to deal with their own feelings.

The most reliable and sympathetic listeners proved to be other nurses and physicians doing the same kind of work. Informal support groups were usually divided along disciplinary and hierarchical lines. Residents were most comfortable talking with other residents because they feared that the attendings would judge and grade them for what they said. Nurses tended to talk chiefly to other nurses, although occasionally a particularly empathic physician might be included in their group. Attending physicians, except for those in the N I C U, tended to talk only to their spouses, if anyone, and rarely to their colleagues. The reasons for the attendings' isolation were unclear but seemed to involve working alone rather than on teams with their physician colleagues, time and money pressures to produce rather than to deal with one's feelings, and competitive issues between individual attendings. It was rare to hear about attendings' asking one another for help, although some wished that their colleagues would ask them if they needed it.

A nurse's or physician's own children were another important source of support, but more for the love and comfort they provided than for what they said. Many people spoke of going home after a horrible death and hugging their children and losing themselves in them. Of course, having children could also hinder your coping if you saw them in the dying child or you identified too strongly with the dying child's parents. Nothing had the capacity to personalize a child's death more than having children of your own. "Each one of us is just a day away from standing in the shoes of those P I C U parents."

Sharing their emotions with a dying child's parents and family was for many a way to help parents to see that others, too, had cared about their child and a way to comfort themselves by joining the family in the mourning process. Some were uncomfortable about openly displaying their sadness with families, feeling that it was either unprofessional or ingenuous to equate one's own loss of a child patient with the profound loss experienced by the child's parents. Participants' opinions about how much emotion a nurse or a physician should display seemed to be based primarily on how they themselves behaved and on their observations of the behaviors of other nurses and physicians they admired. People who were comfortable experiencing and expressing emotions believed that it was helpful both for the patients and their families and for the physician or nurse to do so. They gave explanations such as "it shows the family that the doctors care," "it helps the other staff to know that it's all right to cry when a child dies," or "it helps me to feel closure if I can mourn with the family." Those who were less comfortable about displaying emotions, primarily the physicians, questioned whether it was professional to show feelings and believed that the physician's role is to remain calm and detached in troubled times rather than "running around like a chicken with its head cut off." All, of course, agreed that you should not become so emotional that your feelings interfered with the performance of your duties. Yet even the most stoic sometimes wondered if it were healthy for them to keep their emotions bottled up all the time and worried that some day they might pay a price for so much unrecognized and unprocessed grief.

Two of the participants had lost children of their own, one as an infant and the other as a teenager, and both felt that their empathy with the parents of dying children had been deepened by their experiences of loss. A NICU nurse (because of space limitations her story was not included) whose son died as an infant felt that it was comforting for parents who had lost a baby to learn that she could indeed understand what they were going through. The hematology-oncology doctor whose son was killed believed that he had a unique perspective on how long the parents' mourning process really takes, knowing that it would be many years before they felt whole again. He also emphasized that spouses may differ in the time it takes to mourn their child and that because of this, and the need of some to have a target for their anger, it is often a challenge for couples to stay together after the loss of their child.

Most of the nurses and a few of the physicians were helped to cope with children's deaths by their religious beliefs. "Why should a child have to die? It's just not fair" was a sentiment expressed in one way or another by all of those I interviewed. Having the capacity to understand the child's death as part of God's plan, to believe that the child would earn "a free ticket to heaven" for all its suffering, and to think that the child would never be alone was a great comfort for those that believed in a just God and a hereafter. Many of the nurses did not think that it would be possible to work in hematology-oncology or in the intensive care units if you did not believe in God or a continuing life for the spirit. None of those I interviewed, whether believers or not, could completely accept the view that "once you're dead you're dead and that's it." Even the unbelievers seemed to be hedging their bets on an afterlife or a continuing life for the spirit.

One of the residents who was very interested in the psychosocial aspects of medicine wondered aloud why physicians no longer appear to accept their traditional role of being "midwives of death." My interviews, both with attending physicians and physicians in training, and my observations of their behavior on the wards suggested that many physicians no longer feel comfortable in this role. When it is clear that a child is going to die, they are likely to leave the work of caring for the psychosocial needs of the child to nurses and Child Life specialists. Time, or the perceived lack of it, was the most frequent obstacle cited by physicians for their limited involvement in the patients' and their families' emotional lives.

Another factor that may play a role in keeping physicians from becoming more emotionally involved with their patients was their tendency to compartmentalize their feelings. Much more often than the nurses, the physicians I interviewed acknowledged that from an early age they had learned to keep out of their awareness emotions that they did not like. While this trait was not uniformly present among physicians or universally absent among nurses, physicians were more likely to consciously and unconsciously detach themselves from their feelings. They were also much less likely than the nurses to have been drawn to medicine by a desire to provide individual care to others, but instead were attracted more by the science, prestige, and financial rewards of medicine. Thus, in addition to external constraints of time, physicians' tendency to detach themselves emotionally from children's deaths may also reflect internal issues surrounding the way they deal with strong emotions, their discomfort with unacknowledged death anxiety, and their expectations for their professional lives.

Dying Children and One's Own Mortality

The effects of working with dying children on participants' conscious views of their mortality were variable. For most, the reality of the work shattered that bubble of denial that surrounds all of us and keeps us from being aware of how fragile and transient life really is. "I realized that anyone I love could die at any time." Most worried less about their own dying and death and more about the deaths of their loved ones. People without children were concerned about the loss of their parents, siblings, nieces, and nephews. Those who were parents worried most about the deaths of their children. At times those worries could become extreme and even disabling. Some were afraid to have children because they felt they would worry so much. Others took every sign of illness in their child as an indication that he or she had cancer or some other dread disease. A bee-sting might lead to anaphylaxis, a swollen lymph node might be the first sign of Hodgkin's disease, and one nurse wondered if she should enter psychotherapy because her worries about her child were so extreme. When they did think about their own deaths they were more troubled by the thought of a protracted, painful death or leaving their children or spouses behind than by the thought of death itself. Most were, however, careful to add that they were still young and needn't worry about death yet or hoped they would live for a long time.

As adults and often parents themselves, the nurses and physicians were likely to identify with the parents' pain in losing their child and with the years of suffering they knew would lie ahead for them. Several commented on how comforting it was to later encounter the parents of a dead child and to learn that they were doing all right. Others recognized that many couples do not survive the loss of a child and that in the years to come many will have moved on to other partners.

"Good" and "Bad" Deaths for Children

Participants were united around what constitutes a "good" and a "bad" death for a child. Key to a good death was having the time to bring the parents and family to the realization that their child was going to die and that there was a good and a bad way for that process to unfold. The parents' recognition that their child was going to die enabled the physicians and nurses to switch from an aggressive therapeutic mode to a palliative one of making the child comfortable and pain-free. If the child were old enough, it allowed him time to say good-bye and to be an active participant in the dying process, planning a final trip, organizing his or her funeral, and giving away treasured objects to loved ones. Time also enabled the staff to answer children's and parents' questions about death. "Will it be dark or cold?" "What will it be like to die?" "How will we as parents know that our child is dying?"

Many commented that it appeared to be difficult for children to let themselves die if they sensed that it was not all right with their parents or that their parents would fall apart without them. There were a number of stories of children seemingly waiting to die until their parents had given them permission or were out of the room, as if in death they wanted to spare their parents the pain of watching them die. This seemed to suggest that dying could have a voluntary component, a conscious decision to move from holding on to letting go.

It was felt to be very important that parents and other loved ones be present during the dying process. Some thought it was better for children to die at home surrounded by the people and things they loved, while others believed that the children's pain and the parents' questions could be better managed in the hospital.

The worst deaths were those that were sudden and unexpected; that were protracted, painful, and filled with controversy and conflict, both between the parents and the staff and the staff with one another; and that came as the result of adverse effects of treatment. Dying alone and unloved was perhaps the worst fate they could imagine for a child. There were a number of touching stories of nursing and physician staff members trying to stand in for an absent parent, holding and speaking lovingly to the child so that she would not have to die alone and comfortless. One physician even brought his own dog into the PICU so that a child could satisfy a wish to spend his last night with his puppy.

Colleagues' Abilities to Cope with Children's Deaths

Assessments of one's colleagues' abilities to cope with children's deaths were generally positive and respectful but varied strikingly from group to group. Hematology-oncology attendings found it difficult to evaluate their colleagues because they work serially and rarely observe one another's work. There was a perception that colleagues were skilled and compassionate and generally shared the same values, but there was also acknowledgment of a surprising lack of awareness about how they coped internally with children's deaths. "We just don't talk about it." PICU attendings recognized large stylistic differences among their colleagues in how they dealt with dying children and their families. Some wondered at times if a particular colleague might be so focused on the child's care as to neglect the family, or if another might use the families' admiration and dependency to meet his own needs. They, too, seemed to have little knowledge about their colleagues' inner lives and did not know how they managed their feelings in the face of so much death. The one NICU attending I interviewed described her NICU colleagues, nurses and physicians, as a very close-knit group that had grown up together professionally and knew each other well. She described her colleagues as very supportive emotionally, unlike the P I C U and hematology-oncology attendings, and believed that they were able to share and discuss their work openly and honestly.

From my point of view as a senior physician, I find it unfortunate that we appear to be so often walled off from one another. One of the great joys and privileges of being able to interview physician colleagues for this book was to learn that so many of them, and especially some who had seemed to me to be hard-bitten and in complete control on the job, were not at all that way beneath their professional veneers.

Unlike the attending physicians, whose emotional isolation from one another was striking, the nurses generally expressed a great deal of satisfaction with their nursing colleagues' abilities to share their feelings with one another and to gain mutual support. They did identify some of their colleagues, generally the older and more experienced ones, as appearing to maintain an aloofness and distance from patients and families that they could not relate to, but most had no trouble finding a few colleagues who shared their sensitivities and values. Nursing management was sometimes perceived as unsupportive and at times hostile and was viewed with suspicion. Part of this perception undoubtedly reflects the intense feelings generated by the nurses' strike. However, it may also mirror the thoughts expressed by some of the younger nurses that nurses go into management when they are burned out with patient care and no longer share the intimate and loving attachment to patients and families that attracts and motivates them at the beginning of their careers.

Like the nurses, the pediatric residents found their greatest source of support among their resident colleagues. These were the people they trusted and believed could fully understand their feelings and concerns. While they might open up occasionally to a sympathetic attending physician, most were suspicious of the attendings and wary that any acknowledgement of emotion or weakness could lead to a lowered performance evaluation. Still in the process of forming their professional identities, they tended to value those traits in their colleagues that reflected their understanding of how a physician should behave. Those who believed that physicians should be emotionally available to patients valued openness in their colleagues and wondered about those residents who kept their feelings to themselves and appeared aloof. Those who did not share their emotions with their colleagues wondered if the others were perhaps too open and did not maintain an adequate professional distance. At the same time, this latter group wondered if their emotional isolation was desirable or healthy over time; some seemed to envy their colleagues' ability to enlist one another's support. "They talk about how they're doing and afterwards they seem to feel better."

One of the surprising features about each of the professional groups—attendings, nurses, and residents—was their emotional isolation from the other groups, despite their close and often intense working relationships. Attendings frequently expressed great admiration for the nurses' strong affective connection with patients and families, and for their ability to share their feelings with one another about their work, but with two exceptions, both women, they did not turn to the nurses for support. Unlike the attendings, who were often emotionally isolated both within their own group and from the other groups, the nurses' and pediatric residents' within-group support was high, yet they seldom sought support from the other groups. One resident did comment on a very helpful interaction with a nurse, and a couple of the nurses expressed admiration for supportive attending physicians, but as a rule most looked to peers within their own discipline for emotional support and understanding.

Participants' Reactions to the Interviews

Participants seemed to be grateful for the opportunity to have someone listen to their feelings about their lives and work in a non-judgmental, empathic fashion and often described the interviews as "therapeutic." Most had never spoken with anyone in such depth and over time about their powerful and at times overwhelming emotional reactions to the deaths of children and to the grief of the children's parents. Interestingly, the parts of the interviews that everyone enjoyed the most were those that dealt with their growing-up years and their early family relationships, and for the younger participants, those deaths of children that had been especially painful and troubling.

Many asked if their reactions to the deaths of children were "normal" or if others processed these tragedies differently. Several of the nurses wondered if people could work in a field like theirs that is so beset with loss and the inscrutable actions of fate if they did not have a deep religious or spiritual conviction. Others wanted to know more about the impact of children's deaths on peoples' abilities to interact with their own children and families. A number commented on how painful it had been to reflect on unhappy moments in their early lives and on the loss of especially memorable child patients. However, they also acknowledged that revisiting those memories had been helpful to them and had taught them something about themselves and how they interact with dying children. Several confessed that they had worked hard to maintain an emotional distance during the interviews so that they would not feel overwhelmed. "I can't afford to fall apart here and then have to put myself back together before returning to work."

Most agreed that some kind of on-the-job support about coping with children's deaths would be helpful, especially if it involved one-to-one counseling in a setting in which confidentiality could be assured. Peer support groups were valued, but there was always the worry that others would think less of you if you said "the wrong thing" or appeared "weak." Also, some feared that confessing mistakes in a group setting could lead to professional and legal repercussions.

If there is a bottom-line message to this book, it is that physicians and nurses, and especially those who are new to the field or feel isolated in their roles, need frequently available, voluntary opportunities to talk with skilled and trained listeners in a confidential, preferably individual setting. While these meetings may well have therapeutic effects, they should not be viewed as "therapy" for people who are having trouble functioning but rather as necessary components of ongoing training and workforce preservation. Nursing managers, hospital administrators, and administrative physicians should provide nurses and physicians with these opportunities but should not be present during the sessions, set their agendas, or require reports about them. Every participant must know and believe that whatever is said is strictly confidential and will in no way affect their job performance evaluation. If there are costs involved, they should be borne by the hospital and not by the individuals' private insurance. Many physicians and nurses worried that if they entered into formal therapy to discuss their concerns and then billed their insurance, this might have a negative impact on their careers, or they worried that the medical or nursing board might think they were "unstable." While this should not be the case, it is a widespread belief among the people with whom I have come in contact and, unfortunately, can often lead to protracted and untreated pain and sometimes death.

As medical care accelerates in its technical and scientific sophistication, and consequently its costs, the human side of caregiving seems at times to be increasingly devalued. We as physicians and nurses may experience ourselves as too busy serving the machines, the medical records, and the bottom line to open ourselves to our patients' and their families' deepest concerns. Our patients and their families, however, need providers who have the time and energy to offer compassion, support, and explanations through frightening and sometimes discouraging evaluations and treatments. At the end, death awaits us all, but it is the warm hands and hearts along the way that enable us to treasure the incomparable gift of life. Hopefully, this book will contribute to the efforts of those who strive to retain and strengthen the human side of health care.

INTERVIEW QUESTIONS

Personal background

1. Subject's age and gender.
2. What was the makeup of your immediate family while you were growing up?
3. What were your parents' occupations during your growing-up years?
4. How often were you separated from your mother and/or father for more than three months during your growing-up years?
5. What were the reasons for those separations?
6. How did those separations affect you?
7. What was your immediate family's ethnic and/or religious background?
8. How did your immediate family's ethnic and/or religious background affect you during your growing-up years?
9. How openly was death discussed within your immediate family?
10. What were your immediate family's views about death?
11. What were you taught happens to a person after his or her death?
12. How did your immediate family suggest that one should cope with the deaths of other people?
13. What were your personal views during your growing-up years about what happens to people after they die?
14. What were your personal views about how one should cope with the deaths of other people?

15. What experiences did you have with death while you were growing up?
16. How did that/those experience(s) affect you at the time?
17. How did you cope with those experiences?
18. How do those experiences affect you now?
19. How do you cope with them now?

Professional background

1. Subject's profession—attending staff physician, pediatric resident, hematology/oncology nurse.
2. What first attracted you to medicine/nursing?
3. What first attracted you to pediatrics/hematology/oncology nursing?
4. How satisfied are you with your career choice?
5. What are the positive aspects of your career choice?
6. What are the negative aspects of your career choice?
7. What type of pediatric/nursing practice do you see yourself doing in the future?
8. What are your reasons for that choice?
9. How satisfied are you with your medical/nursing school preparation for dealing with the deaths of patients?
10. How were you taught in medical/nursing school to deal with the deaths of patients?
11. What else do you wish you had been taught?
12. How satisfied are you with what you have been taught on the job since your graduation from medical/nursing school about how to deal with the deaths of patients?
13. What else do you wish you had been taught?
14. How well-prepared are your professional colleagues to deal with the deaths of patients?
15. What are their strengths in dealing with the deaths of patients?
16. What are their weaknesses in dealing with the deaths of patients?

17. How well-prepared are you to deal with the deaths of patients?
18. What are your strengths in dealing with the deaths of patients?
19. What are your weaknesses in dealing with the deaths of patients?

Professional experiences with the death of children

1. What do you remember about your first professional experience of dealing with the death of a child?
2. How did that experience affect you at the time?
3. How did you cope with the experience?
4. How does the experience affect you now?
5. How differently did the deaths of subsequent child patients affect you compared to the death of that first child patient?
6. How did you cope with the deaths of subsequent child patients?
7. What is the most difficult thing for you professionally about the death of a child patient?
8. What is the most difficult thing for you personally about the death of a child patient?
9. How well do your professional colleagues cope with the deaths of child patients?
10. What are their strengths in coping with the deaths of child patients?
11. What are their weaknesses in coping with the deaths of child patients?
12. What helps you to cope with the deaths of child patients?
13. What hinders your attempts to cope with the deaths of child patients?
14. How much support do you get from your colleagues in coping with the deaths of child patients?
15. What more could your professional colleagues do to help you cope with the deaths of child patients?

16. How much support do you get from your spouse/partner/ friends in coping with the deaths of child patients?

17. What more could your spouse/partner/friends do to help you cope with the deaths of child patients?

18. How do the deaths of child patients affect your views of your own mortality?

19. How do they affect your views of the mortality of your family members?

20. How often do you think about the mortality of your family members?

21. How do those thoughts affect you?

22. How often do you think about your own mortality?

23. How do those thoughts affect you?

24. What are the characteristics of a "good death" of a child patient?

25. What are the characteristics of a "bad death" of a child patient?

26. How much do you think that terminally ill children understand about their own deaths?

27. What could be done to increase terminally ill children's ability to cope with their own deaths?

28. How helpful are your colleagues in helping terminally ill children cope with their deaths?

29. What are their strengths in helping terminally ill children cope with their deaths?

30. What are their weaknesses in helping terminally ill children cope with their deaths?

31. How helpful are you in helping terminally ill children cope with their deaths?

32. What are your strengths in helping terminally ill children cope with their deaths?

33. What are your weaknesses in helping terminally ill children cope with their own deaths?

34. What do you say about death to children who are terminally ill?

35. What questions do terminally ill children ask you about their mortality?
36. How do those questions affect you?
37. What questions do the parents of terminally ill children ask you about their child's mortality?
38. How do those questions affect you?

Reactions to interview

1. How do you feel about the interview we have just finished?
2. What was the best part of the interview for you?
3. What was the most difficult part of the interview for you?
4. How could the interview have been made more effective?
5. What other questions might I have asked?
6. How has talking with me about the death of children affected you?
7. What were the positive aspects of talking with me about the death of children?
8. What were the negative aspects of talking with me about the death of children?
9. What else would you like to tell me?

SURVEY OF PRIOR RESEARCH

The present large and well-developed literature about the dying process dates back to the seminal work of Elisabeth Kübler-Ross in *On Death and Dying* (1969). It addresses the psychological adaptations and needs of the dying person and his family and the characteristics of normal and pathological grief (Billings and Block 1997; Field and Cassel 1997; Goldman 1998; Horsburgh, Trenholme, and Huckle 2002; Kübler-Ross 1969, 1975; Maddocks 2003).

The literature describing the grieving of physicians and nurses for their dying child patients is fairly limited (Hilden et al. 2001; Hinds et al. 1994; Kaplan 1998; Khaneja and Milrod 1998; Lenart et al. 1998; Papadatou 1997; Rabow et al. 2000; Sack et al. 1984; Sahler, McAnarney, and Friedman 1981). This is due, in part, to the fact that in developed countries the death of a child is rare and usually occurs in a hospital (Andresen, Seecharan, and Toce 2004). It is generally agreed that caring for dying children is even more stressful than caring for dying adults because of the relative rarity of children dying and the sense that a child's death is a contradiction of the natural order (Khaneja and Milrod 1998; Papadatou et al. 2001; Schowalter 1970). Some have even argued that caring for a dying child is one of the most, if not the most, stressful of events in medical and nursing practice (Hinds et al. 1994; Khaneja and Milrod 1998; Knazik et al. 2003; O'Connor and Jeavons 2003; Schowalter 1970; Vachon and Pakes 1984).

Despite the difficulties inherent in working with dying children and their families, few nurses and physicians are trained to do so (Andresen, Seecharan, and Toce 2004; Bagatell et al. 2002; Behnke,

Setzer, and Mehta 1984; Papadatou 1997; Sack et al. 1984). This deficiency has prompted calls to increase training around end-of-life care for doctors and nurses who work with children (American Academy of Pediatrics 2000; Behnke, Setzer, and Mehta 1984; Davies et al. 1996; Hilden et al. 2001; Hinds et al. 1994; Khaneja and Milrod 1998; Papadatou 1997; Rashotte et al. 1997; Sack et al. 1984; Sahler, McAnarney, and Friedman 1981).

The following sections describe studies that have examined the specific experiences, perceived training needs, and training programs around children's end-of-life care for pediatric residents, attending physicians, and pediatric nurses.

Pediatric Residents

While caring for the dying and their families is viewed as a core competency for physicians (American Academy of Pediatrics 2000; Field and Cassel 1997), many forces appear to operate against their acquisition of such skills (Billings and Block 1997). Several decades ago Kenniston (1967) suggested that medical students display a "propensity to counter, master, and overcome sources of anxiety, a tendency to react to stress and anxiety by an active effort to change the environment, and a highly developed ability to respond intellectually to troublesome feelings" (pp. 348–49). He noted that in medical school students learn to repress or suppress their anxieties about confronting death, pain, and suffering and to channel that anxiety into learning as much about their field as possible. He concluded that the combination of medical students' personal coping strategies around affective issues and the cultural traditions of medicine may lead them to become detached from their own emotions and from those of their patients.

Schowalter (1970) identified a child's death as potentially the most stressful experience in medical practice, but noted that pediatric residents nevertheless receive little formal death education. Within the hierarchy of a teaching hospital, the stress associated with a child's death is often translated into blame, some of which may be assigned to or assumed by the pediatric resident. Schowalter divided the experience of treating a dying child into three phases: impact (diagnosing a potentially fatal illness), battle (attempting to cure the disease), and defeat (recognizing that the child is going to die). It is during this last period, when active, curative treatment has been discontinued and the child is acknowledged to be dying, that pediatric residents may withdraw from the child's care and from their own feelings in order to protect themselves from the pain of the child's death.

In a study of pediatric interns, Adler, Werner, and Korsch (1980) suggested that internship has "deleterious effects on interns' sensitivity to patients and on their personal life" (p. 1000). The interns described the most difficult groups of patients as those who are "hostile and demanding" or "noncompliant," followed by those who are chronically ill and not responding to treatment. Although interns grew in confidence in their medical abilities during internship, their interpersonal skills deteriorated. They identified their greatest sources of stress as fatigue, not having enough time for their personal lives, and making mistakes. They coped with these stresses by turning for support to their families and to their fellow interns.

Sahler, McAnarney, and Friedman (1981) assessed the factors that influenced the relationships of pediatric interns with dying children and their parents. They found that interns were unlikely to develop relationships with patients less than one year of age and with those who were unresponsive or comatose. Their relationships with the parents of dying children were influenced primarily by how long the child had been in the hospital, with interns more likely to develop relationships with parents whose children had been in the hospital for a long period of time. Interns were least likely to develop relationships with neonates and their parents or with the parents of children who died shortly after admission to the hospital. Of the thirteen interns studied, seven were noted to be upset during and after the death of a child they had cared for, and two were noted to function less effectively during that time.

Sack et al. (1984) interviewed thirty-six pediatric residents about

289

their experiences caring for chronically ill and dying children. Twenty-seven of thirty-six had been involved in caring for a dying patient as medical students, but most did not believe that their medical school experience of caring for a dying patient had prepared them to deal as residents with children who were dying. Two-thirds reported having personally experienced the death of a family member and most found that that experience had helped them to feel empathy with the parents of dying children and to make them less avoidant of them. On average, each resident reported having told the parents of thirty-three children that their child had a life-threatening illness. Their initial experiences of doing so were emotional and left them with a feeling of inadequacy. Most had not had the experience of talking on their own with a child about his or her life-threatening illness.

The residents in Sack et al.'s study reported caring for an average of thirty-five dying children during their first two-and-a-half years of residency. In recalling a difficult experience around a child's death, most selected examples from their first year of training. Shock and guilt or blame were the feelings most often reported in connection with these memories. Some expressed anger or frustration if the death was caused by a colleague's error, while others reported identifying with the dying child's parents.

Despite the frequency and emotional intensity of residents' experiences with the deaths of children, Sack et al. noted that training during residency about how to deal with children's deaths was minimal. End-of-life training usually consisted of a few lectures and some readings (few of which the residents could remember), informal educational experiences with faculty, and discussions with peers.

The authors suggested that the residents' experiences of children dying and parents grieving and their emotional responses to them were influenced by several factors. One was the motivation of many young physicians to enter medicine to save lives and their resultant defensiveness when this proved to be impossible. A second was the perceived coping strategies of people who chose medicine as a career. Rather than avoiding or living with anxiety-provoking situations, residents were likely to attempt to master them. They were also more likely to focus on changing the environment than changing themselves, and to deal with anxiety intellectually. These strategies for coping with stress were felt by the authors to be potentially unhelpful in residents' dealings with patients and families. The authors recommended that pediatric residency programs coordinate teaching about the coping and defensive reactions of parents, children, and physicians to a child's death throughout the curriculum. This teaching should include both peer support groups and opportunities for individual meetings with a faculty member to examine one's reactions to children's deaths and to discuss one's own emotions. Also emphasized was the importance of acknowledging that caring for dying children generates distress in physicians.

Behnke, Setzer, and Mehta (1984) evaluated pediatric residents' medical school and residency training in death counseling and their comfort level in providing psychosocial support to dying children and their families. Only 22 percent of the residents had received any training in death counseling, although 67 percent of children and 85 percent of families had approached them requesting such support. Only seven of the twenty-six felt qualified to counsel dying children and their families, and almost all expressed a need for education in how to do so.

Billings and Block (1997) suggested that medical schools have been slow to introduce death education as a major part of their curricula. They found that while 89 percent of schools offer some end-of-life teaching, only 11 percent offer a full-term course on dying and death. In most cases, medical students' exposure to death education is brief (one or two lectures) and occurs primarily in their first two years of school, when they have little patient contact and are least likely to encounter a dying person. Residency offers even less exposure to education in end-of-life care, with only 26 percent of residency programs providing such courses despite the fact that resident physicians experience death routinely, witnessing an average of twenty-eight deaths per resident per year. The study's authors suggest that the gains in humanistic attitudes and skills that medical students acquire during their first two years of medical school are often "untaught," both during their final two years and during their residency, when education about how to deal with dying and death is minimal.

Based on a survey in one New York teaching hospital of pediatricians' perceptions of their coping skills in dealing with dying children, Khaneja and Milrod (1998) recommended several steps for improving pediatricians' training in end-of-life care. These included a didactic curriculum on the care of dying children that would extend through all three years of pediatric residency, a debriefing after each child's death, the introduction of hospice rotations, and encouragement for residents to attend children's funerals.

Vazirani, Slavin, and Feldman (2000) made a longitudinal evaluation of pediatric residents' attitudes toward dying and death. They found that pediatric residents begin their training feeling uncomfortable about end-of-life issues, but that by the end of training they are more comfortable and confident in dealing with them. The key factor that residents identified as having helped them to become more comfortable in dealing with dying and death was a personal experience with deaths among their own family members. Clinically, the most helpful experiences in this regard were meetings with the families of dying or dead patients. Residents felt that death education was not adequately addressed in either medical school or residency and expressed a need for more of it. Interestingly, while residents felt comfortable early in their training administering pain medications to dying patients, by the end they were less comfortable doing so, reflecting the fears of their attending physicians that medicating too heavily to relieve pain might hasten death.

Despite the widely perceived and expressed need for more training during pediatric residency about how to deal with dying children and their families, I was able to discover only two articles that described experiences with such programs. Berman and Villarreal (1983) established a seminar program at the University of Colorado that was intended to train pediatric interns in how to provide pediatric end-of-life care. To help the interns deal with the deaths of children, the authors developed a daylong seminar away from the hospital in which interns could discuss their experiences in the delivery room, intensive care nursery, ward, and emergency room. In discussing an unsuccessful resuscitation in the delivery room, interns identified feelings of failure, guilt, and inadequacy and acknowledged that these feelings had prohibited them from being supportive and compassionate with the child's parents. In the neonatal intensive care nursery, the interns described considerable discomfort when members of the treatment team were not able to reach a consensus about how to manage an infant with a severe birth defect. On the wards, they experienced problems caring for dying adolescents because they overidentified with them and had to deal with their own fears of dying. They recognized how difficult it can be to make the transition between actively treating a child to providing supportive care once it was recognized that the child was dying. They also expressed frustration that they did not have enough time to spend with dying patients. They admitted that they had difficulty coping with angry and demanding parents and with those parents who kept asking the same questions even after they had answered them. They acknowledged that they often experienced a grief reaction after the death of a child and that their grieving could be affected by a number of factors. These included having the child remind them of themselves, their own children, or earlier losses in their lives; experiencing feelings of failure, guilt, and inadequacy; and feeling angry with the parents when a child's death was the result of an accident or abuse. Reflecting on the formation of their attitudes toward death, the interns reported that their childhood experiences of death usually involved those of grandparents or great-grandparents. Only 32 percent remembered talking with their families about death. Their present attitudes toward death were shaped primarily by their religious upbringing and by introspection or meditation. Most thought only rarely about their own deaths.

Bagatell et al. (2002) reported on a six-session seminar they conducted for pediatric residents at the University of Arizona to discuss end-of-life issues in children. The seminar topics included declaring death, medical management of dying children, and case discussions with experienced local physicians about the care of dying children and their families. The participants also had individual discussions with their family members about an important death, group discussions of their personal experiences with death and dying, and a meeting with their significant others to reflect on how dealing with dying children affected their professional and personal lives. By the end of the seminar participants reported feeling more confident in their skills for dealing with dying children and for coping with their own feelings about them.

Attending Physicians

Behnke et al. (1984) examined the problems that pediatricians confront when dealing with dying children. Because they focus on healing and strengthening the living child, they may experience incurable or dying patients as personal failures. Pediatricians have also focused increasingly on the technical aspects of healthcare, often neglecting their patients' emotional needs. Dying children may provoke death anxiety in pediatricians, who may then deal with it by focusing exclusively on patients as clinical problems and losing interest when a child begins to die. Conversely, they may become overinvolved emotionally with the dying child and his family. The authors argue that for pediatricians to deal successfully with dying children and their families, they must overcome their own death anxiety, resolving their personal concerns through either religious or secular training.

Seravalli (1988) also addressed the dilemma of the dying patient and his physician. The terminally ill patient has "a heightened sense of life . . . and an almost overwhelming need for human contact and communication" (p. 1724), including ongoing contact with his physician. The physician, on the other hand, may see her patient's death as a failure and may also identify with the dying person and experience fears of her own mortality. These emotions may cause the physician either to continue therapies that have no purpose or to withdraw from the patient. The author concludes his essay with a poem written by a woman whose grandchild had died: "when he died / my eyes were dry / and gods wearing white coats / turned away" (p. 1730).

The perception that physicians may emotionally abandon their patients once there is no more hope of cure is mirrored in Sharp, Strauss, and Lorch's survey (1992) of parents who had received bad news about their children. The parents expressed a preference that in such situations physicians would give them more information and show their own feelings. They especially wanted physicians to show caring by allowing them as parents to talk and express their feelings.

In a survey of emergency room physicians, Ahrens and Hart (1997) found that 66 percent reported that communicating with the parents of a dead child was the most difficult aspect of their work, much more difficult than communicating with the family of a dead adult. After an unsuccessful pediatric resuscitation, 64 percent of physicians felt guilty or inadequate and 47 percent reported that these feelings continued for the rest of their shift. Only 14 percent reported that they had received training in notifying parents that their child had died, while 92 percent said that such training would be helpful.

Bartel et al. (2000) reported that earlier studies of pediatric intensive care units (P I C U s) had documented several areas where parents had preferences for involvement in their child's care. Parents wanted to be on the unit with their child, to receive truthful and accurate information about their child's condition, to know that their child's pain was well controlled, and to be able to sleep near the unit. In light of these findings, the authors interviewed physicians on a pediatric intensive care unit to determine how they approached the care of families whose children had become suddenly and acutely ill with life-threatening conditions. Because these families had not had time to adjust to their children's illnesses, they were often overwhelmed. The physicians described both contextual and relational factors that are essential for the optimal care of such families. Contextual factors include parental denial and the time lag between the onset of the illness and the parents' acceptance of its seriousness. There are also the time pressures experienced by PICU physicians in caring for numerous acutely ill children, the need for all team members to communicate the same message to the families, and the desire of both parents and staff for a private space on the unit. Relational factors included holding regular meetings with the family, with one team member functioning as the spokesperson for the team, and employing good interpersonal skills when delivering bad news. These skills consisted of behaviors such as introducing oneself, shaking hands, being careful of one's body language, maintaining eye contact, and pacing the tempo of information. The authors concluded that most PICU physicians interviewed were empathic and recognized the importance of psychosocial issues and interpersonal skills in dealing with the families of children with acute and life-threatening conditions. Many recalled learning how to break bad news in medical school and residency. They acknowledged the emotional toll of working in pediatric intensive care units and emphasized the delicate empathic balance between building good relationships with families and feeling emotionally overwhelmed. They also recognized the special role of PICU nurses in having the closest relationships with both patients and their families and being in a position to help the team communicate clearly and effectively with parents.

Hilden et al. (2001) surveyed pediatric oncologists around end-of-life care for children. They found that most felt they had little formal training in this area and that they tended to learn about caring for dying children through trial and error. They stressed that role models in caring for dying children are needed and acknowledged that communication problems exist between parents and oncologists, especially at the point when treatment is shifting from attempting to cure the child to end-of-life care.

Knazik et al. (2003) addressed the issue of how a child's death in an emergency department (ED) affects the unit's staff and how the staff may best prepare to deal with such events. The authors reported that few ED physicians are trained to deal with the death of a child, and that after a child's death their subsequent emotions often impair their performance. While deaths are common in the ED, physicians there often do not acknowledge the emotional impact of the deaths and may be at risk of developing post-traumatic stress disorder (PTSD). It is especially important that physicians deal with their feelings of failure, guilt, and incompetence by talking or writing them out and by engaging in general wellness activities like crafts and exercise. The authors conclude by outlining the normal process of grief in parents after the death of a child. Initially there is a "psychic pain spike" that lasts from five to fifteen minutes, during which feelings of disbelief, numbness, and shock are experienced. Then there is a period of denial that the death has occurred, followed by feelings of anger and then guilt. Guilt can be especially severe for parents because of parents' protective role in child rearing, and it can be very helpful if the physician is able to exonerate the parents from such guilt. If grieving is prolonged or especially intense it may develop into pathological grief that can severely impair the person's functioning. Risk factors for pathological grief include the death of an infant or a child, sudden death, death by suicide or homicide, and deaths in which the parents' feelings of guilt are justified, such as after an accident or child abuse in which the parent may have contributed to the death.

Nurses

The nursing literature has focused more intensively than the medical literature on the grief experienced by nurses caring for dying children. It has developed a theoretical and descriptive understanding of the emotional and coping processes employed by nurses to deal with their grief and has offered suggestions on how to resolve that grief in a healthy and productive manner (Davies et al. 1996; Papadatou et al. 2001; Rashotte et al. 1997).

Friedman, Franciosi, and Drake (1979) described the reactions of nursing staff to a SIDS (sudden infant death syndrome) death in a hospital. A previously healthy child that had been hospitalized for psychosocial reasons died suddenly. The nursing assistant who had cared for the child experienced the most stress, including feelings of guilt, fear of handling other infants, tearfulness, and problems with appetite and sleep. She also reported bad dreams and a new sense of human frailty and helplessness, becoming more watchful of her own two-year-old. Her husband had difficulty understanding why this death should bother her more than others did and wished that she would talk less about it at home. Other nurses experienced guilt relative to their degree of contact with the child. Some also converted their guilt and anger into blame, especially for the child's mother, whose behavior had led to the child being hospitalized.

Vachon and Pakes (1984) provided a comprehensive outline of the types of stress that staff members caring for critically ill and dying children are exposed to. They suggested that working with dying children can lead to substantial emotional stress and to feelings of anxiety, frustration, and guilt. If these symptoms are not acknowledged openly they may result in dysfunctional emotional symptoms and behaviors that may affect patient care, staff relationships, relationships with one's family members, and one's own physical and mental health. They identified stresses that are specific to the child's illness, to the trajectory of that illness, to the care environment, and to the staff member's occupational role. Illness-specific stresses include exposure to sicker and sicker children because of advances in medical care, working only with critically ill children, dealing with iatrogenic (treatment-induced) disorders, and getting too close to long-term patients and their families. Illness-trajectory stresses consist of sudden or unexpected deaths; deaths that take too long or are uncontrolled, especially in regard to pain; deaths of "special" patients; diagnoses that are perceived as "death sentences"; and trying to ensure a "good death" for the patient. Environmental stresses involve the need to constantly develop new technical skills, working in a "fishbowl-like" setting where everyone knows how everyone else is doing, experiencing children as depersonalized by highly technical care and equipment, and having no time to relax in the face of constant demands.

The authors suggest that these stresses can be mediated (increased or decreased) by factors such as the staff member's age, social class, marital status, and history of previous stress. Younger staff may have had little previous exposure to death, middle-aged staff may have an intellectual acceptance of death but continue to deny it emotionally, and older staff may no longer appreciate and feel sympathetic with younger staff members' concerns about death. Staff with children of their own may be vulnerable when caring for patients the same ages as their own children. Being married can be protective if one's spouse is a supportive confidant who can listen empathetically, but it can become an additional source of stress if one's partner does not want to listen or encourages one to find another profession. One's own past losses, if incompletely resolved emotionally, can become a source of stress and may lead to depression in settings where one must deal frequently with death.

The authors identify a variety of physical, psychological, social, and occupational symptoms that may result from the stresses inherent in working in intensive, highly technical, acute-care settings. These range from various somatic complaints including sleep disturbances to depression and thoughts of suicide, denial, anxiety, and anger; overidentification with patients; substance abuse; feelings of dehumanization; marital problems; and overconcern for the health of one's own children. At work these responses may lead to feelings of being overwhelmed or detached, repetitive accidents, overinvolvement with patients and their families, cynicism, and decreased satisfaction with one's profession. What is key to dealing with the manifestations of stress that result from caring for critically ill and dying children is prevention, as well as learning healthy coping strategies such as taking time for oneself, sustaining a good social support system, and having opportunities at work to discuss one's feelings in a safe, confidential setting.

Hinds et al. (1994) reported that the most stressful experience for a pediatric intensive care unit nurse is the death of a favorite patient, and that the accumulated grief from such experiences may lead the nurse to leave the PICU, change specialty, or leave nursing altogether. The authors suggested that the negative consequences of grief are more likely if the nurse's grieving is not recognized, acknowledged, and facilitated. Acknowledged and facilitated grief can benefit the nurse by helping her to reinvest in new patients and to think more globally about life and death. Techniques for facilitating grief include attending memorial services, receiving education about grief and loss, and participating in staff support groups.

Davies et al. (1996) examined the reactions of twenty-five nurses once they had recognized that the death of a child they were caring for was inevitable. The nurses struggled to resolve their grief and moral distress around the child's dying and death. Grieving was complicated for some nurses by a perception that crying was "unprofessional" or would not be tolerated by their colleagues. Thinking and reflecting actively about one's practice, and about life and death issues generally, assisted successful coping with grief. Bringing closure to the nurse's relationship with the patient and family through internal or external mourning processes and attending funerals or memorial services helped the nurses move on and prepare to reinvest their energies in other patients. Moral distress included those feelings of anger, sadness, helplessness, and frustration that nurses felt when they were compelled to carry out painful, active treatment for a child they knew was going to die. These feelings could be dealt with by achieving balance in one's personal and professional life, working to achieve some measure of control in the child's care, talking with peers, and helping to comfort the patient. Ineffective strategies for dealing with moral distress included becoming sarcastic, crying, and withdrawing.

Rashotte et al. (1997) analyzed the grief reactions of six pediatric intensive care unit (PICU) nurses who had cared for at least three children that died. The study confirmed that the grief experienced by PICU nurses differs from the common experience of grief because it occurs repeatedly and on an ongoing basis. The nurses coped with their grief in five ways. First, they expressed or venti-lated their feelings. Second, they found ways to nurture themselves by doing something special like shopping or gardening. Third, they found ways to experience closure with the dead child and his fam-ily through such activities as attending the funeral or wake, writing the family a letter, or making a home visit. Fourth, they attempted to gain control over certain aspects of their practice—for example, by following a personal mourning ritual, determining how much they would cry, and suppressing their feelings until they could be expressed in a safe place. Finally, they sought to establish a balance in their caregiving relationships between detachment and emotional involvement.

Kushnir, Rabin, and Azulai (1997) described the experience of run-ning a Balint-type group for nurses working on a pediatric oncol-ogy unit in Israel. Balint groups, originally developed for work with general practitioners, provide a supportive forum for discussing problems in the patient-professional relationship, and especially problems that presently bother participants. Their goal is to increase personal awareness and to provide a supportive atmosphere for acknowledging and changing defensive reactions to clinical situa-tions. The overpowering issue for the authors' group was the issue of death and dying. This theme pervaded the lives of the nurses both at work and at home. The nurses saw themselves as fighters in a war against disease, in which recovery was victory and death was defeat. They felt themselves isolated from medical staff at work and from friends and family at home, both of whom often questioned how they could work in such painful surroundings. Many felt inferior pro-fessionally to the medical staff and saw themselves as insignificant in the eyes of the administration. They described emotional overin-volvement with patients and families, believing they should give their all, work long hours, and attend funerals. They also believed that they should not get angry with patients or their families because "they had suffered enough." The medical and administrative staff became the targets for their anger. The authors recommended that in order to decrease burnout, job stress should be reduced, peer group support should be increased, and nursing leaders should receive supervision to help them deal with their own emotional reactions so that they could better support the staff nurses.

Kaplan (1998, 2000) described a study of fifteen pediatric nurses who worked with dying children. She reported that the nurses strove to achieve a delicate balance between their emotional responses to their patients and the need to be competent professionals. The closeness of their relationship to the patients and the manner of the children's deaths influenced the strength of the nurses' emotional reactions.

Papadatou et al. (2001) compared nurses' differing experiences of grief around the care of dying children in Greece and Hong Kong. They found that regardless of the cultural setting caring for dying children increased the nurses' stress. This derived from their sense of helplessness in adequately ameliorating the children's pain, and especially because of the patients' and families' distress. They also found that during the grieving process nurses appeared to fluctuate between experiencing and avoiding the pain of loss. This was thought to be healthy, as it allowed them to continue to focus on their work and yet still grieve. Nurses attributed the children's deaths either to divine forces or to the seriousness of the child's illness. Finally, the nurses appeared to derive a sense of satisfaction from their work because of their sense that they were making a meaningful contribution. Their major sources of dissatisfaction were conflicts with physicians over the child's care and staffing shortages.

Papadatou et al. (2002) compared the processes of grieving for children dying of cancer as these were experienced by Greek physicians and nurses. Both professional groups experienced the death of a child patient as highly stressful emotionally and one that triggered a grief reaction and a sense of helplessness. Both groups derived satisfaction from being able to ensure that the child died a pain-free and dignified death. They also described a fluctuation between active grieving and avoiding grief, a process that allowed them to grieve while continuing to function in their jobs. Nurses and physicians differed from one another in several ways. Physicians found it emotionally distressing to be in the room with the dying child because of the help-lessness they experienced, and appeared to be grieving primarily for the loss of their professional goal of curing the child. They tended to grieve privately and not to seek or receive support from their medical colleagues. Nurses felt a sense of satisfaction from the close relationships they were able to develop with children and their families and experienced the child's death as a personal loss that triggered a grieving process. Unlike physicians, nurses were more likely to seek and receive support from their nursing colleagues.

Several avenues for future research are suggested by this work. First, prospective studies might focus on the development of physicians' and nurses' coping skills in dealing with the deaths of children. Of special interest would be those factors that either help or hinder healthy coping, such as unconscious ego-defense mechanisms, social support, and cognitive strategies for dealing with difficult situations (Vaillant 2000). Second, randomized, controlled studies of different psychosocial interventions to assist residents and new nurses, such as the availability of individual versus group counseling, might explore the development of depression and post-traumatic stress disorder in treated versus untreated groups. This would address the question of how effective, and ultimately cost-effective, such services can be. A final area to explore is whether and how the provision of easily accessible, confidential settings for physicians and nurses to discuss and examine their reactions to children's deaths affects the care of their patients. The treatment that health professionals provide to their patients will, I suspect, reflect the ways in which they are treated by the health care systems within which they work. A health care system that develops a caring and supportive environment for its health care providers is likely, in my view, to create an atmosphere of more supportive and empathic care for its patients.

ABBREVIATIONS

ALS   Amyotrophic lateral sclerosis, also know as "Lou Gehrig's Disease." This is a progressive degenerative disease that destroys the body's motor nerve cells and that ultimately results in paralysis and death.

AML   Acute myeloid leukemia. A cancer of the blood in which malignant cells (myeloblasts) invade the bloodstream and bone marrow and interfere with the body's ability to generate new red and white blood cells.

ARDS   Acute respiratory distress syndrome. A condition characterized by the sudden onset of shortness of breath, low blood-oxygen levels, and lung injury, which lead to respiratory failure.

DNR   Do not resuscitate. A physician order indicating that efforts to revive a patient whose heart and/or breathing have stopped should not be made. Typically, such orders are given for patients with terminal illnesses and a low quality of life.

ECMO   Extra-corporeal membrane oxygenation. This is a form of mechanical ventilation for patients, especially newborns, whose lungs are not functioning properly.

ECT   Electroconvulsive therapy. This treatment involves
         the passage of a brief electrical current through the
         brain; it can be helpful in the treatment of certain
         forms of depression. ECT is known popularly as
         "Shock therapy."

EEG   Electroencephalogram. A mechanical tracing of
         the electrical impulses generated by the brain as
         detected by electrodes attached to the skin of the
         skull. EEGs are often used to detect the presence
         of a seizure disorder.

EMG   Electromyelogram. This procedure involves placing
         a needle electrode in a muscle and measuring its
         electrical potential at rest and during contraction.
         It is used to distinguish between diseases of the
         muscles and of the nerves.

ICU   Intensive Care Unit. A unit within a hospital with a
         high staff-to-patient ratio of nurses and physicians
         who are specially trained in the care of severely ill
         patients who require close and around-the-clock
         monitoring and treatment.

IV   Intravenous treatment. This involves the adminis-
         tration of fluids and medications directly into the
         veins.

M and M Morbidity and mortality. M and M conferences
         are used to review cases in which diagnostic and
         treatment problems have occurred, or that involve
         a patient's death.

NICU   Neonatal Intensive Care Unit. This is an ICU that
         delivers specialized care to newborns.

PICU   Pediatric Intensive Care Unit. This is an ICU that
              delivers specialized care to child and adolescent
              patients.

RSV   Respiratory syncytial virus. This virus is the major
              cause of lower respiratory disease in infants.

BIBLIOGRAPHY

Adler, R., E. R. Werner, and B. Korsch. 1980. "Systematic Study of Four Years of Internship." *Pediatrics* 66(6):1000–08.

Ahrens, W. R., and R. G. Hart. 1997. "Emergency Physicians' Experience with Pediatric Death." *American Journal of Emergency Medicine* 15(7):642–43.

American Academy of Pediatrics. 2000. "Palliative Care for Children." *Pediatrics* 106(2):351–57.

Andresen, E. M., G. A. Seecharan, and S. S. Toce. 2004. "Provider Perceptions of Child Deaths." *Archives of Pediatrics and Adolescent Medicine* 158(5): 430–35.

Bagatell, R., et al. 2002. "When Children Die: A Seminar Series for Pediatric Residents." *Pediatrics* 110(2):348–53.

Bartel, D. A., et al. 2000. "Working with Families of Suddenly and Critically Ill Children: Physician Experiences." *Archives of Pediatrics and Adolescent Medicine* 154(11):1127–33.

Becker, E. 1973. *The Denial of Death*. New York: Free Press.

Behnke, M., E. Setzer, and P. Mehta. 1984. "Death Counseling and Psychosocial Support by Physicians Concerning Dying Children." *Journal of Medical Education* 59(11):906–8.

Behnke, M., et al. 1984. "The Pediatrician and the Dying Child." In H. Wass and C. A. Corr, eds., *Childhood and Death*, pp. 69–93. Washington, D.C.: Hemisphere Publishing.

Berman, S., and S. Villarreal. 1983. "Use of a Seminar as an Aid in Helping Interns Care for Dying Children and Their Families." *Clinical Pediatrics* 22(3):175–79.

Billings, J. A., and S. Block. 1997. "Palliative Care in Undergraduate Medical Education: Status Report and Future Directions." *Journal of the American Medical Association* 278(9):733–38.

Davies, B., et al. 1996. "Caring for Dying Children: Nurses' Experiences." *Pediatric Nursing* 22(6):500–508.

Field, M. J., and C. K. Cassel. 1997. *Approaching Death: Improving Care at the End of Life.* Washington, D.C.: National Academy Press.

Friedman, G. R., R. A. Franciosi, and R. M. Drake. 1979. "The Effects of Observed Sudden Infant Death Syndrome (SIDS) on Hospital Staff." *Pediatrics* 64(4):538–40.

Goldman, A. 1998. "ABC of Palliative Care: Special Problems of Children." *British Medical Journal* 316:49–52.

Hilden, J. M., et al. 2001. "Attitudes and Practices Among Pediatric Oncologists Regarding End-of-Life Care: Results of the 1998 American Society of Clinical Oncology Survey." *Journal of Clinical Oncology* 19(1): 205–12.

Hinds, P. S., et al. 1994. "The Impact of a Grief Workshop for Pediatric Oncology Nurses on Their Grief and Perceived Stress." *Journal of Pediatric Nursing* 9(6):388-397.

Horsburgh, M., A. Trenholme, and T. Huckle. 2002. "Pediatric Respite Care: A Literature Review from New Zealand." *Palliative Medicine* 16:99–105.

Kaplan, L. J. 1998. "The Emotional Experiences of Treating Dying Children: Nurses Speak Out." *Dissertation Abstracts International: Section B: the Sciences & Engineering,* 59(4-B), p. 1854.

———. 2000. "Toward a Model of Caregiver Grief: Nurses' Experiences of Treating Dying Children." *Omega: Journal of Death & Dying* 41(3):187–206.

Kenniston, K. 1967. "The Medical Student." *Yale Journal of Biology and Medicine* 39:346–57.

Khaneja, S., and B. Milrod. 1998. "Educational Needs Among Pediatricians Regarding Caring for Terminally Ill Children." *Archives of Pediatrics and Adolescent Medicine* 152(9):909–14.

Knazik, S. R., et al. 2003. "The Death of a Child in the Emergency Department." *Annals of Emergency Medicine* 42(4):519–29.

Kübler-Ross, E. 1969. *On Death and Dying.* New York: MacMillan.

———. 1975. *Death: The Final Stage of Growth.* New York: Touchstone.

Kushnir, T., S. Rabin, and S. Azulai. 1997. "A Descriptive Study of Stress Management in a Group of Pediatric Oncology Nurses." *Cancer Nursing* 20(6): 414–21.

Lenart, S. B., C. G. Bauer, D. D. Brighton, et al. 1998. "Grief Support for Nursing Staff in the ICU." *Journal for Nurses in Staff Development* 14(6): 293–96.

Liechty, D. 2000. "Touching Mortality, Touching Strength: Clinical Work with Dying Patients." *Religion and Health* 39(3):247–59.

Lyon, J. 1985. *Playing God in the Nursery.* New York: W. W. Norton.

Maddocks, I. 2003. "Grief and Bereavement." *Medical Journal of Australia* 179(6 Suppl):S6-S7.

Miller, A. 1997. *The Drama of the Gifted Child: The Search for the True Self,* trans. R. Ward. New York: Basic Books.

O'Connor, J., and S. Jeavons. 2003. "Nurses' Perceptions of Critical Incidents." *Journal of Advanced Nursing* 41(1):53–62.

Papadatou, D. 1997. "Training Health Professionals in Caring for Dying Children and Grieving Families." *Death Studies* 21(6):575–600.

———, et al. 2001. "Caring for Dying Children: A Comparative Study of Nurses' Experiences in Greece and Hong Kong." *Cancer Nursing* 24(5):402–12.

Papadatou, D., T. Bellali, I. Papazoglou, and D. Petraki. 2002. "Greek Nurse and Physician Grief as a Result of Caring for Children Dying of Cancer." *Pediatric Nursing* 28(4):345–53.

Rabow, M. W., G. E. Hardie, J. J. Fair, and S. J. McPhee. 2000. "End-of-Life Care Content in 50 Textbooks from Multiple Specialties." *Journal of the American Medical Association* 283:771–78.

Rashotte, J., F. Fothergill-Bourbonnais, and M. Chamberlain. 1997. "Pediatric Intensive Care Nurses and Their Grief Experiences: A Phenomenological Study." *Heart and Lung* 26(5):372–86.

Sack, W. H., G. Fritz, P. G. Krener, and L. Sprunger. 1984. "Death and the Pediatric House Officer Revisited." *Pediatrics* 73(5):676–81.

Sahler, O. J., E. R. McAnarney, and S. B. Friedman. 1981. "Factors Influencing Pediatric Interns' Relationships with Dying Children and their Parents." *Pediatrics* 67(2):207–16.

Schowalter, J. E. 1970. "Death and the Pediatric House Officer." *Journal of Pediatrics* 76(5):706–10.

Seravalli, E. P. 1988. "The Dying Patient, the Physician, and the Fear of Death." *New England Journal of Medicine* 319(26):1728, 1730.

Sharp, M. C., R. P. Strauss, and S. C. Lorch. 1992. "Communicating Bad News: Parents' Experiences and Preferences." *Journal of Pediatrics* 121(4): 539–46.

Shem, S. 1978. *The House of God*. New York: Dell.

Vachon, A. L. S., and E. Pakes. 1984. "Staff Stress in the Care of the Critically Ill and Dying Child." In H. Wass and C. A. Corr, eds., *Childhood and Death*, pp. 151–82. Washington, D.C.: Hemisphere Publishing.

Vaillant, G. E. 2000. "Adaptive Mental Mechanisms: Their Role in a Positive Psychology." *American Psychologist* 55(1):89–98.

Vazirani, R. M., S. J. Slavin, and J. D. Feldman. 2000. "Longitudinal Study of Pediatric House Officers' Attitudes toward Death and Dying." *Critical Care Medicine* 28(11):3740–45.

INDEX

Acute Myelogenous Leukemia
(AML)', 305
Acute Respiratory Distress Syndrome (ARDS), 305
afterlife, beliefs about, 26, 27, 45, 117, 164, 194, 208, 221–22, 259
American Journal of Nursing, 236
Amyotrophic Lateral Sclerosis (ALS), 305
anger, 23, 24, 34, 42, 47, 218, 219
attending physicians, 91–94, 185, 294–95; career plans of, 101, 153–54, 165–66, 179; career satisfaction of, 101, 119, 138–39, 152–54, 165, 178–79; emotional needs of, 121, 123, 129; reasons for career choice of, 100–101, 118–19, 136, 152, 164–65, 177–78, 265; and research, 294–97, 303. See also coping strategies, attending physicians' assessment of; death, experiences of, prior to medical school of attending physicians; death, impact of subsequent on; death of child patients, attending

physicians' views on; deaths, first in career; medical school, as preparation for coping with patient deaths; mortality, concerns of attending physicians; social support for attending physicians
Awakenings (movie), 85

"Baby Doe" era, 162
Balint groups, 301
Becker, Ernest, 15
bereavement care, 206–7
blaming others for deaths, 34, 154, 172
burnout, 215–16

"Celebration of Life," 206, 211
Chediak-Higashi syndrome, 147–48
child abuse, 23, 24, 47
Child Life: ceding responsibility to, 64; helpfulness of, 107
code: failed, 127–28, 244; full, 18, 214; versus do not resuscitate (DNR), 18, 54–55

deaths, 104, 199–200; and identification with patient or patient's
parents, 33, 93, 97, 133, 231,
263, 266; and inexperience, 38,
77, 107, 200, 239; and lack of
support, 21, 38, 104, 168; and
lack of time, 37, 59, 65–66, 75,
273; and lack of training, 37,
65–66, 146, 154–55; as professional failure, 41, 65, 129, 148–
49, 199, 202, 263–64; professionally versus personally, 10,
56, 97, 110–11, 248; and religious beliefs, 211, 218, 248, 273;
and support, 167, 203–4, 212,
224, 253, 254, 300. See also coping strategies

death: children's awareness of
impending, 56, 61, 63, 182, 226,
242; children sparing parents
from, 107, 158, 225; children's
questions about, 51, 141, 158,
243, 258; children's understanding of, 36, 63, 77, 88, 106–7,
126, 144, 158, 213, 256–57; in-
hospital versus in-home, 220,
225; models of coping with, 57,
175, 293; parents' awareness of
impending, 56, 91–92, 97–98;
parents' questions about,
51–52, 64, 108–9, 126–27, 141,
158, 170, 182, 202, 214–15, 226–
27, 258–59; planned, 128, 225;
preparing children for, 91, 213–

14; talking with child patients
about, 51, 52–53, 61, 63–64,
89–90, 108, 140–41, 182, 243,
257–58; talking with parents
about, 52, 64–65, 77–78, 108–9,
158–59, 214; unexpected, 125,
231. See also coping with child
patient deaths

death, experiences of, prior to
medical school of attending
physicians: and development
of empathy, 290; and family
members, 98–100, 114–17, 134–
36, 150, 164; and other children,
150–51; and pets, 99; and public
figures, 116

death, experiences of, prior to
medical school of residents: and
family members, 26–27, 28–30,
44–45, 57–58, 69–72, 83; and
friends, 27–28, 72–73; and other
children, 70; and pets, 27, 45;
and public figures, 70

death, experiences of, prior to
nursing school of nurses, 194;
and family members, 221, 232–
33; and friends, 208–9; and
pets, 249–50

death, factors affecting reactions
to, 56, 61–62, 68, 124

death, impact of subsequent on:
attending physicians, 95–96,
139, 262–63; nurses, 193, 206,
262–63; residents, 24–25, 40,
55–56, 262–63

death, questions from professionals about, 73, 83, 96, 97–98, 117, 119

death and dying courses, 32, 48, 84, 103, 136–37, 197

death anxiety, 6, 15, 18–19, 63–64, 88, 105–6

death of child patients: as relief, 33–34, 266; characteristics of, 275–76

death of child patients, attending physicians' views on: "bad," 97, 106, 125, 144, 157–58, 169–70, 182; "good," 97, 106, 125–26, 143–44, 157, 169, 182

death of child patients compared to deaths of: adults, 32, 124, 229–30; babies, 168; own family members, 33, 266

death of child patients, nurses' views on: "bad," 201, 213, 225–26, 242, 256; "good," 201, 213, 225, 241–42, 255–56

death of child patients, residents' views on: "bad," 17, 36, 51, 63, 77, 88; "good," 16–17, 35–36, 50–51, 63, 76–77, 88

deaths, first in career, 3–5, 6, 261–62; of attending physicians, 95–96, 112–13, 131–32, 147–48, 161–62, 174–75; of nurses, 7–10, 189–93, 205–6, 217–18, 229–30, 246–48; of residents, 23–24, 39–40, 54–55, 67, 80

debriefing sessions: barriers to openness in, 48, 78–79; effects of, 204, 293; lack of, 32; need for, 32–33, 172–73, 268–69, 279–80

denial of death, 14, 36–37, 158

DNR (do not resuscitate), 18, 305

The Drama of the Gifted Child (Miller), 114

dreams of death, 30

dying process, 8–9, 56, 104, 140. *See also* death

education. *See* medical school; nursing school

Electroconvulsive therapy (ECT), 306

Electroencephalogram (EEG), 306

Electromyelogram (EMG), 306

emotions: dealing with one's own, 103, 120–22, 129–30; expression of, 78, 271–73; at patient's death, 78–79. *See also* coping strategies

Extra-corporeal membrane oxygenation (ECMO), 113, 305

funerals, attending, 9–10, 55, 132, 155, 171, 191

"gomer," as defined by Shem, 18

grief: factors complicating, 12, 14, 299, 300; literature describing, 287, 297–99, 300–301; of physicians versus nurses, 302–3; pro-

nurses, 185–88; career plans of, 210, 222–23, 235–36; career satisfaction of, 187–188, 195–96, 209–10, 222, 234–35, 251–52; "eating their young," 236; overstepping bounds, 144, 202, 260; as patient advocates, 186, 252–53, 257; and political views, 230; and research, 297–303; reasons of career choice of, 185, 194–95, 109, 222, 233–34, 250–51, 165; roles of, 12, 185. See also coping strategies, nurses' assessment of; death, experiences of, prior to nursing school of nurses; death, impact of subsequent on; death of child patients, nurses' views on; deaths, first in career; mortality, concerns of nurses; social support for nurses

nursing school: desires for changes in, 252, 268; as preparation for coping with patient deaths, 197, 210–11, 223, 236, 252, 267–68

nursing strike, effects of, 17, 133, 234, 251

On Death and Dying (Kübler-Ross), 102

organ donation, 24, 238–39

"people like us" (PLU's), 93, 123–24, 173

perfectionism, 44, 50

PICU, 10–11, 37, 103, 107, 113, 218, 231, 239, 300, 307

Playing God in the Nursery (Lyon), 162

postmortem care, 9, 163, 171, 190–91, 198–99, 241–42, 243

psychological defenses: development of, 12–13; effects on coping strategies, 14; healthy 15. See also coping strategies

religious beliefs, 185–86, 200, 211, 232, 237, 248–49, 254, 265–66, 273, 279

residents, pediatric, 21–22; career plans of, 47–48, 59; career satisfaction of, 30–31, 47, 59, 66, 74, 84; interpersonal skills of, 289; reasons for career choice of, 30, 45–46, 58–59, 60, 72, 73–74, 84; and research, 288–94, 303. See also coping strategies, differences in; coping strategies, residents' assessment of; death, experiences of, prior to medical school of residents; death, impact of subsequent on; death of child patients, residents' views on; deaths, first in career; medical school, as preparation for coping with patient deaths; medical school, desires for changes in; mortality, concerns of residents; social support for residents

Respiratory syncytial virus (RSV), 307